God Grant Me . . .

God Grant Me...

More Daily Meditations
from the Authors of *Keep It Simple*

Hazelden Publishing
Center City, Minnesota 55012
hazelden.org/bookstore

Library of Congress Cataloging-in-Publication Data

God grant me— : more daily meditations from
the authors of Keep it simple.
p. cm. — (Hazelden meditations)
Includes bibliographical references and index.
ISBN-10: 1-59285-158-4 (pbk.)
ISBN-13: 978-1-59285-158-4 (pbk.)
1. Substance abuse—Patients—Prayer-books and devotions—English.
2. Twelve-step programs—Religious aspects—Meditations.
3. Devotional calendars. I. Hazelden Foundation. II. Series.
BL624.5.G63 2005
204'.32—dc22
2004060654

Editor's note
In the process of being reissued in 2018, *God Grant Me...*
has undergone minor editing updates and been
retypeset in the Whitman font family.

22 21 20   3 4 5 6

Interior design: Terri Kinne
Typesetting: Hillspring Books, Inc.

Dedication

We dedicate this book to our parents,
Gene, Mixie, Gladys, and Martin.
They gave us faith, love, challenges, and hope,
which carry us through the hard times
and help in our recoveries.

About the Authors

These anonymous authors are a married couple who live in Minneapolis, Minnesota. Both are longtime recovering people and clinical experts who work in the addiction treatment and therapy fields.

Introduction

In 1989, we published our first daily meditation book, *Keep It Simple*. Now we offer up *God Grant Me...*, a volume of entirely new meditations that we hope reflect years of growth and recovery experience since our first book.

Like *Keep It Simple*, this book reflects our belief that a recovery program requires us to meditate, pray, and take action. On each page, you'll find three sections. The first section has a quote followed by a few paragraphs on the spiritual message we have found within the quote. We suggest reading the quote and our thoughts on it, then take a few minutes to reflect on what it means for your own spiritual journey.

Next you'll find a Prayer for the Day. Prayer is the act of reaching outside ourselves to ask for help in being good human beings. We suggest you read the Prayer for the Day, and if it fits for you, repeat it throughout the day. If it doesn't fit, make up your own prayer or use the prayer suggested in Step Eleven, "Thy will be done."

Finally you will find a section named Today's Action. Our active addiction was fed by our destructive actions; our recovery also depends on the actions we choose each day. Most of us need a lot of practice taking positive actions. We suggest that you take action each day—either the one we suggest or some other action that fits better for you. Stay in touch with your sponsor about the new actions you practice.

Thank you for letting us join your recovery fellowship as you use this book. We see it as an honor. We hope you find this book helpful in building your relationship with your Higher Power, your sponsor, your recovery community, and all the people in your life. Most especially, we hope this book benefits your own healing.

— *THE AUTHORS*

JANUARY

We admitted we were powerless over alcohol—
that our lives had become unmanageable.
                    —*Step One of Alcoholics Anonymous*

By admitting we are powerless over our addictions, we embrace the spiritual principle of honesty. Honesty—truth—is how we release the death grip we had on the bottle, the bag of dope, the pipe, the syringe.

We now use that same hand—the one with the tight grip—and reach out to recovery. We use that hand to reach out to the Steps, our groups, our sponsor, and especially our Higher Power. We hold on like children hold onto the loving hands of their parents. We change our dependency on alcohol, drugs, gambling, sex, or food to reliance on other humans and our Higher Power. If we do this, we acquire the power to begin sobriety. Hold tight.

PRAYER FOR THE DAY
I admit I need your help, Higher Power. I admit I am
powerless over my addiction and that my best efforts created
a life of unmanageability. Thank you for today's sobriety.

TODAY'S ACTION
Today as I live the first day of a new year, I will spend it giving thanks for my new life. I will also connect with one of my recovery friends to talk about my gratitude.

God, grant me the serenity
To accept the things I cannot change,
courage to change the things I can,
And wisdom to know the difference.
　　　　　　　　　　　　—*The Serenity Prayer*

This is the prayer we turn to for patience, courage, and guidance. It teaches addicts to stop, reflect, and make better decisions.

Our addictions trained us to be too quick to act. We tried to be our own Higher Power. Our addictions also convinced us we couldn't change anything. We tried and tried to stop the craziness, but still it went on until we gave up believing in ourselves.

However, we can change many things, especially our behaviors, our attitudes, our view of life. We can also accept the things we cannot change, thus giving us energy to change those things we can.

If we get our egos out of the way and partner with our Higher Power, we will receive the gift of serenity.

PRAYER FOR THE DAY
Higher Power, remind me that you are my partner
and I need not be alone ever again.

TODAY'S ACTION
Today I will list the things I cannot change and those I can. Then I will make a third list of the actions I will take to change the things I can.

God, grant me the serenity
To accept the things I cannot change . . .
                                    —*The Serenity Prayer*

The Serenity Prayer starts by having us ask our Higher Power to grant serenity that leads to acceptance of the unchangeable. We reach out. We let our Higher Power put an end to our struggle.

As using addicts, we refused to accept our illness; we struggled against chains that we could not remove. The good thing about acceptance is that it saves energy. When we accept our illness, energy that went to our illness and defenses is freed up to be used for our recovery, our healing.

Prayer is always about reaching outside of ourselves, about stepping outside of our egos, our instincts, our all-consuming troubles. The Serenity Prayer is about us reaching out for our Higher Power's peace, grace, and healing.

PRAYER FOR THE DAY
Higher Power, touch me with your peace and grace.
Help me to accept my illness and the things I can't change.
Please use the energy that acceptance frees up
to help me be the person you want me to be.

TODAY'S ACTION
Today I will make a list of all the things I am now struggling against that I can't change. Throughout the day, I will ask my Higher Power to help me accept the things I can't change.

. . . Courage to change the things I can . . .
　　　　　　　　　—*The Serenity Prayer*

Courage is a wonderful spiritual principle. When we use it, it helps us step into new worlds. When we use it in our Fourth Step and our Tenth Step—looking at our behavior—it helps us to become more than we ever thought we could become. As addicts, we became trapped and controlled by our illness. Over time, fear became strong inside us. Many of us changed this fear to anger—we raged against the world or anyone who got in our way.

The Serenity Prayer helps us seek our Higher Power's courage. This courage can help us face reality and reach out to others. Reality and fellowship team together into a force that we use to create a new life. This new life is not one that fears change but sees change as our ally. We change behaviors and attitudes, and in so doing, we become more—more than we ever thought we could be.

PRAYER FOR THE DAY
*Higher Power, I ask for courage so often—every
time I say the Serenity Prayer—but I often forget
to use it. Help me remember to use the courage
you give me to change the things I can.*

TODAY'S ACTION
Today I will call my sponsor and ask if he or she can sit down with me and make a list and plan for things I will confront and change during this year.

. . . And wisdom to know the difference.
—*The Serenity Prayer*

Some of us once thought that using alcohol or drugs made us smarter and more creative. In reality, it lowered our inhibitions and our standards, and was much more likely to lead us to the destruction of wisdom than its creation.

True wisdom reflects and responds to our Higher Power's rules of order. Wisdom is about order and creating, about movement and flow, about ideas and principles coming together. Wisdom is something we like and want, and changes us from the inside out. It is a treasure.

When we were controlled by our addiction, we couldn't find and respond to the order found in principles, which provide the basis of wisdom. We found only chaos and destruction. Our recovery brings us back to the natural order of things, back to the flow and rhythms of nature and our Higher Power.

PRAYER FOR THE DAY
Higher Power, help me notice the wisdom that surrounds me today. Help me see and hear the order in things that makes them beautiful and wise.

TODAY'S ACTION
Today I will sit down and write out five to ten pieces of wisdom that I've learned in recovery. How will I use these pieces of gold to help me and others have a better life?

Compassion is the ability to see how it all is.

—Ram Dass

Compassion means caring about other people. When we remember to ask others how it is for them—right now—that is compassion. We listen. We "Live and let live." We keep on caring. We try to understand. We accept.

As compassionate people we accept each other, even though we all see things in different ways. We have different ideas about spirituality, family life, and politics. We have different things happening in our lives that bring us joy or pain. We are in different times of our lives—being students, being parents, being together with another person, being alone, learning what to do with our strength and energy, or learning how to survive our weakness and depression.

When we see these differences, we learn to give to others when we can. We learn to ask for help when we need it. We learn to listen to others, to be there for them. And we learn to share our troubles and let them be there for us. That's how compassion works.

PRAYER FOR THE DAY

Higher Power, let me be there for others today with compassion. Help me to treat others with the same dignity and compassion that you treat me.

TODAY'S ACTION

When I hear about other people's troubles today, I will really listen, treat them with compassion, and say a little prayer for them.

Nobody can make you feel inferior without your permission.
—Eleanor Roosevelt

Some of us don't want to believe that we are just as good as everyone else. As long as we believe we are less than others, we have a reason to hold back or be lazy. We can hang on to fear and anger. After all, we never got a break. We were born to be losers. And sometimes that's okay with us, because being a loser is easy.

The truth scares us. The truth is this: we are just as important as every other person on this earth. Just like every other person, we are here for important reasons. Our souls have lessons to learn. Our hearts have people to love. There are others around who need our attention and friendship. We have work to do. We need to do our share of loving, helping, teaching, caring, working, and having fun.

PRAYER FOR THE DAY
Higher Power, I believe that you don't make junk. That means I'm not junk. Help me make you proud of me today.

TODAY'S ACTION
I will list five worthwhile things to do today. They can be big or small.

*Surround yourself with only people who are going
to lift you higher.*

—Oprah Winfrey

As we live within the recovering community, we will meet many types of people. We will meet some who take their recovery very seriously and others who don't. We must remember that this is our life we're fighting for. Addiction is a very dangerous and deadly illness. We need to surround ourselves with the best. We deserve it. An AA saying tells us to "Stick with the winners." Why? So we, too, can be winners.

During our active addiction, we helped to bring out the worst in others. We supported our using friends in doing things that were dangerous and destructive. We argued and fought with our families until all sides were operating from the worst parts of their being. Now we learn attitudes and skills to support each other in being the best we can be. And the reward: we get to be the best we can be.

PRAYER FOR THE DAY
*Higher Power, please lift me higher. Please surround
me with your love and with people who will give
me love even when I don't believe I deserve it.*

TODAY'S ACTION
Today I will make a list of the winners I see in my recovery community. I will make a commitment to get to know them and let them help me be a winner.

All are related.

—Lakota Saying

We are all related. What a powerful idea. Every living thing and every part of nature was made by the same Higher Power that made us. We are all part of the same family. Trees and rivers, beetles and puppies, clouds and stars, people of all colors and shapes—these are our relatives.

We are part of life, of nature. There is a place for us. We already belong. The more we accept that fact, the happier we will be.

Who are these relatives? What is this life we are given? How do we belong? These are the gentle questions we will answer as we work our program. The Twelve Steps teach us how to walk in balance with all living things. The fellowship gives us the support of relatives who understand us. All the love and help we need is there for us. We only need accept it.

PRAYER FOR THE DAY
*Higher Power, thank you for making me part
of your universe. Thank you for the life that flows
through me and through all your creation.*

TODAY'S ACTION
I will take a minute today to get to know a relative. This could mean studying a tree or a pet or a person. I will ask myself, "What are three things we have in common?"

We never know the timber of a man's soul until something cuts into him deeply and brings the grain out strong.
—Gene Stratton-Porter

We do not know ourselves until drugs and alcohol bring us to our knees. Our first prayers are those of a broken person begging for mercy and relief. Addiction cuts deeply into a human's soul; it convinces many of us that we are evil.

But we are not evil. We have a disease that controlled our actions and choices. We can regain control over how we act—good or bad—and when we stay sober and work for our recovery. Recovery cuts into addiction just as a surgeon's knife cuts into the tumor that is threatening life. In recovery we come to know ourselves.

When we work the Steps, our true grain is exposed. We find pride in the part of us that is good; we develop tools and friends to help us with our flaws. In recovery we stay sober and get well.

PRAYER FOR THE DAY
*Higher Power, help me use the challenge
of addiction to come to know myself better.*

TODAY'S ACTION
As a start on Step Four, I will make a list of what I've learned about myself, including things I like and don't like about myself.

*Your talent is God's gift to you. What you do with
it is your gift back to God.*
—Leo Buscaglia

Every one of us has a special gift deep in our soul. Some
of us have already found it. But some of us don't yet see
the gift that makes us special. Maybe it's time to find it.

When we were in our active addiction, all our best
energy went into the wrong goal—getting high. Now that
we are sober and have a life that is more sane, we have
energy for good things. The time is right. We can put
some of that extra energy into finding our talent.

Our program has taught us how to look at ourselves in
Step Four, Step Eight, and Step Ten. We have learned to
listen to feedback to improve ourselves in Step Five and
Step Eleven. We can use these skills to find our talent.

It's scary to be special. It means being different. But
that is why the world needs all of us—we each bring
something different. And now we have the energy, we
have the skills, and we have people who care about us
who will help guide us. Isn't it exciting?

PRAYER FOR THE DAY
*Higher Power, I have made a decision
to turn over my life and my will to your care.
Please show me how to use my talent.*

TODAY'S ACTION
Today I will find one thing I'm good at. I will talk with my
sponsor and a friend about how I can use this talent.

Wheresoever you go, go with all your heart.
—Confucius

Our program asks us "to be fearless and thorough from the very start." We are warned that some of us will hold on to old ideas and that the result will be nil unless "we let go absolutely." Recovery asks that we put our heart into our programs. How? By working the Steps. By calling group members to see how they're doing or to let them know how we're doing. By meeting with our sponsors so they can get to know us and guide us in working the Steps.

This is just what we need. We must not sit on the sidelines of the program. We should not settle for the illusion of commitment that we got by drinking and drugging. We need to surrender, to let go absolutely and enjoy the ride.

PRAYER FOR THE DAY

Higher Power, I give my heart and soul to you to do with as you want. Place me where I can do the most good. I pray for willingness to let go absolutely.

TODAY'S ACTION

For today I will work at stepping into the day with all my heart. I will work at having the attitude and actions of letting go absolutely.

Faith is the strength by which a shattered world shall emerge into the light.
—Helen Keller

We live in a broken, shattered world. This has been true for a long time—maybe for as long as people have lived on the earth. There are people who lie, fight, and steal from others. Thousands of people on this earth starve to death every day while others live in luxury. People are spoiling the lands and waters of the earth. The mean and ruthless have grabbed too much power in the world.

These problems are way too big for us. Fixing them is not our job. But we can help heal the part of the world where we live. Step Twelve tells us how. When we work the first eleven Steps, we wake up spiritually. Then "Having had a spiritual awakening as the result of these steps, we tried to carry this message to alcoholics, and to practice these principles in all our affairs." What principles? Faith, for one. Faith, first.

PRAYER FOR THE DAY
Higher Power, please help me have faith today.
Let faith replace my fear so that I am open to your energy.
Help me give it away to others. Use me to spread a bit
of healing energy in my part of the world today.

TODAY'S ACTION
Today I will believe in the healing power of recovery principles. I will notice my actions that help heal the world: when I smile at another person, when I pick up a piece of garbage, when I hold a door open for someone.

Every night the river sings a new song.
—*Eva-Lis Wvorie*

Ours is a program of twenty-four hours. We are to live "One day at a time." We are to live in the moment, for only in the moment can we connect with our Higher Power. How? By bringing life to the spiritual principles our Higher Power has given to us. By choice.

By choosing to live by spiritual principles, moment by moment, we stay connected to our Higher Power. We work to keep the channel open in order to receive the gifts our Higher Power wants us to embrace. To stay open and to live by spiritual principles is hard. Our instinctual side wants us to take the easier, softer way. In addition, we addicts are afraid of the future. We tend to focus on the entire journey instead of what is right in front of our face.

But our recovery program tells us, "Just today, live by spiritual principles today." Focus on today's song, for tomorrow life will teach you a new song.

PRAYER FOR THE DAY
Higher Power, help me to live by the spiritual principles you gave me through recovery. Help me to learn your lessons and help me stay open to the gifts they will give to me.

TODAY'S ACTION
Today I will work to be mindful of the moment and to see choice in the moment. I'll work to remember that the quality of my life depends on the choices I make.

The only real mistake is the one from which we learn nothing.

—*John Powell*

Most of us hate to admit our mistakes. That's too bad. Why? Because we all make them, but only some of us learn from them. Whenever we set a goal to master something new, we start out as beginners. We will make mistakes. That is true in sports, art, work, relationships— and almost everything else in life. Most of the time, a mistake has something to teach us if we look at it clearly. In fact, learning from our mistakes is one of the ways we grow and stretch as human beings.

Our program of recovery teaches us to handle our mistakes well and learn from them. It also teaches us to expect mistakes because they are sure to happen when we live full and loving lives. That's why the program recommends we practice. We should go ahead and try living in this new way and learn from our mistakes, and as we practice, we get better and better at it.

PRAYER FOR THE DAY
Higher Power, please give me the courage to work my program today. I know that means I will see some mistakes—old ones and new ones—but that is okay. I'm not afraid of mistakes anymore.

TODAY'S ACTION
Today I will face my mistakes and fix them the best I can. In doing this, I am learning and practicing a new way to live.

Love truth, but pardon error.
—*Voltaire*

During our active addiction many of us said we loved the truth but in reality we were afraid of it. Family and friends would bring us the truth and tell us we had a problem, and we would argue with them. We had become afraid of the truth. Truth meant we'd have to give up alcohol and drugs, give up our addictive life.

Our error was that we were afraid of the wrong thing. We thought we knew better than those who loved us. We refused to accept the reality that we couldn't use like normal people.

However, in recovery, we can't afford to beat ourselves up for the errors of our past. We need to put this energy into our recovery. We need to learn from the errors of our past, make amends when possible, and embrace the truth that recovery offers us. We can heal our guilt by fixing our mistakes.

PRAYER FOR THE DAY

*Higher Power, help me to forgive myself for the errors
I have made, to learn from them, and to embrace the truth.
For in truth, I am able to find you.*

TODAY'S ACTION

Today I will reflect on where I am in my recovery. Are there any errors I haven't forgiven myself for? If so, I will list them and think of actions I need to take to forgive myself. I will then share this list with my sponsor.

We need four hugs a day for survival. We need
eight hugs a day for maintenance. We need twelve
hugs a day for growth.

—*Virginia Satir*

Virginia Satir was an internationally acclaimed therapist. She knew a lot about what people need to be healthy and happy, and to live in good relationships with each other. She was very smart, and most of her advice was pretty simple.

Take hugs, for example. What could be more simple? One person reaching out to touch another person with safety and care. Very simple. But what do hugs give people? Comfort. Acceptance. The basics we all need no matter where we are at today.

PRAYER FOR THE DAY
Higher Power, help me ask for the hugs I need and want
today. Remind me today to offer hugs to the people around
me. And help me feel the big hug you have for me, too.

TODAY'S ACTION
Today I will talk with my sponsor about this question: "What is easier for me—to get a hug or to give a hug?"

True life is lived when tiny choices are made.
—*Leo Tolstoy*

Dependency is about losing the ability to say no. Recovery gives us back the gift of choice. Recovery by itself doesn't make us good people, but we will become good people by the choices we make.

We create our new authentic life by choosing to place principles before personality. This means we make choices based on good values. During our active addiction, if it felt good, we did it. In recovery, we choose based on doing the next right thing. Recovery is choosing to go to a meeting even when we don't feel like it. Recovery is choosing to keep our mouths shut when we are invited to gossip. Recovery is thousands of little choices, all of which must be guided by our values. We must choose wisely. We must choose as if our life depends upon it, for it does.

PRAYER FOR THE DAY
Higher Power, guide my choices. Help me to place principles before personality, even when I don't want to.

TODAY'S ACTION
As I walk through the day today, I will be mindful of the choices I make. I will slow the day down enough so I can watch to see if my choices match my values.

The bluebird carries the day on his back.
—*Henry David Thoreau*

What a happy thought. Imagine a bluebird building its home in a nest box, chattering away to tell the world, "I'm here, and I'm busy!"

The bluebird does not think about yesterday or tomorrow but only about doing the next right thing to make the present day a good one. The bluebird listens for an inner voice—the voice that tells it when to start building a nest or when to begin its flight south for the coming winter.

We can learn from the bluebird. When we do our activities of the day, one at a time, we put together a good day—a day that is just what it is supposed to be.

PRAYER FOR THE DAY
*Higher Power, help me be true to myself today
and to live my life just the way it is supposed to be.
Help me feel the joy of it!*

TODAY'S ACTION
Today I will talk with my sponsor or a friend in recovery about how my days need to be at this time in my life. I will be happy that I know how to live well today.

Every passage has its price.
—*Meredith Ann Pierce*

Our life of active addiction had a price, and we paid it. It asked for our dignity, and we gave it up. It asked for our relationships, and we gave them up. It asked for our self-respect; we gave that up, too. We did whatever our addiction asked of us. We paid any price it asked.

Recovery will also ask us to ante up. We will need to surrender our wills and lives over to a Higher Power. We will need to go to meetings even when we don't want to. We will have to work and help those who still suffer. We will have to make lists of wrongs done and make amends to those we have harmed. Yes, every passage has its price, even recovery.

PRAYER FOR THE DAY
*Higher Power, I pray for willingness to show up
whenever and wherever recovery needs me to.*

TODAY'S ACTION
Today I will do something nice for someone. Freely doing for others helps me be more willing in the future.

When it is dark enough, you can see the stars.
—*Charles A. Beard*

We human beings seem to prefer to be in the light. Most of us rely on the daylight to move around safely and do our work. In the light we feel like we have more control. At night, when the world is dark, we feel less in control. We do two things: we turn on the lights so we can continue our daytime activity, or we go to sleep.

But darkness has gifts for us—different gifts than we get from light. Darkness changes how we see things. In the dark we see less, but we pay better attention. As we let go of our fears and let our eyes adjust to the dark, we find that we can see more than we first thought. We can see enough to take the next step. There are some things, like the stars, that we can see better in the dark.

PRAYER FOR THE DAY
Higher Power, let me learn the lessons of loving the dark. Let me learn to really see the gifts that surround and support me, and the beautiful possibilities that life holds for me.

TODAY'S ACTION
Tonight as I get ready for bed, I will get a different view of my surroundings. I will sit up in the dark for a few minutes. I will feel the floor or bed supporting me, and I will let my eyes adjust to the dark.

*Self-made men are most always apt to be a little
too proud of the job.*

—*Josh Billings' Farmer's Allinax*

Ego gets us in trouble. Ego tells us that we are special
and different. We are not *that* special. We are not *that*
different. We are creatures who need relationships with
others and with a Higher Power. Ego tells us the only
relationship we need is with ourselves. There is fear
behind the ego. Yes, an inflated ego comes from being
afraid of others, of our Higher Power. This is why our
egos grew so large during our active addiction. They
were equal to our fear.

Recovery asks that we place ego and fear aside. We are
to replace them with relationships and being of service
to others. Why? For one thing, it keeps us sober. It also
pushes us to learn from others. As we learn from others,
we get closer to the truth, the home of our Higher Power.
Truth lowers fear and demands that we put aside ego.
These are aids to living. We must remember, truth before
fear, relationships before ego.

PRAYER FOR THE DAY
*Higher Power, help keep my ego in check. Help me to
use the energy of my fear to reach out to others, to deepen
my relationship with you. With you by my side, there is
nothing to be afraid of. I choose you instead of my ego.*

TODAY'S ACTION
Today I will watch for how my ego gets me in trouble.
I will beware of placing myself before my Higher Power.

The more we give of anything, the more we shall get back.

—Grace Speare

When we first hear this advice, it doesn't seem to make sense. How can we get more of something by giving it away? Yet we hear the same advice in Step Twelve of our recovery program: we must "Give it away" in order to keep it.

What does this mean? Maybe it means that when we pay attention to living in this way, we change our whole value system and our behavior. For example, we can choose to lay our anger and whining on others, but that doesn't really get rid of it. In fact, we find that people tend to join in our negative behavior and feed it. We end up with more.

But if we give to others the feelings we really want to keep—understanding, honesty, kindness, patience, and humor—they will share their good stuff with us, too. And that helps us stay sober.

PRAYER FOR THE DAY
Higher Power, help me share the important things today—the things I want more of.

TODAY'S ACTION
Today I will be aware of what I am giving others with my behavior. If I need to share negative comments or ideas, I will balance each one with five positives. I'm making life better for others and for myself, too.

*We must be willing to get rid of the life we've
planned, so as to have the life that is waiting for us.*
— *Joseph Campbell*

Over and over we tried to drink or use in ways that
wouldn't hurt us or those we loved. The harder we tried,
the more out of control we became.

Recovery asks us to surrender and accept. We surrender to the reality that we were powerless over our addiction and that our lives were unmanageable. In order to
step into our new life, we have to let go of the life we had
wanted and the life we had planned. We step into a life
our Higher Power has waiting for us. We must accept that
there is nothing back there for us. We must look forward
with anticipation.

PRAYER FOR THE DAY
*Higher Power, help me live the life you want for me.
Help me to surrender my will and life over to your care.*

TODAY'S ACTION
I will spend some time today reflecting on what type of
life my Higher Power wants for me. I will then ask myself,
"Am I working with my Higher Power or against my
Higher Power's plan for me?"

It's the most unhappy people who most fear change.
—*Mignon McLaughlin*

It's an odd fact, isn't it? If we are unhappy, it seems like we would want change. The hitch is, when we are unhappy, we are also very often afraid. We may fear things will get worse, not better, if anything changes.

We have good reason to fear change. Some of the changes we made in our life, such as starting to use alcohol and drugs, led to big trouble. When we were using, we made more bad choices about changes in our behavior—choices that could have killed us.

The changes we make in recovery are different. They bring us happiness. We choose our changes with the help of our Higher Power and healthy people in recovery. Then we act out our changes with the same help—help we can trust.

PRAYER FOR THE DAY
Higher Power, help me turn over my life and my will to your care. Help me remember that I can trust you.

TODAY'S ACTION
Today I will be aware of my moments of fear. Then I will ask for help and move ahead in spite of my fear.

Who dares to teach must never cease to learn.
—*John Cotton Dana*

Part of recovery is being there for those who still suffer and for those who have yet to walk through the doors. We teach others how to get sober, how to stay sober, and how to build a new life. We teach when we share our stories, experiences, strength, and hope. We teach through our successes and failures.

This means we also have a responsibility to continue our learning. We must study literature that feeds our souls. We must study life and be open to new ways. Learning demands that we open our minds and hearts, that we develop a questioning, not a cynical, mind. If we do this, life will always hold new adventure and gifts for us. So we continue to study the Steps and life, do our homework, and show up for class.

PRAYER FOR THE DAY

Higher Power, I pray for your help to stay open to the lessons of the day even when my fear wants me to close the book. May your voice come through me as I teach and help others.

TODAY'S ACTION

I will make a list of the people who have been my main teachers in recovery. I will offer up a prayer of gratitude that they were willing to learn their lessons.

Stop a moment, cease your work, and look around you.

—*Thomas Carlyle*

This is what we do in Step Ten. We stop for a few minutes each day. We look around us. We look at the events of the day and at our actions. Did we pay attention to the important things today? Did we do the next right thing?

What did we give to the world around us today? Did we add to the good energy by sharing a smile? Did we help things go smoothly by taking care of our responsibilities? Did we take care not to hurt anyone? Did we lend a helping hand?

Or did we upset the peace with our angry tantrums? Did we leave messes behind us that will bother others? Did we give a hurtful look or say an unkind word to someone who got in our way?

PRAYER FOR THE DAY
Higher Power, help me look at my behavior every day, because every day I do things that make a difference in my world, good or bad. I want to make a good difference.

TODAY'S ACTION
Today when I do my Step Ten, I will take note of the areas where I need more practice working my program. I will talk about these areas with my sponsor.

Believe more deeply. Hold your face up to the light, even though for the moment you do not see.
—*Bill Wilson*

At times, despair, sadness, and hopelessness fill us. None of us will get out of this world without experiencing tragedy. At these times, we turn to our Higher Power and the spiritual principles as guides. At these times especially, we turn to the fellowship. We are here to help each other, comfort each other, and offer sanctuary to each other. We are to be each other's gifts.

During our active addiction, when troubles came, we turned inward, pretending everything was okay. We acted as if we needed no one—mainly because we trusted no one. We were surrounded by darkness, inside and out. Recovery teaches us to trust in the "light," to believe it is there even when we can't see it. It may be as close as our next meeting or a phone call to our sponsor. In this, we must believe deeply.

PRAYER FOR THE DAY
Higher Power, I look to you when I can't see. Show me the light. I look to you for the guidance I cannot give myself. Show me the way and give me hope. Higher Power, thank you!

TODAY'S ACTION
Today I will remember a time during my active addiction when I felt hopeless. I will reflect on what I learned from this and share my thoughts with a recovery friend.

A single grateful thought toward heaven is the most complete prayer.

—*Gotthold Ephraim Lessing*

Thank you is one of the most important things we can say to anyone. *Thank you* packs a lot of meaning into two little words. *Thank you* says, "I see you. I see what you have done for me. You have been kind to me. I know it takes work to be kind. I feel special that you did the work of being kind to me. I am grateful."

Sometimes it is hard for us to say thank you because we are too busy feeling shame or sadness or anger. So what? No excuses. Those feelings are our own problems, and we know what to do about them now that we have a recovery program. No matter what is going on with us, we can always find help. And we can always be kind to others. Saying thank you is an easy way to start.

PRAYER FOR THE DAY
Thank you, Higher Power. Thank you for the gift of life, for a world of natural beauty and power to live in, and for the people around me who love me and accept my love. Thank you for caring about me and helping me every day in my recovery, and please help me ask for the gift of your help each day.

TODAY'S ACTION
Today I will practice thinking "Thank you, Higher Power" every time I receive a little help or a lucky break.

*For everything that has happened, thank you. For
everything that is to come, yes.*

—Dag Hammarskjöld

In recovery, we are to embrace an attitude of gratitude
and openness. We are to be open to learning from our
past and to the lessons the future will give us. The Big
Book tells us, "No matter how far down the scale we
have gone, we will see how our experience can benefit
others." This is our way of saying, "For everything that
has happened, thank you." Our experiences become our
stories, and through our stories, we teach each other
about life. We teach each other what mistakes to avoid,
what successes to embrace. We teach each other that
there is hope.

The Big Book also says, "We will intuitively know how
to handle situations which used to baffle us. We will
suddenly realize that God is doing for us what we could
not do for ourselves." This is our way of saying, "For
everything that is to come, yes." We say yes to the future
because we know the future will bring us closer to our
Higher Power.

PRAYER FOR THE DAY
*Higher Power, today I stand before you and say, "Thank you
for my past and for my future. Use them as you wish."*

TODAY'S ACTION
I will think of five ways my past can be of help to others.
I will list my present challenges and what gifts may be
found within them.

*Oh, what a tangled web we weave when first we
practice to deceive.*
—*Walter Scott*

To deceive means to fool people into believing things that
are not true. As addicts, we did this in many ways. We
lied. We hid facts. We were sneaky. While we were trying
to fool other people, we also fooled ourselves. Every lie
was like a knot. Pretty soon we were a tangled mess.
Our lives became unmanageable, tangled webs of life.

Our recovery program—an honesty program—tells us
how we can untangle our lives. In the First Step, we admit
we are all tangled up in our life of addiction. Second, we
realize we can fix it. Third, we decide to take on the job
of fixing it, no matter how much work it takes. In Steps
Four and Five, we find the knots with the help of another
person. In Steps Six to Ten, we untangle these knots.

Without the tangles, our life is free and ready to be
used for whatever we decide. Steps Eleven and Twelve
help us find good ways to use the gift of life.

PRAYER FOR THE DAY
*Higher Power, thanks for giving me my life, strong as
a good rope. Please help me keep it straight by being
honest today with myself and others in everything I do.*

TODAY'S ACTION
Today I will work on straightening out one knot—just one.

FEBRUARY

Came to believe that a Power greater than our-
selves could restore us to sanity.
—*Step Two of Alcoholics Anonymous*

The Second Step pushes us to start believing in some-thing other than ourselves. After facing that we are powerless in Step One, we feel vulnerable. What we do with our vulnerability is very important.

Hope is a power greater than us. We see others healing in the groups we attend, so we start to believe in a healing power. The power of the group is greater than us.

As we start to believe in hope, in our group, and in ourselves, we are slowly restored to sanity. When we were using alcohol and drugs, we knew our thinking and behavior were not balanced and sane, but we gave in because we had no hope. Now we have hope because we see that recovery creates a healthy life of sanity.

PRAYER FOR THE DAY
Higher Power, I see you in the smiles and serenity
of people in recovery. Please restore me to sanity.

TODAY'S ACTION
Today I will make a list of the ways my active addiction made my thoughts and actions insane and off-balanced.

Freedom is the will to be responsible for ourselves
—*Friedrich Nietzche*

As we work a recovery program, we regain and experience freedom. Freedom from craving. Freedom from shame. Freedom from our self-centered desires. Freedom to choose what type of people we will be.

But with freedom and new choices comes responsibility. We are responsible for our sobriety. We need to get ourselves to meetings. We need to work the Steps, not just talk about them in meetings. We call our sponsors and others from meetings who may need encouragement. We do our service work.

Our program also tells us that we are responsible for those who still suffer, for those who will come after us. We are to conduct ourselves in a manner that would attract people to recovery.

PRAYER FOR THE DAY
Higher Power, thank you for setting me free.
Help me to fulfill my responsibilities,
as a person and as a recovering person.

TODAY'S ACTION
Today I will have gratitude for the new freedom I have been given. I will spend fifteen minutes thinking about and writing down my recovery responsibilities.

It is much more difficult to judge oneself than to judge others. If you succeed in judging yourself rightly, then you are indeed a person of wisdom.
—Antoine de Saint-Exupéry

Judging ourselves rightly gives us a huge edge in life. When we really know ourselves—our strengths and our weaknesses, our quirks and our beauty—then we are ready to really live.

In Steps Four and Five, we judge ourselves. In Step Four, we dig through all the stuff we carry around—our feelings, thinking, behavior, and skills—and judge what to keep and what to leave behind. In Step Five, we tell another person what we have found and make sure we are judging rightly.

Once we really know what helps and what hurts us, we can make wise choices. Once we know how we help and hurt others, we can make wise choices. Working the rest of the Steps helps us follow through on our choices. As we work Steps Six through Twelve, we become wiser and wiser.

PRAYER FOR THE DAY
Higher Power, please help me become wise by really knowing myself. Help me learn easily so the lessons can be gentle.

TODAY'S ACTION
Today I will make myself wiser by working on Step Four or Step Ten. I will write down at least two things I am carrying around, and I will tell them to my sponsor.

Desire is the very essence of man.
—*Benedict de Spinoza*

There is nothing wrong with desire. It is part of being human. During our active addiction, our desires directed our lives. Our desires made our choices for us. If it felt good, well then, "Just do it!" We placed our desires ahead of our values and spiritual principles. This is the mistake we made.

Desires are like children; they need to be guided. In recovery, we use the Steps to guide and direct our desires. We now desire to do the right thing. We desire to get close to people. We desire to be good family members and good citizens. Why? Because this is what we've wanted all along. We desire to be good people with good lives.

PRAYER FOR THE DAY
Higher Power, help me guide the energy
of my desires toward what you want me to do.
Help me to place principles before desire.

TODAY'S ACTION
I will make a list of five times I've placed my desires ahead of what is right for me and others. I will call and share my list with someone in recovery.

All his thinking could not make him understand,
but his singing heart could.

—*Laura Adams Armer*

Now that we are sober, we are pretty good thinkers. Clear, sober thinking is great. But thinking is not the whole story. We human beings are only part mind; we also are part body, part heart, and part soul.

We need to use all of these parts in our recovery from addiction. Our recovery program asks us to think, of course. It also feeds our hearts as we relate to other people in the fellowship of our groups. It teaches us to take care of our bodies by staying sober, eating better, and sleeping like normal people. Spirituality in the program feeds our soul as we learn ways to relate to our Higher Power.

We become healthier and more whole—mind, heart, body, and soul—as we work the Twelve Step program. Life is meant to be lived on all of these levels. And when one part of us doesn't get it, we have three other parts of us to help us understand.

PRAYER FOR THE DAY
Higher Power, please help me use all of me to live life
fully—my body, mind, heart, and soul.

TODAY'S ACTION
Today I will spend five minutes just sitting and relaxing. I will notice how I am aware of thoughts, emotions, and daydreams.

Caring is the greatest thing; caring matters most.
—*Friedrich von Hirgel*

The Third Step clearly asks us to turn our wills and lives over to the *care* of our Higher Power. Care is to become our guide when we choose our actions. Is it caring for an alcoholic to drink? No. Is it caring for an addict to turn to drugs instead of people? No. Is it caring for us to not seek help when we need it? No. Whenever we are at a crossroad, let us stop and look for the caring path. If we can't find the caring path, we ask our sponsors or those who have gone before to help us find the way.

Care is the path of our Higher Power; it is the path of recovery. We will learn in recovery that care is the greatest and best guide we could ever have. It is our Higher Power's gift to us.

PRAYER FOR THE DAY
*Higher Power, help me to seek out and find
the caring path. Help me to care again for others
and myself. Let my last words of the day,
and especially my actions, be those of care.*

TODAY'S ACTION
I will list five ways I can act in caring ways toward myself and others today. Then I will put this list into action.

The purpose of life is a life of purpose.
—Robert Byrne

When we first get sober, our main job for the first couple years is just to get well. It's a big job because our disease has taken a lot out of us in every way. We have to heal our body, mind, heart, and soul. We learn to take it easy, work the Steps, talk with our sponsor, and go to meetings. In early recovery, we try to keep the rest of life simple.

Once we are healthy and settled into our new sober way of life, we can live even more fully. We will be ready to give of ourselves in new areas. We can put more energy into doing the work we are here for. That may be raising children, finding a career, or even getting involved in politics.

We are all here to help make the world a better place in some way or another. Once we are sober and stable, we will have a special purpose. We will find it by practicing Step Eleven.

PRAYER FOR THE DAY
Higher Power, help me practice the idea
of "First things first" in my recovery.
After I am healthy, help me find your purpose for me.

TODAY'S ACTION
I will talk with my sponsor today about where I am with finding my purpose. Am I ready, or am I still healing?

I accept the universe.

—*Margaret Fuller*

Recovery asks that we surrender our will—that we accept life on life's terms. During our active addiction, we fought the universe or tried to bend the universe to fit our wishes. We fought, not to surrender, but to keep using alcohol or drugs as long as we could. Surrender tells us to let go, to stop fighting, and to let our Higher Power and others in.

Recovery teaches humility. Humility is about acceptance and working to find our right place in the universe. We accept help when it is needed or offered. Humility is also about accepting the fact that we are unique but not special. We accept hope instead of hopelessness. As we find our place in the group we attend, we start to accept the universe on its own terms and to find our place within it.

PRAYER FOR THE DAY

I accept the fact that I have an illness, and I accept that I need help. I will work with the universe instead of fighting it. To do this, Higher Power, I need your strength.

TODAY'S ACTION

Today I will sit down and write about five ways I have fought the universe instead of accepting it. I will share this list with my sponsor or a recovery friend.

Wherever there is a human being, there is an
opportunity for kindness.

—*Seneca*

In today's world, it seems like kindness is not in style. It can feel more relevant to be tough or sassy, to have an attitude that "no one can touch me."

This worked during our active addiction. As using addicts, we treated other people like objects. We ignored them, pushed them out of our way, or used them. No one got into our hearts. That's the way addiction works. It separates us from our human support and feeds us alcohol and drugs.

In our recovery program, we stop being separate from everyone else. We join with them in creating support and caring for each other. We learn to be kind. First we ask for help and stop the insanity. Then we learn kindness to ourselves in Steps Six and Seven. Steps Eight, Nine, Ten, and Twelve teach us to be kind to others. Where does all this kindness lead us? To fairness, honesty, and having nothing to hide. To being a real person.

PRAYER FOR THE DAY
Higher Power, remind me today to be kind to others.
Even when I have nothing else to give,
I can offer a smile. I can listen.

TODAY'S ACTION
I will list three unkind behaviors I still use and three kind ones I will practice instead.

It is better to begin in the evening than not at all.
—English Proverb

At times, we addicts feel bad that we lost years to our illness. We've wasted time, money, and energy on our addiction. Those days are gone. Let us not look behind except when our program and the Steps ask us to. We only look behind to see the mistakes we made for one reason—in order to not make them again.

Today we look forward. Today is a day to celebrate and live our sobriety to its fullest. We should embrace each moment of sobriety and live it with dignity and integrity. When we do this, we increase our chances of being sober tomorrow. Each day that we act from care instead of from self-pity, we learn how to be caring. If we are thankful this evening for today's sobriety, we increase our chances of having gratitude follow us into tomorrow.

PRAYER FOR THE DAY
Higher Power, help me to have gratitude for each moment
of sobriety as they add up into days, weeks, months,
and years. Help me to see that my future depends on
how well I surrender to you in the moment. Help me
to use the evenings to look forward, not behind me.

TODAY'S ACTION
I will write out six ways that my life and world will be better as I stay sober one day, one moment at a time.

Anger is a short madness.

—Horace

Madness, or being crazy, means we aren't thinking right. We act however we feel like acting. We don't care about the harm we do. We tell ourselves it is okay to act this way because someone or something "made" us angry.

We may think anger is an excuse to hurt people. Then we think they should not feel hurt or be angry back at us because we are the only ones that have a "right" to be angry. Then, when we are done being mean, we think they should forgive us. How crazy is that?

We can do a lot of damage to ourselves and to others when we are mad. Words hurt people, just like axes cut wood. When we stop, we have left our marks. The impressions of our words don't go away even if we are forgiven.

PRAYER FOR THE DAY
*Higher Power, I don't want to be a mad person,
hurting the people around me. Please help me
to think before I act today. Remind me to be
grateful for the forgiveness of others.*

TODAY'S ACTION
I will ask one person, "How have I hurt you when I was angry? How does that hurt affect your trust for me? Are you afraid of me now in any way?" Then I will talk with my sponsor about how I act when I am angry.

I was as hollow and empty as the spaces between the stars.

—Raymond Chandler

As our illness progressed, we became empty and hollow. We humans need real connections with other people, our Higher Power, our values, and ourselves. Our illness leads us to betray all of these connections. Addiction gives us an illusion of connection as long as we stay in the trance. When the trance ends, the emptiness appears, and we get scared and run back to the high. The end result of addiction is total aloneness, total emptiness. Our addiction pushes away the things that feed our hearts and souls.

Recovery asks that we open up our hearts and souls to be filled again. But to do this, we must face the emptiness of our addiction and then ask for help. We need to ask others and our Higher Power to help and teach us how to be humans instead of addicts.

PRAYER FOR THE DAY
Higher Power, help me be open to the teachings, tasks, and gifts of recovery. Fill me with your presence.

TODAY'S ACTION
Today I will make a list of ways that my drinking or drugging emptied my heart and soul. I will share my list with my sponsor or another recovery friend.

I have had just about all I can take of myself.
—S. N. Behrman

We addicts know the feeling! We had it when we were using alcohol or drugs. We sometimes call it "Sick and tired of being sick and tired." We were sick of ourselves. The feeling kept building, and it got stronger and stronger until we stopped using and entered recovery.

What a relief. We got out from under the alcohol and drugs, and stopped the rotten behavior that our active addiction caused. We found out that we can be good people, with the help of the Twelve Steps and our friends in recovery.

We also learn in recovery that there is more to life than focusing on ourselves. Once we get sober and work on the Steps, especially Steps Eight and Nine, we find that recovery leads us to a new interest in other people. Our lives become busy with friends and family, work and recreation, and our recovery program. We are interested. We have energy. We have value. Life is good.

PRAYER FOR THE DAY
Higher Power, help me remember today that it's not all about me. There is a bigger picture to life, and I have a part to play in making it better for everyone. I will never have to be bored and sick of myself again.

TODAY'S ACTION
When I take my Tenth Step inventory today, I will ask, "How did I get outside of myself today?"

Most people see the problem of love primarily as
that of being loved, rather than that of loving, of
one's capacity to love.
                                        —Erich Fromm

We want others to love us. We search to find love. However, recovery asks that we focus our energies on loving instead of looking for love. We are to work at increasing our capacity to love. Love and loving others help protect us from our addiction.

During our active addiction, we "loved" to drink, do drugs, party, gamble, or casually hook-up with other people. Although we "loved" these behaviors, these are not loving behaviors; these are self-centered behaviors.

We learn in recovery that we need to do the work of love. We see a need, and we work to be of service. We see someone hurting, and we offer an ear to listen. Or maybe we just sit with that person for a time so they know they are not alone. We have looked out for ourselves long enough. Now it is time to give back some of the love the world gave to us, which kept us alive during our addiction.

PRAYER FOR THE DAY
Higher Power, help me stop looking for love
and teach me how to increase my capacity to love.
Provide me with opportunities to be of service.

TODAY'S ACTION
Today I will be of secret service to someone. I will do something for someone and expect nothing in return.

*We do not remember days, we remember
moments.*
—*Cesare Pavese*

I'll never forget peeling potatoes very early one morning preparing for the arrival of twenty-five guests. "We're not just making breakfast," said my friend. "We're making memories."

I don't remember the rest of that day, but I do remember making hash browns and chatting with my friend while the morning was still dark. Laughter filled our crowded cabin as our friends arrived at dawn.

The friendships we develop in recovery change our lives. We can have parties, plan adventures, and take healthy risks with our safe friends. We can make memories with the people we love, too.

In recovery, our wild and fun days are far from over, but now we will remember them!

PRAYER FOR THE DAY
*Higher Power, help me be lively and share
the fun of life with others. I want to make happy
memories with my family and friends.*

TODAY'S ACTION
I will think of a happy moment I shared with someone, and I will reach out to say, "Remember the time . . . ?"

When hope can't be found, seek out a friend and
borrow theirs.

—*Anonymous*

Often we find ourselves feeling down or wondering what it's all about. We may feel sorry for ourselves or angry at the world. This is a dangerous place for us addicts. At these times, we may want to trust alcohol and chemicals more than we trust our Higher Power. At these times, we need to seek out recovery friends.

Our recovery friends help us remember that we are important but not in a grandiose way. We also discover the mutual benefits of recovery friendships. There will be times when we can offer encouragement to friends who are feeling hopeless. In turn, they'll be able to offer the same hope to others or perhaps even to us on a bad day. This is the way of recovery—friends helping friends.

PRAYER FOR THE DAY
Higher Power, please give me the power to reach out
whenever I feel hopeless. Also, help me to provide hope
to others. Help me to honor the "we" of recovery.

TODAY'S ACTION
Today I will make a list of all the people in my recovery groups that I will turn to if I start to feel hopeless or feel like using.

The now never asks what's coming next.
—*Larry Stillday*

We need to spend some time every day in the now. Just being. Just being enough. Relaxing. Enjoying the people around us or enjoying a moment alone. Listening to our heartbeat. Feeling the air enter and leave our bodies as we breathe calmly and deeply. Trusting that, for this moment, all is as it should be. Life is taking care of us. We are in our Higher Power's care.

In this moment, we let go of the past and we let go of the future. We focus on now. Now we don't think. We simply listen. To our heartbeat. To our breathing. To the sounds of life around us. To the quiet voice of our Higher Power.

PRAYER FOR THE DAY
Higher Power, in my old life I used alcohol or drugs
to forget the past and the future. I wanted to be in the now,
but I embraced death instead of life in my search.
Hold me as I enter the now sober, alive, and listening.
Please use these moments to restore my spirit.

TODAY'S ACTION
Today I will practice being in the now. I will freeze-frame two times today. Once, alone as I practice a moment of meditation, and once as I simply stop thinking and truly look around me at life's energy.

There are no shortcuts to any place worth going.
— *Beverly Sills*

The Big Book says, "We thought we could find an easier, softer way. But we could not. With all the earnestness at our command, we beg of you to be fearless and thorough from the very start."

We are making a new life. And we need to make it a good life, one we will be proud of. We need to invest everything in surrendering our ego to the spiritual principles of recovery. Why? If we look around the recovery rooms, we will see many miracles, people who have been transformed by surrendering their wills and lives to spiritual principles.

Surrendering is hard for us and our big egos. It also takes work. It's time to stop looking for shortcuts; we've tried that route. It is time to invest in ourselves.

PRAYER FOR THE DAY
Higher Power, help me to stop looking for the easy
way when it comes to my program. Help me
to see my true value and to invest in myself again.
Help me to be fearless and thorough.

TODAY'S ACTION
Today I will make a list of the ways I have cheated myself by always taking the easier, softer way. If I'm not willing to do this simple task, am I still looking for the easier, softer way?

We ask ourselves, "Who am I to be brilliant, gorgeous, talented, and fabulous?" Actually, who are you not to be? You are a child of God.

— Marianne Williamson

Remember when our parents used to tell us to behave in public? They probably said something like, "What you do makes our family look good or bad, depending on how you act."

Now that we have turned over our lives and wills to our Higher Power, what we do makes our Higher Power look good or bad, depending on how we act.

Our Higher Power does not make junk. Our Higher Power makes beautiful, talented, generous, fabulous people. And each of us is one of them. Is that how we act? What kind of example of our Higher Power's work do we let ourselves be?

That doesn't mean we are perfect; our Higher Power is not done with us yet. But it's our job to practice being the kind of person we are made to be.

PRAYER FOR THE DAY
Higher Power, help me accept all the good things you put into me, and help me act like the person you made me to be.

TODAY'S ACTION
Today I will write a letter to my Higher Power to say thank you for all the good things about myself. I will read the letter to my sponsor.

I am grateful for this minute. My eternity may be in it.
— AA Grapevine, *March 1947*

The present moment is our link to the divine. How we conduct ourselves in the present moment is how we come to know what we believe in. We must never forget that moments are tied together, one moment leading into the next. Thus, by acting from our values in *this* moment, we increase our chances of acting from our values in the *next* moment. If we stay tied to the divine in *this* moment, we increase our chances of being tied to the divine in the *next* moment.

Recovery allows us to choose what we do with our moments and what we choose to be tied to. Dependence, on the other hand, is the loss of choice. Are we grateful for having choices again? Are we grateful to be able to connect with the divine this very moment?

PRAYER FOR THE DAY
I am grateful to have this moment. Higher Power, help me to use it to help others and to do what you want me to do. In reality, it is your moment. Thank you.

TODAY'S ACTION
I will work to live today in the moment. I will work to see and find my Higher Power in the moment. If I can do this, I will stay connected to eternity.

Our deeds determine us, as much as we determine our deeds.

— George Eliot

Who are we, really? It seems like we are one person on the inside, and yet we often act like someone else. Can a good person do bad things? Can a bad person do good things? It's pretty confusing, isn't it?

Our recovery program teaches us that we can change who we are by changing the things we do. We can become the kind of person we want to be by acting as if we are already that person. For example, if we want to be sober, we can act as if we are a sober person; that is, don't drink, and don't hang out in places where people go to drink. If we want to be a caring person, we can do caring actions for others.

We are the person we feel like on the inside. We are also the person we act like on the outside. In recovery, we change how we think, feel, and act. We practice making changes in each of these areas, and every time we do well in one area, we help in the others, too.

PRAYER FOR THE DAY
Higher Power, help me become the person I want to be by changing how I act, how I feel, and how I think. I am sick and tired of acting, feeling, and thinking like an addict.

TODAY'S ACTION
Today I will watch how I think, feel, and act. I will remind myself to think, feel, and act like the person I want to be.

Love yourself first, and everything else falls into line. You really have to love yourself to get anything done in this world.
— *Lucille Ball*

What does it mean to love yourself? Didn't we love ourselves during our active addiction? Loving yourself doesn't means giving in to every desire. This is self-indulgence. Loving yourself means doing what is right and good in terms of self-care.

During our active addiction, we were self-centered, not self-loving. Most of us have to learn how to be self-loving. We have sponsors who teach us how to be self-loving. We learn that saying no is often the most loving thing we can say to ourselves. This is a new concept for us. We have to learn how to direct our energy toward good living. This is a new concept for us, too. When we do these things, everything else seems to fall into line.

PRAYER FOR THE DAY
Higher Power, help me learn about self-care. Help me say no to things that would put distance between you and me.

TODAY'S ACTION
Today I will list of all the things I love about myself. Then I will call my sponsor and share the list with him or her.

It is in the shelter of each other that the people live.
— *Irish Proverb*

In the history of AA, we learn about the famous doctor Carl Jung who wrote that alcoholics are people who live outside "the protective wall of human community." It is true. When we were using, we were outsiders. We may have hung out with other outsiders, but we were not part of a loving group of people who cared for each other in healthy ways.

In recovery, all that changes. We enter loving groups as we join in Twelve Step fellowship, and we form healthy friendships and family relationships. We start to feel like part of something that protects us.

PRAYER FOR THE DAY
Higher Power, help me give up my pride in being an outsider. Help me feel the comfort and happiness of being part of a healthy group of people.

TODAY'S ACTION
I will make a list of the people I feel connected to in my sober life. I will call my sponsor and talk about how I feel about these new relationships.

Fear keeps us from making the journey.
— *Carl A. Hammerschlag*

Fear is a natural by-product of our illness. Fear sets in as we distance ourselves from our family and friends, our Higher Power, and our values. Fear is a warning sign. It tells us that things aren't right and our well-being may be threatened.

As addicts we make mistakes. Mistakes are normal, and our recovery program is teaching us how to correct our mistakes. But our mistakes and fears can seem to overpower us. That's when our fears can trigger us to drink or use drugs. Fear can control us and keep us frozen in addiction.

Recovery is the movement from the darkness of fear back into the light. At first, the light may scare us and hurt our eyes. We just need to keep walking and grab someone's hand. We are not alone anymore.

PRAYER FOR THE DAY
Higher Power, help me keep walking even
when my fear wants me to cower in the shadows.
If I stay in the darkness, I'm choosing my
addiction over you. Push me toward the light.

TODAY'S ACTION
Today I will list the different ways my addiction controlled me with fear. I will share this list with my sponsor or another recovery friend.

Good can imagine evil; but evil cannot imagine good.
— W. H. Auden

Addiction makes us blind. When we were sick with our addiction, we could not imagine being well. We could not even see a healthy way to live, much less reach it in our own lives. We were hopeless.

We needed help from outside ourselves. We got it. We still get help—every day—in our recovery because we need the help of others to keep our vision of recovery alive. With our sponsors and friends in recovery, we not only imagine goodness and wellness in our lives, we even make it happen.

PRAYER FOR THE DAY

Higher Power, help me let go of denial and blindness. Help me imagine goodness and wellness for myself in recovery. Help me believe that even more good things will come as I practice my recovery program.

TODAY'S ACTION

I will talk with my sponsor about the ways my using made me blind to the good possibilities in life. And I will talk about how much more I can see now—both good things and bad things. I will talk about how I can make better choices now that my disease is under control.

I try to take one day at a time, but sometimes several days attack me all at once.

— *Ashleigh Brilliant*

We all need a little humor in our lives and in the way we work our program. For example, one of the first things we learn in recovery is to take "One day at a time." This is very good advice, so we practice living that way. Most days it works pretty well.

But once in a while it seems like we can't even handle one day. We just can't handle everything that happens along the way, plus carry out our own plans for the day. Perhaps we have to stop and change a flat tire. Or a friend calls and needs help. Or one of our kids has a meltdown in the grocery store. Or maybe all those things happen in the same day! That kind of day used to be our perfect excuse to get high.

Now it's a perfect excuse to take a deep breath, call our sponsor or a friend, and have a good laugh about it. Now we realize that our days are not really ours. We can plan them, but we can't really control them. That's just the way it is, and it's okay.

PRAYER FOR THE DAY
Higher Power, please help me to pay attention to the most important things today. And please, send a few good laughs my way!

TODAY'S ACTION
I will find a few things to laugh about today.

All doors are hard to unlock until you have the key.
— *Robert O'Brien*

When we were using alcohol or drugs, our addiction was like a door we could not open. We could not fix our lives until we found the key. The key was simple once we found it. The key was surrender.

Surrender means we give up fighting with our addiction. We stop fighting to control how much we use alcohol or drugs. We stop fighting to control what happens when we use. We admit that these are fights we cannot win. Alcohol and drugs simply beat the life out of us. We need to give up. We need to walk away from the fight.

Once we found the key and surrendered, we started to feel better. We found out that we are not losers in life; we are only losers when we fight with our disease. None of us can control disease, but we don't need to let it control us or beat us up either. We can avoid the fight by staying sober.

PRAYER FOR THE DAY
Higher Power, help me pick my fights in life.
Help me fight for good and right things, to make
the world a better place. Remind me that picking
a fight with my addiction is a stupid choice.

TODAY'S ACTION
I will make a list of the ways I have become a winner since I surrendered in the fight with alcohol and drugs. I will read the list to my sponsor.

People just want to know that they matter.
                                    — *Oprah Winfrey*

In recovery, we do service work. Service work should not just be seen as helping the still-suffering addict, though we are responsible whenever asked. Service work should include our families and our communities. We need to give back to them. Why? First, we have a debt to repay. But more importantly, it is in doing for others that we discover that our lives hold meaning. By stepping outside of the self-centered core of our addiction, we find value again.

During our using years, both our grandiosity and our self-pity were symptoms of how little we valued ourselves, how little we felt our lives counted. We were bent on destroying ourselves.

Remember, we have a basic human need to feel that our lives have meaning, that our lives make a difference to others. Service work is our shortest way to knowing we count. So we should get out there and make a difference. The world needs us.

PRAYER FOR THE DAY
If self-pity or grandiose behavior start to develop in me, Higher Power, please give me service work to do. Help me see the needs of others and give me the power to satisfy those needs.

TODAY'S ACTION
Today I will look to be of service to others, whether these others are in recovery or not. I will work on developing an attitude and lifestyle of service.

Only the educated are free.

— *Epictetus*

Every one of us gets many chances to continue learning in our lives. We miss many of these chances because we just don't see them. It's very easy to stop learning. We get into habits of doing things the same old way. We stop reading about science or literature or geography or politics. We don't know what's going on in our community. We even eat the same kinds of foods every day.

When we stick with what we already know, we stop growing. Our world and our life get very small. We get stuck. We get left behind. We give up our power to be free.

When we were using, we couldn't be free. Freedom takes energy, and all our energy went into feeding our addiction. Now that we are sober, we have energy to pay attention and to learn. We can break out of the little box we lived in. We can make free choices.

PRAYER FOR THE DAY
Higher Power, help me be free today.
I will pay attention to the new things that you
are trying to teach me so I can make new choices.

TODAY'S ACTION
I will list three ways I could be more free if I learned something new. I will talk with my sponsor about what it takes to really be free.

MARCH

*Made a decision to turn our will and our lives
over to the care of God* as we understood Him.
— *Step Three of Alcoholics Anonymous*

Let's cut right to the heart of the matter: we get in trouble if we try to run our own lives. Our ego starts to mess things up. We try to control things we can't control. We think we are smarter than we are. We start to think we can run things just fine by ourselves. What's the end product? We end up alone—spiritually and sometimes physically—and in trouble.

What we need to do is let the care of our Higher Power run our life. We can use care as a guide because care is what a Higher Power is all about. When we put care into action, we get healing love as a result. So let's put our egos aside and ask our Higher Power to help us do the next right thing.

PRAYER FOR THE DAY
*Higher Power, I've made a decision. I am yours to do with
as you want. I know that you will guide my life with care.*

TODAY'S ACTION
I will write down one way that I can be caring to others and myself today. Acting from care is acting for my Higher Power.

You can pay too high for a bit of soft living.
— *Mary Norton*

We didn't become addicts by choice. We thought we had found an easier, softer way. We thought we could squeeze a little bit more fun and excitement out of life by our drinking or drug use. We thought we could control the outcome of our use, but we could not. Soon it controlled us. Oh, we pretended we were still in control, but in our heart of hearts, we knew we were lost.

Our addiction then asked for our dignity, and we gave it. Our addiction asked for our relationships with those we loved, and we paid up. Addiction asked that we betray our values and spiritual principles, and we did. Addiction kept asking for more, and we kept on paying; this is loss of control.

Social users will not give up their dignity, relationships, and values for their use, but addicts do. This is our illness. Now that we are in recovery, we don't have to give them up either.

PRAYER FOR THE DAY
Higher Power, help me do the things I need to do to stay sober, even if I think they are hard to do— for with your help all things are doable.

TODAY'S ACTION
I will do the hard things first. If there is a call I've put off, I'll make it. If there is someone I need to talk with but I'm afraid to, I'll talk with that person today.

Worry is like a rocking chair. It gives you some-thing to do, but it doesn't get you anywhere.

—*Anonymous*

We addicts need to be very careful when we feel worried because it can lead to relapse. So how can we stop worrying? We can take some clear steps.

First, we need to determine the root of our worry. If necessary, it may help to write down our problem. Second, we should answer these questions: How likely is it that this problem will actually happen? How serious is the problem? How much control do we have over it? Third, we need to make a plan. What could we do about the problem? What would this action solve? Sometimes the best thing we can do is let go. Fourth, we should talk it all over with our sponsor, someone who has faced worry and stays sober.

When we take these steps, we usually learn one of two things: there is a smarter way to handle the problem, or there is nothing we can do about it.

PRAYER FOR THE DAY
Higher Power, help me see what's at the root of my worry and fear, and embrace the wisdom of the Serenity Prayer whenever I feel my anxiety getting the better of me.

TODAY'S ACTION
If I have a worry, I will focus on the Serenity Prayer. If I am not worried today, I will call my sponsor and talk about how the Serenity Prayer helps me avoid worry.

Sometimes one must travel far to discover what is near.
— Uri Shulevitz

The journeys of addiction and recovery take us into many different worlds. During our active addiction, many of those worlds were dangerous and ugly. *We* became dangerous and ugly. A group member once described being drunk and sitting in a crack house: "You could feel and smell the decay in the air, and no one cared." Similarly, we traveled into the dark side of our humanity. We used darkness as our guide.

Recovery takes us into the world of the Steps, the world of spiritual principles. It asks that we dig deep and look into our actions and ourselves. In recovery, the *light* of our Higher Power becomes our guide.

What is it we discovered in both worlds? Self. We are both the dark and the light, the ugly and the beautiful. Recovery gives us the gift of free will. We now get to choose what type of people we will be. We discover that if we stay close to our Higher Power, we also stay close to ourselves, our hearts, our souls.

PRAYER FOR THE DAY
Higher Power, when I become afraid and want to turn away from the light, call me to you.

TODAY'S ACTION
Often it is my fears that have caused me to seek refuge in the shadows. I will write down all the things that scare me about living a life of values.

What, then, is your duty? What the day demands.
— *Johann Wolfgang von Goethe*

We live our new lives in recovery "One day at a time." What a relief. Sometimes the changes we are making seem so big we get a little afraid that we can't do it all. We forget that we don't have to do it all at once. "Easy does it."

Recovery is not just about *what* we do every day (or how much we do). It is much more about *how* we do every day. Am I living today as a person in recovery? Am I being honest, kind, sober, and living by my values? Am I willing to help someone else if they need help?

Of course we need to think about the future, too. We need to have dreams about what our life can be. But these will come. They are not supposed to take our energy today. Today's energy is for living today well.

PRAYER FOR THE DAY
Higher Power, help me live today in your grace.
Help me live a strong, healthy recovery as I
learn that life happens "One day at a time."

TODAY'S ACTION
I will list three things that I handled today like a person in recovery would handle them. I will think about how I would have handled these things when I was using alcohol or drugs. I will call my sponsor and talk about the way I lived today.

You can't steal second base and keep one foot on first.

— Unknown

In recovery, we talk about letting go of the past to make way for growth by saying, "Let go, let God!" There are a lot of things to let go of—attitudes, resentments, behaviors, isolation, stubbornness, anger.

All of these are different forms of fear. All are part of an old life that doesn't fit us anymore. The Third Step suggests that we turn our life over to the care of our Higher Power. We are to let *care,* not *fear,* be our guide in this new life. It is through care that we get closer and closer to our Higher Power. We are to let go and fall into the care and love of our Higher Power. This is how we'll find our way home.

PRAYER FOR THE DAY
Higher Power, I give myself to you, to your care.
Help me to be the most caring and loving person
I can be. For when I'm being caring and loving,
I'm the closest I can be to you.

TODAY'S ACTION
I will make a list of five caring things that I will do today. After I do one of them, I will say a prayer of gratitude then do the next. Then I will think of people I know who are good role models of care and will work to be like them.

*The man does better who runs from disaster than
he who is caught by it.*

—Homer

Human beings are born with survival instincts, and one of them is fear. Our instincts tell us when we better run or fight or hunker down in a hole to wait until the danger passes.

The problem is, our instincts don't always work, especially when the dangers are modern ones like old drinking and using buddies.

Our program tells us to be very careful to stay away from persons, places, and things that are triggers for us. They wake up our Inner Addict and make us want to get high. These dangers don't make us want to run away; instead they tempt us. They lure us to walk into danger.

When we can, we should stay away from those persons, places, and things. If we have to face them—by attending a wedding reception or other family event, for instance—we can take a recovery friend along.

PRAYER FOR THE DAY
*Higher Power, help me develop good instincts
about how to stay sober and safe in my recovery.
Help me be smart about facing slippery situations.*

TODAY'S ACTION
I will make a list of persons, places, and things that might be relapse triggers for me. I will read it to my sponsor.

The spiritual life does not remove us from the world but leads us deeper into it.

— Henri J. M. Nouwen

We get into recovery to get our life back. The shame that is often part of our addiction can have us believe we are second-class citizens. We are not. Recovery demands that we go deeper and deeper into the world.

By moving deeper into the world, we deepen our relationship with our Higher Power. As we are given the gifts of recovery, freedom, care, and love, we are to take these gifts out into the world. The world needs them, just as we need recovery.

We who were hopeless must bring hope to those who need it. We who lived in despair must now bring joy into the larger world. We who lived in shame must now bring dignity to those who seek direction. This is the way of the spirit. We are now givers, not takers.

PRAYER FOR THE DAY
Higher Power, help me to stay on the path of the spirit. Help me to go deeper and deeper into your world.

TODAY'S ACTION
Today I will list five ways I can give more to the world I live in. I will then start to act in a way that will make me a giver and not a taker.

*Kindness is more important than wisdom, and
the recognition of this is the beginning of wisdom.*
— Theodore Rubin

It's more important to be kind than it is to be smart.
Being kind means actually doing things that help other
people and make the world a better place. Being smart,
or wise, is really nothing in itself without action.

Notice what happens when someone pays attention to us
with a smile. We experience a wonderful, heart-warming
feeling. And we can do that for others anytime we want.

It's so easy to do kind things. We can smile and say
hello. Hold a door open for someone. Help with the dishes
after dinner. Send a note or make a phone call to brighten
someone else's day. Make the coffee or set up chairs at
our recovery meeting. Sponsor a newcomer.

When we can, we should do kind actions that are a
bit more difficult. We might help out at a food kitchen for
the poor, run errands for a shut-in neighbor, or coach a
children's sports team. No matter if our kind actions are
big or small, they make the world a happier place.

PRAYER FOR THE DAY
*Higher Power, remind me today that I can do a favor
for you. I can make your love real in the world by giving
away a smile, a greeting, or a kind word to someone.*

TODAY'S ACTION
Today I will practice being kind. I will say hello to at least
five people while I look them in the eye and smile. I will
notice what happens when I do this.

Guilt: the gift that keeps on giving.

— *Erma Bombeck*

Often we are confused about the difference between guilt and shame. Guilt can be good. It tells us that we may be acting in a way that betrays our values. Guilt asks that we keep our behaviors in line with our values. Shame, on the other hand, tells us that we are no good, that we have little, if any, value. This is the lie of shame. Addiction thrives through shame. Recovery heals shame by giving us a new perspective based on responsibility for our disease and dignity in our recovery.

To keep us on the right track, we start our meetings with an admission of our disease, "Hi, my name is _____, and I'm an alcoholic," or "Hi, my name is _____, and I'm a drug addict." In order to keep this perspective in our daily living, we strive for conscious contact with our Higher Power; we seek this through prayer and meditation, which can guide us to stay on the path of the spirit.

PRAYER FOR THE DAY
I pray for conscious contact. Higher Power, tell me when I'm acting in accordance with your wishes, and tell me when I need to change. Thank you for your voice of reason and love.

TODAY'S ACTION
Today I will think about what changes I need to make. I will list any ways my behavior does not match up with my values and share this list with my sponsor.

What makes the desert beautiful is that some-where it hides a well.

—*Antoine de Saint-Exupéry*

No matter how sick we became from our active addiction, recovery is the life-giving water in the desert of our life.

When we think about it, it's amazing that we made it this far without dying. Now as we drink from the well of recovery, we have the strength to leave the desert of addiction and step into a new life.

What's in our well of recovery that gives us strength to leave the desert? Acceptance of our disease, surrender to a new way of living, and hope based in a community of healthy, caring people.

The Big Book says that by the time we do the amends of Step Nine, we will be able to remember our days in the desert without shame.

PRAYER FOR THE DAY

Higher Power, you led me to the well of life in my desert.
It was filled with the water of recovery. Thank you.

TODAY'S ACTION

How was my addicted life like a desert? How is my life in recovery like living in a fertile land? I will write down my thoughts. Perhaps I will write a poem.

There is enough in the world for everyone's need,
but not enough for everyone's greed.

— Frank Buchman

Ours is an illness of *more*. More! More! More! The greed of addiction decays the soul and leaves us to desperately try to fill the hole that is left behind, but there is never enough. The greed of addiction also keeps us running from the responsibility of a relationship with our Higher Power. Over time we're left with great spiritual pain.

Recovery asks us to replace greed with gratitude. If we are sober today, that is enough. We should be grateful. If we can make one person smile today, that is enough. We should be grateful. If we have a place to rest our head and food to nourish our body, that is enough. We should be grateful. As our needs are met, we give thanks instead of demanding more.

PRAYER FOR THE DAY
Higher Power, help me become a person who
is thankful for the gift of life and sobriety. Help
me give thanks for the challenges as well as the
easy times. Help me to see that I am enough.

TODAY'S ACTION
Today I will make a list of all the things for which I am grateful. I will give thanks to my Higher Power, especially for my sobriety.

Sleep is the golden chain that ties health and our bodies together.
— *Thomas Dekker*

Sleep is a wonderful gift in our lives. For eight hours, we rest our bodies. We let the thoughts, feelings, and events of our lives tumble through our sleeping minds as they sort themselves through our dreams.

But dreams are not always happy. Some of us are afraid to sleep. Our dreams scare us. We may dream about using again or about bad things that happened. But we shouldn't let our dreams fool us. They are not reality. They are just feelings, thoughts, and memories working themselves out. In early recovery, there are a lot of things to sort out.

We create the reality of our lives by the choices we make when we are awake: how much we trust in our Higher Power, how we care for ourselves, how we treat others, how we work our program.

PRAYER FOR THE DAY
Higher Power, help me listen to the messages of my dreams. Help me understand that my dreams will get better as my life gets better.

TODAY'S ACTION
I will listen to my dreams. What is my mind working out in my sleep? If I remember my dreams, I will talk about them with my wide-awake friends.

Seriousness is the only refuge of the shallow.
— Oscar Wilde

One of the gifts of recovery is learning to laugh again, especially at ourselves and our silly little problems. Our egos make us take ourselves way too seriously. They tell us we are the center of the universe. This is not true.

When we find ourselves taking ourselves too seriously, we have lost perspective. We need to get to a meeting and call our sponsor.

Recovery teaches us what is important. We learn that spiritual principles are much more important than petty conflicts and concerns. The program tells us to put "Principles before personalities." If we can do this, we'll gain perspective and humility. We'll also lighten up, smile, and laugh again.

PRAYER FOR THE DAY
Higher Power, help me keep problems in perspective.
Allow me to be a humble servant. Remind me
to place spiritual principles before ego.

TODAY'S ACTION
Today I will write down five examples of times when I took myself too seriously. What spiritual principles could have helped me do things differently?

The body is like a piano. It is needful to have the instrument in good order.

— Henry Ward Beecher

Why does our body matter? Because it's where our thoughts, feelings, and spirit all reside. We need a healthy brain in order to think well. We need balanced hormones in order to have balanced emotions. We need strong and limber arms and legs, and a strong back if we want to play well with others.

Now that we are sober, we can take good care of our body. We can eat healthy food, get enough sleep, and exercise. We can deal with an addiction to tobacco or sugar that can lead to lung disease or diabetes.

We have been given back our life. Let's keep our body in tune so we can make pretty music with our life.

PRAYER FOR THE DAY

Higher Power, thank you for saving me from my addiction to alcohol and drugs. Help me keep my body in tune so I can live well and love well with this life you have given me.

TODAY'S ACTION

I will take a look at how I care for my body. Do I neglect it? Abuse it? How can I take good care of my body so that my mind, feelings, and movements stay healthy and strong? I will do one good thing for my body today.

It got to the point that I felt even my own shadow was against me.

— *Anonymous*

Often during our active addiction, we trusted no one. We felt everyone was out to get us, out to cheat us. We became the kings and queens of self-pity. The reality was, we *were* being cheated, but not by others. An illness called addiction cheated us out of our dignity and integrity. It brought out the worst in us. It was very unpleasant, and we became very unpleasant to be around.

Recovery asks us to step past the blaming and self-pity, and see our illness as the cheat. We do inventories in order to see past the denial and see the values we believe in. We work to better ourselves in order to have a pleasant life and be pleasant people. We stop seeing ourselves as entitled. Instead we see what needs to be done.

PRAYER FOR THE DAY
*Higher Power, help me be of service
and move past my self-pity.*

TODAY'S ACTION
Today I will list my favorite ways to feel sorry for myself. I will read this list to my group members and ask them to confront me if they see me using any of these.

A knowledge of the path cannot be substituted for putting one foot in front of the other.

— *M. C. Richards*

Once in a while we meet someone who hangs around recovery but does not really step into it. These people know all about the Twelve Steps. They sound very wise. They might even go to meetings. But they don't stay sober.

Why not? Because knowing about something is different from doing it. "Doing it" means more than going to meetings and learning the lingo of recovery. It means asking a strong role model to be our sponsor and staying in close touch with that person. It means working the Steps with our sponsor's help.

Every day we put one foot in front of the other. We go to meetings. We read the Big Book. We pray or meditate. We ask for our Higher Power's help. We call our sponsor. We fill our time with good things—work, healthy relationships, and self-care.

PRAYER FOR THE DAY
Higher Power, please help me really work a good recovery program. I know it takes practice every day to live in this new way. Recovery is a practice.

TODAY'S ACTION
Today I will work on a Step. I will call my sponsor. I will spend a few minutes in prayer or meditation. I will be of service to someone else.

The purpose of life is life.
— *Karl Lagerfeld*

Our active addiction took us away from a life connected to our Higher Power, family, friends, community, and spiritual principles. During our active addiction, our primary relationship was with alcohol or drugs. Addiction is an illness of mistaken relationship. We believed we could get emotional needs meet through a relationship with chemicals. We can't.

Now, in recovery, we get back to living instead of dying. We work to heal the wounds our illness created within our families. We see trust being created. We no longer avoid police officers, for we are respectable citizens again. We regularly pray and meditate. We feel the presence of our Higher Power again in our life.

PRAYER FOR THE DAY
Higher Power, you gave me life for a purpose.
Help me live that purpose to its fullest. When I
want to avoid life, place me back in the middle of it.
When I feel like I can't go on, give me strength.

TODAY'S ACTION
Today I will do at least one task that I have been avoiding. I will remind myself that avoiding tasks takes more energy than doing them.

Looking for happiness is like clutching a shadow or chasing the wind.
— *Japanese Proverb*

We don't enter recovery and find that we are happy right away. Our program tells us that if we really work on the Steps, we will know a new freedom and a new happiness after we take Step Nine.

How do we get there? By trying to race straight to Step Nine so that we can get to the happy part faster? No. If we skip some Steps or work them poorly, our program is weak.

Working the Steps is like building a house for ourselves to live in. When we do it right, the house is strong and safe and warm.

Like a solid house, our life becomes a safer place to be when we work the Steps. By the time we work Step Nine, we have straightened out our big mistakes as best we can. We have gotten to know ourselves much better and learned to act in line with our values. We can be proud of ourselves. What do you know? We're happy!

PRAYER FOR THE DAY
Higher Power, I want to be happy. Help me do the things that will get me there, one step and one day at a time.

TODAY'S ACTION
I will list five things I am happy about in my recovery. I will tell a friend what is special about these things.

*What lies behind us and what lies before us are
small matters compared to what lies within us.*
— *Ralph Waldo Emerson*

During our active addiction, we were filled with sadness, frustration, bitterness, and fear. These are the
by-products of addiction. The most spiritual moments
we had were when we felt pain and regret over hurting
others. But our addiction kept us from acting on these
feelings, for to do so meant we would have had to face
the truth we were denying.

Now we go to meetings and read and study spiritual
principles. We are involved in our communities. We go
to sporting events to follow the game, instead of to get
drunk. We invite people to our homes to eat, laugh, and
enjoy each other's good company. We know now that
what we pay attention to grows.

PRAYER FOR THE DAY
*Higher Power, I open up my heart to you. Fill me
with your joy and love. Help me live a life of values.*

TODAY'S ACTION
Today I will be conscious of what I do to nurture a positive
inner life. I will work to pay attention to joy and gratitude.

He who helps a friend in woe is like a fur coat in the snow.
— *Russian Proverb*

We came in from a very hard life when we came into recovery, kind of like coming in from a blizzard in Siberia! The old life was dangerous, cold, and lonely, and it forced us to use all our energy just to survive. Sooner or later it would have killed us. We were definitely in woe.

Someone—a family member, a friend, a boss, a probation officer—offered us a chance to get sober. That person saved our life, as surely as if he or she walked out into a blizzard and wrapped around us like a warm coat. Thanks to our Higher Power, we accepted the help this time.

In the future we will have the chance to help others who are still out there freezing in the blizzard of addiction. We can offer them the kind of help that saved our life. We can't make them accept our help though. We just keep it handy, like a fur coat, in case they reach out to accept it.

PRAYER FOR THE DAY
*Higher Power, I am willing to help another addict.
I will be ready when you put someone in front of me.*

TODAY'S ACTION
Is there an alcoholic or an addict in my life I wish I could help? I realize that my example is the best way to show them recovery. I will talk with my sponsor about this person and how I am best able to help him or her today.

Be not afraid of life. Believe that life is worth living, and your belief will help create the fact.

— William James

One of the most beautiful gifts of recovery is not having to be afraid of life anymore. Our active addiction controlled us and made us live in constant fear. Would we be found out? Were the police going to catch us? Was our spouse going to divorce us? Hundreds of scary questions filled our mind to the point that we wondered if life was worth living. It's no wonder that we lose a lot of fellow addicts to suicide.

In recovery, we meet others with the same illness who are filled with hope and a joy of living. We want what they have. We work the Steps to get it, and over time we start to believe that life is again worth living. This belief helps us through tough times. This belief allows us to push away negative thoughts and other people's negativity. We have replaced a life of fear with a life of joy. This is the essence of recovery.

PRAYER FOR THE DAY
Higher Power, when fear enters into my mind, help me push past it and find my way back into your loving arms.

TODAY'S ACTION
Today I will list things I was afraid of during my active addiction. I will cross out the fears that don't exist anymore. Then I will talk to my sponsor about the ones that are left.

*There's a lot of hope and a lot of faith and love
mixed up in a miracle.*
— Meindert DeJong

A miracle is an event that we can't explain with the laws of nature or science. We believe a miracle is a supernatural happening that some Higher Power played a hand in. For many of us, recovery is our own personal miracle. We were sick. We tried to stop our daily slide into sickness, but we could not. We were hopeless.

Then we found ourselves with new possibilities. We could get sober, get better, and have a good life. A miracle made what was once impossible seem possible.

What happened? We were touched by the hope, faith, and love of our Higher Power and others. And we accepted it. We opened our hearts and let healing in. The light in our spirit was turned on, and we were shown the way to recovery.

PRAYER FOR THE DAY
*Higher Power, thank you for the miracle that
pulled me out of addiction. Thank you for the hope,
faith, and love that showed me a way out.*

TODAY'S ACTION
With hope, faith, and love, today I will further open my heart to allow more change in myself and in my life.

Everyone has inside of him a piece of good news.
— Anne Frank

As we work the inventory Steps, we are pushed to examine our insides, to look for mistakes we have made. We also find the good news inside of us—that our values never left us. We still have them.

We did know right from wrong during our active addiction. We see this when we remember how bad we felt about hurting others and ourselves. This pain was caused by our values trying to get our attention. Through working the Steps in recovery, we transform this good news into a good life. We transform our pain into a new commitment to living a good life. We not only find the good news inside of us, we *become* the good news to others.

PRAYER FOR THE DAY
*Higher Power, help me find the good news inside of me.
Help me carry this good news back into the community
as a living example that recovery works.*

TODAY'S ACTION
When was the last time I did a Fourth Step? Is it time to do another? Am I doing a Tenth Step on a regular basis? I will talk with my sponsor about these questions.

There's a rhythm to flying, and it's the rhythm of the universe.
— William Steig

Nature has a lot to teach us. One of these lessons is to stop trying to control everything and "Let go and let God." Think of a flock of geese flying in a V-formation. What a beautiful sight! How do you think all those geese know what to do? It's all in the rhythm of the universe.

How does a seed know when to sprout? How do our hearts know when to beat and our lungs know when to breathe? It's all in the rhythm of the universe.

We each have a rhythm to our lives. We lost it somewhere along the way—perhaps in our active addiction, perhaps earlier. When we move too fast, we waste a lot of energy. When we move too slow, we miss out. But when we make the decision to put our life and our will into the care of our Higher Power, we will find the right rhythm for us. We just let go, and the timing will come to us as we practice listening to the rhythm of our spirit.

PRAYER FOR THE DAY
Higher Power, teach me to live like the geese fly,
with grace and direction and with my friends.

TODAY'S ACTION
Today I will think of a time I tried to control things, when I had the timing all wrong. Then I will think of a time when everything went well, and the timing was perfect. What am I learning about rhythm and trust?

I have never seen a greater monster or miracle than myself.
— Michel Eyquem de Montaigne

During our active addiction, many of us became monsters. We hurt our family and anyone who dared care about us. Now as we sit in our healing circles and listen to the stories of others, we realize that we weren't alone in our actions. We often hear tales of people destroying everything they ever loved. Then came recovery.

Now we hear and see the miracles. We meet people whom everyone had given up on. They become good, sober people and good citizens again. We see courage replace fear; we see hope replace hopelessness; we see gentleness replace anger. We have the honor of witnessing miracles in the making. We've been given the gift of seeing the healing power of spiritual principles brought to life in the actions of our members.

Recovery doesn't keep us from being monsters, it just gives us the choice: will we be monsters or miracles?

PRAYER FOR THE DAY
Higher Power, help me remember that I am responsible for who I become and how I act. Help me to be a walking miracle and living example of the healing power of your love.

TODAY'S ACTION
On a piece of paper, I will make two columns. In the first, I will write down ways I have acted like a monster. In the second, I will write down ways I am a miracle.

You shall judge a man by his foes as well as by his friends.

— *Joseph Conrad*

Hopefully, now that we are in recovery, we like people who are honest and kind. We like people who stand for values and principles we respect. We are learning to admire and like people who do a good job of living in a way that makes the world a little better for others.

Not everyone is the kind of person we want as a friend. There are people who are misguided. They care more about objects, money, and power than they care for people. Sometimes they do a great deal of harm to others.

It is true that others judge us by who we choose as friends and who we take a stand against. We can learn about ourselves this way, too. We can help ourselves grow into better people by choosing to be around people who are the kind of people we want to be.

PRAYER FOR THE DAY
Higher Power, help me be on the positive side of things. Line me up with people who will help me continue to move my life forward in a positive way, and help me be alert to people who bring trouble.

TODAY'S ACTION
I will list those who seem to be my foe right now and talk with my sponsor about how to handle my feelings and behavior around them.

If you want a quality, act as if you already have it.
— William James

We hear a lot about this in our recovery groups: "Fake it till you make it." When we start out in recovery, we don't know how to do recovery. As active addicts, we only knew how to act like addicts. So the first year or so of recovery is largely learning how to act like and become sober people. We get to be beginners.

What is important is that we work hard to become the people we want to become. If we act respectful, some day we will become respectful. We don't know when, but it will occur. Next, we will become respectable. If we act with dignity, we will become dignified. If we act from love, some day we will become loving. This is the miracle of spiritual principles: when we regularly put them into action, we become them.

PRAYER FOR THE DAY
Higher Power, you have given me spiritual principles. Now help me live them so the power they hold can heal my life.

TODAY'S ACTION
Today I will talk with my sponsor or a recovery friend about what spiritual principles I want to embrace. I will then write down behaviors I can do to help me live these principles.

*Each thing she learned became part of herself, to
be used over and over in new adventures.*

— *Kate Seredy*

We started working our recovery program for one reason:
to stop our disease from controlling our life. Once we
recover our ability to live in a sane way, a funny thing
happens—we discover that we're learning so much.

First we learn we have a disease that we can recover
from. Then we learn about ourselves—our strengths and
weaknesses, and our values. Next we learn how to live
better. Then we learn how to have healthy relationships.
Finally we have a spiritual awakening.

These are huge changes. We learn things in recovery
that we will use in all areas of our life. We now have the
skills and courage to follow the lead of our Higher Power
into new adventures as we develop our relationships and
our talents, and find a way to make a difference in our
own corner of the world.

PRAYER FOR THE DAY
*Higher Power, help me learn what you
want me to know and to be who you want me to be.
Then help me do what you want me to do with my life.
I'm getting ready for the adventure.*

TODAY'S ACTION
I will think about the limits I put on myself in the past
because I didn't know any better. I will talk with my sponsor or a recovery friend about how my horizons are broad-
ening already.

Either this man is dead or my watch has stopped.
— *Groucho Marx*

Recovery is about getting busy and getting a purpose. We didn't get sober just to sit in meetings. We get sober to get back into the busyness and joy of living. We go on picnics and laugh with our family. We volunteer and help our community. We show up at our job and add our ideas and creativity. (We've called in sick often enough!) We do hobbies, take care of ourselves, and learn to enjoy our own company.

Sobriety asks that we keep walking into life. As active addicts, we backed away from life and unknowingly were backing into death. Sobriety asks that we fall in love with living again. The world needs more people in love with living. So let's get busy living! The world needs what we have to offer.

PRAYER FOR THE DAY
*During my active addiction, I often acted as if
life weren't important. Higher Power, accept my apology,
for you are life, and I acted as if I didn't need you.*

TODAY'S ACTION
Today I will practice acting with purpose. I will be busy in ways that improve my sobriety and increase my joy of living.

The reason most people are bad is because they do not try to be good.

— *L. Frank Baum*

Many of the best people you'll ever meet are addicts in recovery. "Normal" people just don't pay as much attention to how they live their lives. Recovering addicts really work at being good people, and it shows.

Our program not only asks us to pay attention to being good—doing the next right thing—it also gives us many ways to practice and learn. We do service at our meetings. We talk openly about what is going on in our life and listen to the feedback others give us. We try to live in line with our values.

We learn discipline, too. We don't drink or use drugs. We go to meetings. We stay in touch with our sponsor. We work the Steps. We are not lazy, because recovery keeps us busy.

PRAYER FOR THE DAY
Higher Power, I'm willing to work at being a good person today in order to stay sober and get well. Please guide me gently and help me do the most important things for today.

TODAY'S ACTION
What do I like about how I act today that is different from what I used to do? I will write down five things.

APRIL

*Made a searching and fearless moral inventory of
ourselves.*
— *Step Four of Alcoholics Anonymous*

Who, exactly, are we? We have admitted in Step One
that we are addicts, dependent on alcohol or drugs. We
know that we are not exactly the same persons we were
before this disease took hold of us; it has changed us.

Step Four suggests that we take a long hard look at ourselves. What are our values? Our feelings? Our behaviors?
What can these things tell us about the persons we are
inside? The Big Book or a Fourth Step guide can help us
make this inventory.

Some of what we find will be good. A lot of what we
find will be things we really don't want to admit and take
responsibility for. That's because our disease has changed
the way our brain works, making it harder to be true to
ourselves. Step Four is strong medicine to help us get well.

PRAYER FOR THE DAY
*Higher Power, help me be fearless and thorough in
doing my Fourth Step. Help me remember that, although
I may not like it, I need to do it in order to get well.*

TODAY'S ACTION
Have I taken my Fourth Step? If not, I will ask my sponsor
to help me do a fearless and searching moral inventory.
The sooner I do this work, the faster I will heal.

*It's the friends you can call up at 4 a.m. that
matter.*
— *Marlene Dietrich*

A recovery friend once said, "There have been only two
people in my life that I've called up at 4 a.m.: my mom,
to get me out of jail, and my sponsor, to help keep me
from drinking and ending up in jail."

Many of us may also remember calling up a recovery
friend in the wee hours of the morning and hearing a
calm, caring voice on the other end of the phone. Or we
may have had the experience of having a recovery friend
call us in the middle of the night and perhaps even spend-
ing the night on our couch.

We create safety for each other when we can't create
it for ourselves. This is the nature of recovery. Having
friends and fellowship that will be there for us whenever
there is a need is a gift and a privilege. We should honor
it well.

PRAYER FOR THE DAY
*Higher Power, thank you for the fellowship and
for friends who will be there for me during the best
of times and especially during the worst of times.*

TODAY'S ACTION
I will take time and think about which of my recovery
friends have helped me the most. I will call and thank
them for their care and kindness.

Nature has given us two ears, but only one mouth.
— *Benjamin Disraeli*

We've all heard that we should listen twice as much as we talk. That's pretty good advice. Listening is how we learn what works for other people like us. Listening is how we hear the experience, strength, and hope that others share with us. If we don't listen, we won't know how to change and grow.

But we also need to talk. We need to share what we are thinking and doing each day, and how we are feeling. There are many good things we get from talking. For example, we get a chance to listen to ourselves, and that helps us know ourselves better. We also get care, attention, and understanding. This is how we make friends. And when we talk with others, they give us feedback that can improve our ideas.

In recovery, we listen and we share. We get and we give. We find that we learn something every time we agree or disagree with someone else's ideas. Most important, we learn how it works for others and what we can try for ourselves.

PRAYER FOR THE DAY
Higher Power, help me listen carefully and often today.
And remind me to share my thoughts, too.

TODAY'S ACTION
I will list ten helpful things I learned today by listening.

*A real friend is one who walks in when the rest of
the world walks out.*
— *Walter Winchell*

Most of us walked into the healing circles of recovery
after the rest of the world had walked out on us. It was
here that many of us found a home and new friends. We
told these new friends why we couldn't ever like ourselves again, and all they said was, "Welcome." We told
them of how we came mainly because we had no place
else to go; they offered us a chair and a cup of coffee.

These new friends made room for us. They made
room for us to heal and find our spirits again. If they had
judgments, they kept them from us and taught us about
the Steps instead. They taught us much and did it with
patience. In return, they only asked that when we see
others in need, we make room for them.

PRAYER FOR THE DAY
*Higher Power, thank you for those who had the courage
to walk before me. Thank you for those who walked
with me when I had given up on myself. Help me to be
there for the still-suffering addicts who will follow.*

TODAY'S ACTION
Today, tomorrow, or when I go to my next meeting, I will
seek out the newest members and ask them how they are
doing. I will ask them if I can walk with them for a bit.

Those people are earthbound. They heap too many goods. They have not learned the trail of beauty.
— *Laura Adams Armer*

If we want to walk the trail of beauty, we are better off bringing a backpack than a moving van to carry our stuff. We need to travel light.

The point is, stuff—things, belongings—can tie us down if we become too attached. We can pass up wonderful adventures because we can't let go of stuff.

There are some things we need, of course. And it's okay to have more than we need as long as it doesn't get in the way of our lives. Our lives are for loving and learning and serving others, not for taking care of our things. When our things take too much of our time and energy, we have too much.

We can do with our stuff what we do with our thoughts and our feelings—look them over, see if they still work for us, and decide whether to keep them or let them go.

PRAYER FOR THE DAY
Higher Power, I don't want to get stuck in my emotional, mental, or physical stuff. Help me sort through it and keep only what adds service or beauty to my life.

TODAY'S ACTION
I will think for a few minutes about how I think and feel about having my own things. What things are important to me? Why? I will talk with someone about this topic and listen to how it is for that person, too.

He that shuts love out, in turn, shall be shut out
from love.
— *Alfred Tennyson*

Addiction caused us to turn away from love. We started to feel things weren't right; this feeling was a message of love from our Higher Power. We used denial or blame to turn away. Our family members told us they were worried; this was another message of love. We argued and blamed them. Our friends expressed concerns, still another message of love. We dumped them and got new friends. And then we wondered why we felt like love had turned its back on us.

Recovery pushes us back toward love. People treat us with care and kindness; these are messages of love. They ask that we turn to a Higher Power, a further message of love. We used to shut out love because our addiction demanded this of us. Now we must embrace love because our recovery requires this of us.

PRAYER FOR THE DAY
Higher Power, help me to do what love asks of me,
even when I'm scared.

TODAY'S ACTION
I will list the ways I shut out love during my active addiction. Am I doing any of these today? I will use my Tenth Step to keep track of my relationship with love.

*If you can learn from hard knocks, you can also
learn from soft touches.*
— *Carolyn Kenmore*

At our meetings, we often hear recovering addicts say,
"It seems like I never change until it hurts too much not
to." Or "No one could help me until I hit bottom." Why
is it that we see ourselves as people who have to learn
the hard way?

Wouldn't it be nice if we could learn the easy way for a
change? After all we are smart people. We could always
figure out a way to get what we wanted as long as it was
something bad for us.

Now that we are sober, we can put our brains to use in
better ways. We can learn without having to suffer first.
When we see a behavior that needs changing, we can
change it. We don't have to wait until it gets us in big trouble. Sometimes we might need our Higher Power's help to
change, and we ask for it in Steps Seven and Eleven. Our
recovery program teaches us to change with grace and
joy, not always with pain and problems.

PRAYER FOR THE DAY
*Higher Power, if something needs to be changed,
help me see it and change it. Help me see it clearly
and quickly so my lessons can be gentle.*

TODAY'S ACTION
I will take an inventory of my behavior and thoughts over
the last day. If I see something that is a problem, I will talk
with my sponsor about how to change it.

Live courage, breathe courage, and give courage.
— *Dhan Gopal Mukerji*

Courage relates to self-confidence. Self-confidence is tied to our relationship with power. As we attached more and more to alcohol, drugs, and self-defeating behaviors, we lost power. We lost the courage to face the world and others. We ran deeper and deeper into the black hole of our addiction. Fear was chasing us. It was hard to face what we were becoming.

Recovery asks us to attach to spiritual principles—to place "Principles before personality," to "Practice these principles in all our affairs." Why? First, because they keep us sober, but also for the power these principles hold. They have power beyond our knowledge.

As we let their power into our being, we become more powerful. We get the power and courage to handle situations that used to baffle us. Fear leaves us. More courage is given to us. Feelings of uselessness and self-pity disappear. We find courage to face the world.

PRAYER FOR THE DAY
Higher Power, help me to place your principles
before my ego. Help me to live courage, breathe
courage, and give courage to others.

TODAY'S ACTION
Today I will examine how fear controlled my life during my active addiction. I will ask myself, "Am I acting in a more courageous way now that I'm in recovery?"

If you were going to die soon and had only one
call you could make, who would you call and
what would you say? And why are you waiting?
— *Stephen Levine*

When we were in the depths of our addiction, we could
not be truly present in our relationships. We could not
do the work of being caring and responsible. We were
too focused on using alcohol or drugs to change our
own feelings.

Now that we are sober, we can change. We clean up
our messes when we work Steps Eight and Nine. We list
the people we have harmed, think about it, and then we
make amends to them.

Cleaning up our old messes makes us free to start over.
We keep a better eye on our own behavior as we take our
inventory every day in Step Ten, and we become decent,
real human beings. We make real friends. Family members
begin to trust us with their love. Our new sober life
gradually fills up with people.

PRAYER FOR THE DAY
Higher Power, help me be a real human being today.
Help me understand my importance to others and
treat my relationships with the respect they deserve.

TODAY'S ACTION
I will imagine that I don't have long to live and have only
one call I can make. Who will I call, and what will I say?
And why am I waiting? I will make that call today. If I
need support, I will get it from a friend.

In three words I can sum up everything I've learned about life: it goes on.

— Robert Frost

Most of us addicts are afraid of anything we can't control. Life is one of these things. During our drinking and drugging days, we had checked out of life. We were sitting on the sidelines, pretending we could get back into it whenever we wanted. But life went on without us. Friends built careers and loving families, and we fell behind. Friends built deeper intimate relationships. They become skillful at living a life of values and communicating with their Higher Power. We fell behind.

Working the Steps requires us to get working. Ours is a program of action. At times we will want to stop and sit on the side of the road again. But we must go on! Go and be of service. Go talk to a friend. Go to an extra meeting. We got sober to have a life, not to sit on the sidelines. We must be recovery in motion, living a program of action.

PRAYER FOR THE DAY
Place me in the middle of life, Higher Power.
Help me be a person of action. When fear says, "Stop!"
please whisper in my ear, "Go on, go on!"

TODAY'S ACTION
Today I will be active and involved in my program and in life. I will be a doer not a watcher.

It is as hard to see one's self as to look backward
without turning around.
— *Henry David Thoreau*

Getting to know ourselves is hard work. We spent years
in our addiction trying not to see what was really going
on with us.

Now we have a new way to see things. We understand
that we have a disease that tries to fool us—and makes
fools of us. But we can change the foolishness by facing
the disease. We now face it, and we do what we need to
do every day to stay in recovery.

To get to know ourselves and face our disease, we ask
our sponsor and our recovery friends to give us feedback.
We tell them about everything that goes on in our lives so
that they can get to know us well. Then they can help us
get to know ourselves.

This could be very self-centered, except for one thing:
we do the same for them. That's how we help each other
learn to act like the decent and loving human beings we
want to be.

PRAYER FOR THE DAY
Higher Power, help me pay attention to myself and my
friends in recovery. Help me give and accept feedback.

TODAY'S ACTION
I will think of one behavior I do that I want input on. I will
call two of my recovery friends and ask them about how
they see me when I do this behavior and how they think it
affects my recovery.

We need to listen to one another.
— Chaim Potok

Listening is an important skill to cultivate. We need to sit in our healing circles, and lovingly listen and learn from each other. We are each other's teachers. Our sponsors listen to our troubles, and we listen to their suggestions. We pray to our Higher Power and then meditate, a form of listening, from which we develop conscious contact with our Higher Power.

Listening is one of the gifts we give to each other. Listening is also one of the gifts we give to ourselves. As we listen to others and learn from them, we stop thinking we are the center of the universe. Listening to others—to truly hear what they say, to learn from them—helps keep our egos in check. We should frequently ask ourselves, "Am I practicing the skills of active listening?"

PRAYER FOR THE DAY
Higher Power, today I pray that I may open myself
to hearing your voice in the words of others.
Allow me to see the people around me as teachers.
Help me stay open to being taught.

TODAY'S ACTION
Today I will listen. I will notice those times when I stop listening and start judging. I will bring myself back into listening mode. Today I will be a learner.

*There are some people that if they don't know,
you can't tell.*
— Louis Armstrong

We all know people like that. In fact, most of us used to be people like that. Nobody could tell us anything we didn't want to hear without facing our defenses.

We all had our own favorite defense mechanisms that we used to push people away when they tried to tell us something. For some of us, our favorite defense was denial. We simply said, "No, that's not how it is." Others of us said, "Yes, it's a problem, but it is caused by someone else, not me." Or we used this one: "I know I shouldn't act that way, but I am just no good, and I can't do anything about it." Or we said, "It's not that bad."

In recovery, we don't have to put up our defenses anymore. Now we can listen to what others tell us and think about it. We can check out new ideas. In the end, we can take what we like and leave the rest.

What a relief. We don't have to be know-it-alls anymore. We can relax and learn. Life can be interesting again.

PRAYER FOR THE DAY
*Higher Power, help me enjoy learning from others.
Help me listen well, think clearly, and ask for advice.*

TODAY'S ACTION
I will list the three favorite defenses I used when people tried to tell me something I didn't want to hear. Then I will talk with my sponsor or a recovery friend about how I am changing these defenses.

Learn by practice.

— *Martha Graham*

We were practicing addicts. We were working to perfect our craft; we were *good* at being addicts. Let us practice recovery with the same intensity. We need to practice the Steps. We need to work to deepen our relationship with them. We must practice patience and tolerance with ourselves and others.

Remember we're working to be in this for the long haul. We seek humility not perfection, progress not perfection. We seek to learn and better ourselves at being ordinary people. We seek to enjoy the journey, knowing it will never be over. And as we practice and learn, we step deeper into life and sobriety.

PRAYER FOR THE DAY
*Higher Power, each day help me show up for practice
and enjoy the process of learning.*

TODAY'S ACTION
At the end of today, I will take some time and ask, "What did I learn today that will help me live a good, sober life? What will I practice at tomorrow?"

*Appreciation is a wonderful thing; it makes what
is excellent in others belong to us as well.*

— Voltaire

Appreciation is a big word for a big idea. To appreciate a thing means to really look at its value, its goodness, its beauty and to be glad about it. When we can do this, it changes our life. We become grateful.

It used to be that we felt jealous when someone else was attractive or smart. We felt envy when we saw people who were having fun or who seemed to be in love with each other.

Now that we are sober, we know that we can enjoy the beauty other people create. We can be happy that some people are smart and good at problem-solving. We can be glad that people are in love and raise good kids who will make the world a little better.

When we see these things around us, we know that life holds good things for us, too. There is enough for everyone.

PRAYER FOR THE DAY
*Higher Power, help me turn my envy and
jealousy into appreciation. I want to find joy
and hope in the good things that others do.*

TODAY'S ACTION
Today I will list three qualities I appreciate in others. Do I want to find these things in myself? How can I do that? I will talk about it with my sponsor.

Go to the truth beyond the mind. Love is the bridge.
— *Stephen Levine*

Our best thinking often got us in trouble. We convinced ourselves that doing the absolutely wrong thing was right. We thought we knew what was real and true. We fought to defend our truths. We became self-righteous, arrogant, and full of ego. These attitudes kept us from the truth. Why? Because what was missing was love. We replaced love of people and love of spiritual principles with love of alcohol and drugs, and love of self. We rejected divine love and chose self-centeredness instead.

Recovery asks us to risk telling the truth again. We start our meetings by stating the truth of why we are there: "Hi, my name is _____, and I'm an addict." We do inventories to discover truths about ourselves. The love we show each other and the love of our Higher Power help nurse us back to health. Love is the bridge that makes us willing to face the truth. We use the Steps to cross this bridge and find the truths that will set us free.

PRAYER FOR THE DAY
Higher Power, you are both truth and love.
Help me to see you in the challenges of my day.

TODAY'S ACTION
Today I will call a member in the program whom I respect and ask that person to tell me how love has helped him or her get to the truths needed to stay sober.

Assume a virtue, if you have it not.
— *William Shakespeare*

Our recovery program tells us to "Act as if." If we wish we had more faith, we will act as if we had it and see what happens. If we wish we were more honest, we will tell the truth and see what happens. If we wish we were brave, we will take the actions a brave person would take and see what happens.

Face it. Few of us are as good, kind, brave, generous, honest, and loyal as we would like to be. But the way we become who we want to be is simple. First think about how we will act in a difficult situation, then do it. In the beginning, it feels a little phony, but that's okay. Our program also says it's a good thing to "Fake it 'til you make it."

Hey, we can do that! We can't remake ourselves and fix everything all at once, but we can fake it a little. We can act like a kind person. We can do what a brave person would do. We can say what an honest person would say. Let's just call it practicing the program.

PRAYER FOR THE DAY
*Higher Power, help me recognize times to practice
"Acting as if" today. Help me act as if I were
already the kind of person I hope to be some day.*

TODAY'S ACTION
I will be aware today of the chances to act the way I would like to act instead of the way I am used to acting. I will write a sentence or two about what I learned.

*He who is devoid of the power to forgive is devoid
of the power of love.*
— Martin Luther King Jr.

We heal through forgiveness and love. We learn to forgive others by learning to let go of resentments. We learn to forgive, often by watching how others forgive us for the wrongs and hurt we have put on them. The Ninth Step is very helpful in showing us how other people are willing to forgive us even before we are willing to forgive ourselves. Over time we also come to learn how to forgive ourselves for the pain and damage we created during our active addiction.

Forgiveness is a powerful spiritual principle. It helps us accept that the past will never be different. Forgiveness frees up lots of our energy so we can direct it toward building our new sober life. We come to see that forgiveness—of others and of self—is an act of love.

PRAYER FOR THE DAY
*Higher Power, help me to forgive others and myself
for our weakness. Help me see weakness as
humanness and our reason for needing you.*

TODAY'S ACTION
Today I will make a list of the people toward whom I have resentments, and I will pray for each person.

It's often safer to be in chains than to be free.
— *Franz Kafka*

Some days we wish we could have stayed in a nice, safe detox unit or treatment center forever. Our choices and decisions were easier, and the temptations were farther away. Freedom is a challenge for us. We can do anything we want with it. But we had better choose a path and do what we really want to do, or our freedom will be our downfall.

Why? Because living with our freedom is like riding a bicycle. As long as we are willing to pedal our bike, we can go many places. If we stop pedaling, sooner or later we will fall over. We can do many things with our lives as long as we are willing to do the work. We can coast a bit to rest, but too much coasting means we fall over or go downhill.

Our recovery program teaches us to pedal—to do the work we need to do to stay free—and to use our freedom in the best possible ways.

PRAYER FOR THE DAY
*Higher Power, thank you for the freedom to choose
what I make of my life. Please guide me as I pedal
and help me find my pace and my path.*

TODAY'S ACTION
Today I will think about the times in my life when I enjoyed the ride. What choices was I making about how to use my freedom? What happened? I will talk about it with a friend and ask how it was for him or her.

When all else is lost, the future still remains.

— *Christian Bouee*

Ours is a program of hope. We sit in meetings and give each other hope. For no matter how long we have been sober—five days or thirty years—there will be times when we feel horrible. This is life. In everyone's life there are times of wonderful joy, but also times of incredible pain.

If we act from our values and the spiritual principles given to us by our Higher Power, pain will be transformed into growth and new understanding. Pain is transitory and softens with time.

These are the lessons of recovery. Bad times can be transformed into growth and joy.

PRAYER FOR THE DAY

Higher Power, I give you my pain and I ask you to show me the lessons I'm to learn. I ask for your help in holding on to hope. Help me to never forget that you and others are with me.

TODAY'S ACTION

Today I will list the times during my active addiction that I felt most hopeless. Then I will think of what lessons I learned from these moments. How did others, my Higher Power, and I transform these moments?

Character is simply habit long continued.

— *Plutarch*

Addiction changed us. It ate away at our character—
the inner backbone of morals and ethics that make us
strong. We still wanted to be good people, even in the
depths of our illness. We just could not seem to behave
that way. Our disease was stronger than our moral backbone. We were powerless over alcohol and drugs, and
they controlled our behavior.

Now that we are sober we are practicing new behaviors—behaviors guided by our morals and ethics, not
by our addiction. As we continue to practice these new
behaviors, they will become habits. And after a while,
we will find that these good habits have made our moral
backbone strong again. As we become healthy and strong
in our recovery, we build our character.

PRAYER FOR THE DAY
*Higher Power, help me become a person of good character.
Help me act in ways that match my new values, morals, and
ethics. I need your help to stay sober and practice recovery
behaviors that become a habit and build my character.*

TODAY'S ACTION
Today I will think of some people I have met in the program whom I admire because they are solid in their goodness. I will call at least one of them and ask how he or she
got that way.

Like a horse breaking from the gate, my life has begun.

— *Scott Spencer*

A fellow addict once shared his attitude about life. He almost died twice during his active addiction, once in a car accident and once of an overdose. He talked of how grateful he is for the fact that addiction and recovery have taught him to embrace life in a whole different way. He once saw life as something to be endured, but recovery has taught him to celebrate and have gratitude for each day of life, even the bad ones.

Sometimes when we come close to losing something, it pushes us to view it in a different way. This man saw his dry date as the day that his life began. His joy is contagious and makes others automatically smile. He is a living example of gratitude in motion.

PRAYER FOR THE DAY
Higher Power, you have given me this day. Help me embrace it, live it, and have gratitude for it. All of it!

TODAY'S ACTION
Today I will think about how I shy away from life. For today I will live life like a horse breaking from the gate. I will embrace life and work to live happy, joyous, and free.

Unthankfulness is theft.
— *Martin Luther*

Many of us have experienced a guest who tracked in dirt, ate our food, dirtied our dishes, took our time, whined and complained through the whole visit, and left without saying thank you. Such experiences leave us feeling angry and ripped off. We aren't eager to invite that person back to our home or to do any favors for him or her.

Let's make sure we don't act like that bad guest. Let's be aware of the kind things people do for us every day—from greeting us with a smile or opening a door to preparing a meal or washing our clothes. Let's remember that we've been given the gift of sobriety and to daily offer prayers of gratitude. Let us look around the group and be grateful for those who offer us their stories and their hope. Higher Power, thank you! To my group, thank you! To life, thank you!

PRAYER FOR THE DAY
Higher Power, thank you for inviting me into your house and for the many wonderful gifts you have given me. Thank you for your love and the gift of sobriety.

TODAY'S ACTION
Today I will call three group members and thank them for what they have given me.

The more you obey your conscience, the more it
will demand of you.
— C. S. Lewis

Conscience is our Higher Power working to steer us toward our authentic life. It has great gifts to give us. But it asks that we not just live by principles, but that we live to *become* these principles. Conscience makes us responsible for bringing life, through action, to spiritual principles. We are to act respectfully, to be respectable. We are to treat others with dignity and to live with dignity. By living according to spiritual principles, we experience transformation. Ours is a program of transformation. All we need to do is look around the recovery rooms to see it.

We are the soil, and spiritual principles are the seeds. As these seeds grow into beautiful trees, we must nurture them and give to them what is needed for their growth. This means placing principles before personality. If we do this, we will receive abundance.

PRAYER FOR THE DAY
Higher Power, I pray for conscious contact.
Help me to listen to your sweet whisper and then
give me the power and willingness to obey your wishes.

TODAY'S ACTION
Today, during my daily meditation, I will work to listen for the voice of my conscience. I will then do what it asks of me.

I'm really a very good man; but I'm a very bad wizard.

— *L. Frank Baum*, The Wonderful Wizard of Oz

No matter how well we get, we can't be our own Higher Power. When we were sick and in trouble, we knew we needed help from a power outside ourselves—one that had more than we did to help us get well. It was very clear then.

But when we begin feeling that our lives are under control again and things are going well for us, beware. It's tempting to think we can take the controls back from our Higher Power and run our own lives without help. After all, we are good people, and we are well now.

We need to remember that we are here to play our part in a much bigger picture of the world. And our Higher Power sees this picture better than we can. No matter what we call our Higher Power—God, Nature, Great Spirit, Allah, Buddha, The Goddess, our recovery group—that Higher Power gives us vision and power we cannot have by ourselves.

PRAYER FOR THE DAY
Higher Power, thank you for blessing me with knowledge of your will for me today and the power to carry that out. I know that your will for me is the best possible plan for my day.

TODAY'S ACTION
Today I will think about the surprises my Higher Power has had for me in recovery. I will list three things that made my life better than I thought it could be.

My dependency meant demand—a demand for
the possession and control of the people and the
conditions surrounding me.

— Bill Wilson

As our addiction increased its control over us, we began
trying to control everything and everyone around us—
like an animal caught in a trap, chewing off its own
leg in an attempt to be free. It was an indication of our
ever-increasing sense of powerlessness.

Little did we know that surrender was the way out of
this trap. We had to surrender to the reality of our illness,
surrender to our Higher Power, surrender to a program,
surrender to the Steps of recovery. Control is an illusion.
Surrender asks us to face reality and use our energies
more wisely. Do we still believe in the illusion of control?

PRAYER FOR THE DAY
Higher Power, today I surrender myself into your
loving arms. Help me to turn to you and others
whenever I want to control life and others.
Teach me to follow your rhythm, not mine.

TODAY'S ACTION
I will reflect on yesterday. How did I try to control others?
I will ask myself, "What could I have done differently?
What was I afraid of?"

Remember, Bill, let's not louse this thing up. Let's keep it simple.
— Dr. Bob to Bill W.

The two men who started Alcoholics Anonymous were different from each other in many ways. But they were alike in one important way: they were both alcoholics. They were also both smart men—one a doctor, the other a stockbroker. It would have been easy for them to let AA get very complicated if they let their brains get too busy.

However, they both knew one very important thing: being smart never helped them stay sober. And if they were not sober, it didn't matter how smart they were, their lives were going to fall apart. So it all rested on one thing really: don't drink.

But how can an alcoholic keep from drinking (or an addict keep from using)? Go to meetings. Our fellow addicts will help us learn how to stay sober by changing the way we live.

There's nothing very complicated about what we are doing. All we need to do is do it.

PRAYER FOR THE DAY
Higher Power, please help me "Keep it simple" today. There is no good reason for me to drink or use drugs today and no part of my life that it wouldn't make worse. Help me stay sober.

TODAY'S ACTION
I will talk with my sponsor about what happened the last time I drank or used drugs and about how my life is different now.

Anger was spreading through me like a malignant tumor.
— Isabel Allende

We often hear in meetings, "We addicts can't afford to be angry." The reasons are many. Anger feeds and inflates our egos. Anger disconnects us from our conscience, our values, and the conscious contact we have worked hard to nurture. Anger gives us a sense of entitlement; we believe we can do and say whatever we want. Anger allows us to feel self-righteous and above others, increasing our isolation. Anger creates a separation from the "we" of our program back to the "me" of arrogance.

Anger is often a mask for hurt or fears. If we stay angry, we never learn how to effectively face and deal with these feelings. We stay reactive instead of embracing the serenity that awaits us. We need to question ourselves when we feel angry. We need to stop the cancer of anger from growing in our hearts and souls.

PRAYER FOR THE DAY
Higher Power, I often use anger to cover up my hurts and fears. I am weak; you are strong. Give me the willingness to turn to your strength instead of my anger.

TODAY'S ACTION
Today I will write down five examples of how my anger has gotten me in trouble. I will think about how the outcome would have been different if I had turned to my Higher Power or others to help me.

If what I say resonates with you, it's because we are both branches of the same tree.

— W. B. Yeats

Once we begin our recovery, we have an instant bond with others in recovery; they seem to understand us pretty well even if they haven't known us very long. This is because we have a lot in common. We have the same disease. When we hear other addicts tell their stories, we know what they have gone through because it is a lot like what we have gone through.

The disease does similar things to us all. Yet each of us is unique and different, like the branches of a tree.

The fact that we share so much with our recovering friends is a true strength. It helps us grow strong. The fact that we have our own special talents, thoughts, and dreams is also a gift. In fact, it makes us a gift to ourselves and others.

PRAYER FOR THE DAY
Higher Power, thank you for the people in my life who understand me and love me, both because I am like them and because I am different from them.

TODAY'S ACTION
Today I will make a list of people in recovery I don't know very well. I will reach out to them so they become part of my recovery tree.

*Learning is a skill we develop that leads to lifelong
adventure.*
— *Anonymous*

Recovery asks that we commit ourselves to a life of
learning. We do not turn our backs on our past; we learn
from it. Past mistakes become guides and warnings to
others and to us. As we use the Steps, our sponsor, and
the fellowship, we make sense of how we got so lost. We
gain knowledge of how we were seduced by intensity,
which we mistook for intimacy. We see how we followed
our instincts instead of spiritual principles. We see how
our illness needed us to believe we were of little value.
We see how our pain equaled entitlement to keep using.
If we sit and listen, we learn much.

While listening in our healing circles, we are learning
how to do life, how to do the next right thing. We start
to see how to be of service to others instead of being a
burden. We use this new knowledge over and over in this
adventure we call life.

PRAYER FOR THE DAY
*Higher Power, help me to be open and committed to learning.
Keep me from the arrogance that was part of my addiction.*

TODAY'S ACTION
Today I will write down five things that I've learned during
my sobriety that have helped me have a better life.

MAY

Admitted to God, to ourselves, and to another human being the exact nature of our wrongs.
— *Step Five of Alcoholics Anonymous*

The literature of AA tells us what we will gain by working Step Five. We will get rid of that terrible sense of isolation we've always had. We will be able to receive forgiveness and give it, too. We will gain humility and a clear recognition of who and what we really are, which will be followed by a sincere attempt to become all that we can be.

When we take Step Five, we change the possibilities that life holds for us. After we take Step Five, we belong; we're not alone anymore. We are honest and open now—not filled with secrets and shame. We are fully aware of our strengths and our weaknesses. We get the information we need to live the rest of our life in a very different way.

PRAYER FOR THE DAY
Higher Power, help me use Step Five to unload all the things that hold me back from being the person you want me to be. Speak to me through another human being who accepts me and helps me lay down my burden.

TODAY'S ACTION
If I have taken Step Five, I will talk with my sponsor about what I got out of it. If not, I will make a plan with my sponsor and set a date.

Dealing with him is like dealing with a porcupine in heat.

— *Anonymous*

Some days we wake up angry at the world. Everyone annoys us. We try to tell ourselves that we're spiritual people and need to have a better attitude. But still, sometimes those inner voices keep whispering that the world is out to get us.

This is called *life*. Part of life is having bad days. What is important is how we choose to behave during these bad days. We can't take our negative attitudes too seriously. These voices feed self-righteousness and can drive us back to being self-centered addicts. We can end up believing we are entitled to happiness on demand. We know where these old attitudes and old behaviors will land us.

PRAYER FOR THE DAY
When I feel negative and full of myself,
Higher Power, help me to remember that this, too,
will pass, especially if I don't take it too seriously.

TODAY'S ACTION
Today I will write down a plan for what to do the next time I wake up feeling negative and mad at the world. Who will I call? What will I do to try and turn over my negative attitude?

It's when we're given choice that we sit with the
gods and design ourselves.
— Dorothy Gilman

Some of us addicts have dangerous ideas about freedom. Like everybody else, we want it. That is not the problem. The problem is that we don't really understand what freedom is and how it works.

Freedom means we can make choices about our own behavior. It doesn't mean we can control other people. It doesn't mean we can escape the consequences of our behavior. It doesn't mean that we can do whatever we want and things will turn out the way we want.

Our choices and our behaviors have consequences. That's the part we hated when we were using. When we make a choice, we are using our freedom, and we will get the consequences of that choice, whether we like it or not. Good choices usually result in good consequences. Bad choices usually result in bad consequences.

How can we use our freedom to get the *good* consequences in life? By working the Steps and listening to the advice of people who have what we want.

PRAYER FOR THE DAY
Higher Power, thank you for the freedom I have
had all my life. Thank you for the freedom I have
now. Help me take your advice on how to use it.

TODAY'S ACTION
Today I will think about my choices and their consequences.

I don't believe you! Flowers are weak creatures. They are naive. They reassure themselves as best they can. They believe that their thorns are terrible weapons.

—*Antoine de Saint-Exupéry*

When we are feeling weak and our lives are unmanageable, we grow our own kind of thorns. We act badly to scare people away. We think we are tough.

We do hurt people and scare others away. But that does not solve our problems. Then we are alone, and our lives are still unmanageable. We feel weak and afraid when what we really want is love and intimacy.

We need to remember that we are not just thorns. We are also flowers with the seeds of life in our centers. When we use our goodness instead of our thorns, we get along with others and are true to ourselves.

PRAYER FOR THE DAY
Higher Power, help me trust that in recovery it is safe to be a beautiful flower, not a bush of thorns.

TODAY'S ACTION
I will list three things I did this week to keep people at a distance. Did I ignore people? Was I rude? Did I make jokes at another's expense?

Pride comes before a fall.
—Aesop's Fables

The word *pride* can mean a lot of things, and some of them are good. Pride can mean self-respect, a sense of dignity and joy in the work we do.

Pride can also mean thinking too much of ourselves or our possessions. When our pride is so big that we look down on others, it is bad. When we forget to be grateful for our success and want to take all the credit, pride is bad. This is false pride.

When we are too proud, we think we can do it all ourselves. We forget to ask for help. We forget to pray and meditate. Soon we'll find ourselves all alone, except for our Inner Addict. And when it's just us and our Addict, we know what happens—relapse.

What's the safeguard between good pride and false pride? Gratitude. When we feel grateful, we know that we have had help in doing the things we are proud of. We share the joy with others, knowing they helped us by caring about us and being in our lives.

PRAYER FOR THE DAY
Thank you, Higher Power, for the dignity and success and joy I feel when I know I am being useful in your world.

TODAY'S ACTION
I will list five things I did today that I can feel proud of in a good way. Did I take good care of my health? Did I say a kind word to someone? Did I do my job well?

The soul is here for its own joy.

— *Rumi*

Our Higher Power wants us to find, embrace, and live a life of joy. Our Higher Power created joy as a gift to us. Unfortunately we got lost searching out joy. We thought excitement or intensity would bring us to joy.

Joy comes from living a life of values, hope, and faith. Our souls produce joy when we do the next right thing. Joy comes from knowing that our Higher Power loves us and wants us near. We must remember, as Bill W. said, "We didn't get sober to just go to meetings." We got sober to have good, joyous lives within our healing circles and in our everyday lives. We are to transform pain and challenges into growth and joy. Follow that which feeds your soul, and joy will follow. Joy is not a goal but a by-product.

PRAYER FOR THE DAY
Higher Power, you speak to me through my soul. Whisper songs of joy and love to me. Guide me closer to you.

TODAY'S ACTION
Today I will list all the things in recovery that bring me joy. I will do these things more often.

How unhappy is the person who cannot forgive himself or herself.

— *Publilius Syrus*

One of the most important things we do in recovery is to forgive ourselves. It is so important that it takes the first nine Steps to teach us to do it fully.

Our path to self-forgiveness is a difficult one. First we have to take a hard look at how we have lived and what we have done. Once we face the facts, we can decide to get well.

Why do we find it so hard to let go of blaming ourselves? Because our ego insists that we are in control and so we are to blame. We need to give up that idea and accept the facts. We have a disease that is stronger than we are.

Now we can face the damage, repair it, and move on with our lives. Now we can learn how to manage our disease—with help from our Higher Power and our program—and live a good and useful life.

PRAYER FOR THE DAY

Higher Power, I can't be free to do your will for me when I am bound up in ego and self-blame. Help me let go, accept my disease, and forgive myself.

TODAY'S ACTION

Today I will call my sponsor and talk about the ways I am being responsible for dealing with my disease. Then I can talk about self-forgiveness.

My best friend is the one who brings out the best in me.

— *Henry Ford*

To be a friend involves risk. Friends confront each other when it's needed, but they do it out of love and with compassion. All of us need a friend who will tell us when we are acting out of line, when we are "not able to see the forest for the trees." Friends are there for us in the struggles—rooting us on, maybe teasing us a bit, helping us get past the difficulties and eventually helping us find the gift embedded in them. Friends risk upsetting us, if it means we may become better people.

We need to be grateful for these people. Theirs is not always an easy job. Many of us have big egos; we don't want to be told that we are wrong. However, friends keep seeing the best in us, even when we aren't acting our best. Theirs will be the faces we see when we look back at our lives, especially at the times of crisis and challenge.

PRAYER FOR THE DAY
Higher Power, help me be a friend,
and help me be grateful for my friends.

TODAY'S ACTION
Today I will work to bring out the best in those around me, even if that means saying the hard things. If I must confront someone, I will only do it if I can do it with love and compassion.

In giving advice, seek to help, not to please, your friend.

— *Solon*

We all have a lot to learn in life, and it's difficult enough to figure things out without getting bad advice from others. When we ask for help from someone, we hope to learn something helpful. Yet all too often, we learn nothing. Instead we hear something meant to make us feel good. For example, "I think you're doing fine." Instead of being really helpful, this statement leaves us feeling like there's no help available.

When friends ask us for advice, we should tell them what we know and how we know it. "When I had that kind of problem, here's how I fixed it, and here's how it worked." Or "I can tell you one thing I did that turned out to be a mistake." We don't tell other people what they should do, but we can share our experience, strength, and hope.

PRAYER FOR THE DAY

Higher Power, help me be a good friend to others,
willing to share what I know when someone
asks for my advice. Use me to help others by
sharing my experience, strength, and hope.

TODAY'S ACTION

Today I will talk with a program friend about the difference between helpful sharing and "advice-giving," which is not helpful.

*It is only possible to live happily ever after on a
day-to-day basis.*
— Margaret Bonnano

It is said, "The moment is our link to eternity, to the
Divine." Recovery gives us many messages about living
in the moment: "Easy does it," "One day at a time," and
"Just for today."

As active addicts, we used chemicals to alter our relationship with the present. By getting high, we lived dis-
connected from the moment. Now we are learning that
the present moment is our best point of influence. In
this moment, we can choose to act from our values or to
betray our values. By living in the moment, we stay connected to our Higher Power and our values. With each
new day of staying sober and living a life of principles
before personality, we increase our chances of doing the
same in the future.

PRAYER FOR THE DAY
*Higher Power, you are found in every moment.
Help me seek you out in my everyday life,
not in the past or in the future, but now.*

TODAY'S ACTION
Today I will practice living in the moment. If I find myself
drifting into the past or the future, I will come back to the
moment.

Make new friends and keep the old; one is silver and the other gold.
— Joseph Parry

Friendship is wonderful. But what is true friendship? This is a question we encounter in early recovery, and it will be important for the rest of our lives.

A friend is someone we know, like, and trust. When we first get sober, we should look at the people we call friends. Are the things we like about them important to our healthy self or things our Inner Addict likes?

We become like our friends. That is why it is important to choose friends we want to be like. It takes work to sort this out when we first get sober because we have collected "friends" who are bad for us.

Where do we find good friends? First we can look to the people we knew, liked, and trusted before our addiction. Next we can look in our recovery groups. When we are a friend to the right person, then we will have a friend.

PRAYER FOR THE DAY
Higher Power, help me to choose friends, old and new, who help me be the person I really want to be. Help me be that kind of a friend to them, too.

TODAY'S ACTION
I will list the five people who have been my closest friends in my life. What do I like about each of them? Would I trust them to help me be my best?

It is better to know some of the questions than all of the answers.

— James Thurber

What know-it-alls we were during our using days! We had opinions, answers, and comments about everything and everyone. Most of this was a cover-up. We acted like the big shot, hoping no one noticed how afraid or lost we were. As our sense of powerlessness grew, so did our arrogance.

One of the gifts of recovery is the gift of not *having to know,* but rather *getting to question.* This is one of the reasons why we do inventories. We have questions that we must find the answer to. How did I get so lost? Who did I hurt? How can I right the wrongs of the past? We look to find out the ways we are incomplete. Then we can ask for what we need; we need others to help us be complete. What a gift it is not having to know it all ourselves! What a gift it is to have recovery friends and sponsors to help us!

PRAYER FOR THE DAY
Higher Power, keep me questioning life. Help me remember that an open mind is one that allows you and others in.

TODAY'S ACTION
Today I will make two columns on a piece of paper. On the left side, I will list times when I acted like the big shot. On the right, I will write down what fears or insecurities I was trying to cover up.

The fact that she had a nut for a head did make
new ideas difficult for her to grasp.
— *Carolyn Sherwin Bailey*

In recovery we talk a lot about feelings but not so much
about thinking. During our active addiction, we were
controlled by our feelings. Our thinking started to bend
around our feelings and our addiction. Deluded, we lost
our ability to think clearly. We became experts in the
twisted logic of The Addict.

In recovery, we are learning once more to think clearly.
We know that it is important to face our feelings but not
let them run our behavior and lives.

By talking with others about our thoughts, we ask for
help in thinking clearly. We get feedback on questions
such as: What is the true problem? What are my choices?
What is the best resolution? Which choice fits with my
values? What supports my sobriety?

PRAYER FOR THE DAY
Higher Power, help me think before I act. Help me stop
hurting myself and others by acting too quickly.

TODAY'S ACTION
Today I will face one problem I want to understand. What
is the core of this issue? I will talk with my sponsor about
the problem and my thoughts about it.

Whenever you are confronted with an opponent,
conquer him with love.
— *Mohandas Gandhi*

Think of all the opponents we face in a day: an angry co-worker, bad traffic, a challenging child, or maybe just feeling tired and grumpy. These are situations when our egos can fire up our worst character defects—anger, sarcasm, and impatience.

Love, a spiritual principle of the highest order, is a great weapon to conquer these opponents. Love demands that we see all things as having value, even if the value is merely placing principles before personalities. Love, if turned to, will remove our character defects and allow balance and harmony to be created, even if just for a few moments.

PRAYER FOR THE DAY
Higher Power, you are love in its purest form. Thank you
for all the solutions you will give to me if I stay open to you.
When things seem dark, let your love light my way.

TODAY'S ACTION
Today I will walk through the day with love. I will work to be loving in all situations.

They talk of my drinking but never my thirst.
— Scottish Proverb

Some of us had reasons for our drinking and drugging—not that we needed a reason. We were looking for comfort or courage, to drown our rage, our loneliness, or our hopelessness. We used because we wanted to be somebody, find somebody, or find answers or happiness. Whatever we were looking for, we ended up addicted and out of control.

The end of our drinking and using marked only the beginning of our recovery process. When we sobered up, we still had the same needs, the same thirst. What do we do with those needs when we are sober?

That is why the Twelve Steps were written—to show us how addicts found what they were looking for in their lives. When we work the Twelve Steps, our thirst is quenched. We experience the meaning of life in a way that we could never know when we were using. We find a new freedom and a new happiness.

PRAYER FOR THE DAY
*Higher Power, thank you for bringing me into
this recovery program so I can find the real way
to the peace and happiness I want so badly.*

TODAY'S ACTION
Today I will write down three things I have learned about happiness since I started working a recovery program.

*A very small degree of hope is sufficient to cause
the birth of hope.*

—*Stendhal*

For many of us, when we walked into recovery, we were
without hope. But even at our very first meeting we
were greeted by the smiles, joy, laughter, and hope of
those addicts who began the recovery journey before we
did. We wanted what they had. We had nothing, so their
hope had to be ours until we could create some of our
own. Their joy had to be ours until we could find some
of our own. Their values had to be ours until we could
establish a value system of our own. Their smiles will
always be a part of us.

Now it is our job to greet the newcomers and the old
comers at meetings. We can smile at them, giving them
hope and watching it grow. This is the essence of our
fellowship.

PRAYER FOR THE DAY

*Higher Power, help me to be hope for others. Help me to
make others feel that life, even when tough, is worth living.
Help me to live a life that attracts others to you.*

TODAY'S ACTION

At the next meeting I go to, I will make it a point to greet,
smile at, and say hello to anyone I don't know, as well as
many I do know.

Nothing is worth more than this day.
— *Johann Wolfgang von Goethe*

Life—each day of it, each minute of it—is such a miracle. Let's stop and think about it for a minute. Where does it come from? Why was it given to each of us?

Life is not the same for any two people. Every person has a life that is different from everyone else's. Yet in some ways it is the same for all of us. We are all born, and we all die. We all lose people we love and welcome new people to love into our lives.

The flavor of life today—the exact mix of sunshine and clouds, happiness and sadness, courage and fear, love and loneliness—will never be the same again. Not tomorrow or the next day.

PRAYER FOR THE DAY
Higher Power, help me appreciate the beauty of your world and the richness of my life today.

TODAY'S ACTION
Today I will smile—at everyone.

Dig a well before you are thirsty.

— *Chinese Proverb*

At times, we may feel like picking up a drink or using drugs again. These feelings are normal for us addicts. This is why we go to meetings *today*. This is why we do service work *today*. This is why we work the Steps *today*. *Today* is when we are to prepare for tough times in the future.

The program will teach us many ways to safeguard our future, to prepare for cravings. We save for the rainy day. We learn to surrender and practice the skill of reaching out to another addict. We want connectedness to be as natural as aloneness was to us during our using. We will stay safe in the future through using the skills we develop today.

PRAYER FOR THE DAY
Higher Power, help me put all of my energy into today's sobriety. Help me hold nothing back as I go through the day. My future may depend upon it. Help me see that the work I do today is the work that will keep me sober tomorrow. Thank you for today's sobriety.

TODAY'S ACTION
I will call my sponsor and ask him or her what I can do today to help me be sober tomorrow.

Conceit spoils the greatest genius ... and the great charm of power is modesty.

— *Louisa May Alcott*

Addiction does bad things to our egos. We see ourselves as very different from others. Either we think we are better, with puffed-up egos, or we think we are worse than others, feeling sorry for ourselves. Either way, the rules don't apply to us, of course, because we are *special*.

The Big Book says that the early members of AA realized that they were pretty self-centered, and that was a big part of the problem for them. It's a big part of the problem for most of us in recovery today, too. It seems to go with addiction.

We must get real about who we are and what we have to offer others. We need to accept that life doesn't revolve around us. Rather we are here to work with others, with our talents, and with love to make life better and more meaningful for all of us. That is how we make a real difference in this world.

PRAYER FOR THE DAY
Higher Power, please help me learn more about my talents, my strengths, and my purpose for being here. What part of your work would you like me to do today?

TODAY'S ACTION
Today I will learn about my gifts. I will ask four people who know me in different parts of my life this question: "What positive thing do I bring when I join a group of people?"

*To see how our erratic emotions victimized us
often took a long time. Where other people were
concerned, we had to drop the word* blame *from
our speech and thought.*

— Bill Wilson

During our active addiction, emotions ruled us. Often
we didn't know what to do with them, especially the
negative ones. They became reasons to get high, act out,
and isolate ourselves from others. We often used blame
to deal with these emotions. Blame served our addiction well. Blame kept us feeling either self-righteous or
self-pity.

The function of blame is to deny responsibility. Its secondary function is to push people away. Blame is a very
effective defense mechanism.

As Bill Wilson said, we must drop blame from our
speech *and* thoughts. It is not enough to stop voicing
blame if, in our thoughts, we secretly still blame others
for our troubles. These secrets need sharing. That's why
we talk about them with our sponsors and recovery
friends.

PRAYER FOR THE DAY
*Higher Power, help me to use the Steps to deal with
negative emotions instead of using blame to deal with them.
Help me to drop blame from my speech and thoughts.*

TODAY'S ACTION
Just for today, I will not blame anyone, including myself.
I will choose to be responsible for myself.

There is nothing permanent except change.
— *Heraclitus*

Most of us don't like change very much. Getting sober is like stepping into a rushing river of change that will take us to new places in our lives. We sense that. We are learning to trust it more each day. But even though life keeps getting better for us, we still keep some of that fear inside us about what will happen if we keep working our recovery program and life keeps changing for us.

Maybe we get a good job, and we are afraid we will louse it up. Maybe we make new friends, and we are afraid they will find out what a jerk we really are. Maybe our kids are speaking to us again and want to have a better relationship, and we are afraid of the responsibility.

You know what? It'll be okay. It's okay to have good things happen. It's okay to trust ourselves to handle responsibility. Nobody knows how to do life perfectly— that's why we need our Higher Power to guide us.

PRAYER FOR THE DAY
Higher Power, help me listen for your directions today as I walk through a new day in sobriety. Together we can handle any surprises and changes the day may bring.

TODAY'S ACTION
Today I will write down three ways fear of change is holding me back, and I will talk with my sponsor about these things. What do I need to do to be ready for these changes?

*I shall follow the path to wherever my destiny and
my mission for truth shall take me.*

— *Kahlil Gibran*

We start recovery only when we become willing to
embrace the truth. One bit of truth is this: we have
a dreadful illness called addiction. We are addicts.
Recovery is the mission of dealing with this truth.

We take inventories as we work the Steps to learn
more truths about ourselves. We share these truths with
our Higher Power and other human beings. We ask for
our defects of character to be removed because we can't
remove them ourselves.

In Step Eight, we write down the truths about those we
have hurt and do our best to right these wrongs. We take a
daily inventory of truths in Step Ten and seek more truth
through prayer and meditation in Step Eleven.

We then share our new understanding with addicts
who still suffer, respecting that they will have their own
truths to discover. Yes, recovery is a mission of discover-
ing truths that can free us from the grasp of addiction.

PRAYER FOR THE DAY

*Higher Power, you are the truth, not me. I will follow you
wherever you take me. Your mission is my mission.*

TODAY'S ACTION

Today I will write down five truths I have discovered
in recovery. I must remember that the daily Tenth Step
inventory is the best method to keep looking for truths.

Down in their hearts, wise people know this truth:
the only way to help yourself is to help others.
— *Elbert Hubbard*

Bill W. knew this when he felt a relapse coming on in Akron. He looked for an alcoholic to help. He found Dr. Bob. The rest is history.

Recovery is a "we" deal. We are in this with other people. We can't save ourselves and forget about others; most of us have tried that many times. We change our lives by taking each thing as it comes and handling it in a new, healthy way with the help and advice of our friends.

The key is to call upon and use our sponsors, rely on our groups. When we need help, we know where to go to get it. But here's the other part: when our recovering friends need help, to whom do they come? *To us. We* are part of *their* support group. We need to be there for others and serve as a sponsor for others.

PRAYER FOR THE DAY
Higher Power, help me see when my recovering
friends need help and support. Help me be
there for them as others are there for me.

TODAY'S ACTION
Today I will make a phone call to someone in my recovery group who is having a hard time lately. I will let this person know that I am thinking about him or her.

Let yourself never wander too far from that which
you love; it is your source of strength.
— *Alcoholics Anonymous Member*

As addicts, we loved illusions while rejecting love of humanity and spirit. We claimed to love good things, but our actions were not actions of love.

In recovery, love is always a verb. We seek authentic love through our actions—love that heals wounds and brings us close to others. This love brings smiles and tears of gratitude—and leaves us knowing we are never alone. If we look closely, we can see a glimmer of the Divine in such love. It sees others as spirit; it works to bring out the best in others, not the worst.

The man who spoke the above quotation has been in recovery for over thirty years. He says his long-term relationship with recovery has taught him how to have other long-term relationships. This year he celebrated his twenty-fifth wedding anniversary. His gratitude is enormous for recovery's lessons of love.

PRAYER FOR THE DAY
Higher Power, you have given me spiritual principles.
As I put them into action, the love they hold is released.
Help me to be a person of loving action.

TODAY'S ACTION
Today I will make a list of all the wonderful relationships that recovery has given to me. I will try to see each as a gift of love.

Our deepest fear is not that we are inadequate. It is that we are powerful beyond measure. It is our light, not our darkness, that frightens us.
— *Marianne Williamson*

We addicts scare ourselves when we get well. We find out that we are smart, good people. We find out that other people like us. We find out that the world needs people who are like us. Suddenly we realize that people expect us to share our talents, energy, and wisdom. We have something to give, and we are wanted.

We're not used to that. When we were using, the work of everyday life went better for people when we stayed out of their way. We couldn't help ourselves, and we couldn't help anyone else.

Now, with the help of our Higher Power, we can carry our own weight, and we can help others, too. It's called turning over our life and our will to the care of our Higher Power—accepting care for ourselves and carrying it to others.

PRAYER FOR THE DAY
Higher Power, help me see that it's now part of my job in life to share the light you give me. I can trust that you will give me the strength and wisdom I need to help others.

TODAY'S ACTION
Today I will remember three times when I felt a pull to help out a person or a group in need. What did I do?

*To understand all this a little better, it might help
to look at someone who is quite the opposite.*
— *Benjamin Hoff*

We addicts are a rigid, stubborn bunch. We often
get something in our heads, and it seems to push all
the questions out. Recovery suggests that we work to
develop an open mind that wonders, questions, and is
willing to cast doubts, even on our own motives.

One of the gifts of going to meetings is hearing the
opinions of people whose thinking is directly opposite
of ours. How often it happens that the person we see as
having nothing to offer us ends up teaching us the most.
This is the way of openness. Openness asks that we welcome the truth no matter who the messenger is. Openness
is also an admission that we are incomplete and we need
the new ideas, opinions, and suggestions of others.

PRAYER FOR THE DAY
*Openness allows me to hear the truth. Higher Power,
you are the truth. Help me keep listening for your messages
and guidance as they come to me through others.*

TODAY'S ACTION
Today I will write down three times that my closed mind
has gotten me struck or in trouble.

Dreams are thoughts waiting to be thought.
— Jan de Hartog

Addiction stole our dreams. We used to have dreams about what we would do with our lives, about people we would love, places we would go. But addiction took over, a little bit at a time, and stole our dreams. As addicts, we dreamed addict dreams that took us toward death as we chased the next high.

There was no place for people in these dreams, unless they could help us get high. No place for helping others, unless they would pay us back. No place for pride in our good work—our Addict thought it was a waste of time. Our addict dreams led us to loneliness, fear, and darkness.

With sobriety, there is a return of our sense of self. We once again have dreams that lead us toward life, love, and health.

PRAYER FOR THE DAY
Higher Power, I'd like my dreams back.
I am happy when I go with your flow.
Give me the dreams you want me to dream.

TODAY'S ACTION
I will make a list of three things The Addict dreamed about and three things my real self dreams about. I will read them to my sponsor.

A critic is a man who knows the way but can't drive the car.
— *Kenneth Tynan*

It is easy for us to be critical. It is a way for us to hide the fears and other feelings that we don't know how to deal with. During our active addiction, as our life became more fearful, we became more negative. Instead of admitting we were lost and in trouble, many of us acted as if we knew everything. We acted as if we had chosen this life of addiction, refusing to see it as the illness it is.

Being critical is easy to carry into recovery because in recovery we still have fears. Plus, in recovery, we don't have the chemicals to cover up these feelings of fear. So in recovery, when fears and other negative feelings come along, we need to turn to our friends, sponsor, and Higher Power.

In recovery, we use courage to change fears into deeper relationships with our friends, our values, and especially our Higher Power. When we find ourselves wanting to be critical, we should call a sponsor or say the Serenity Prayer. And we can ask ourselves, "What am I afraid to face?"

PRAYER FOR THE DAY
*Higher Power, help me seek safety in you
and others instead of hiding in fear and cynicism.*

TODAY'S ACTION
I will list my five favorite things to be critical about. Today I will try not to be critical. I will work to embrace gratitude instead of fear.

Character is what a person is in the dark.
— *Dwight L. Moody*

How many of us act differently when no one can see us? During the worst days of our illness, we used to steal, lie, and leave messes for someone else to pick up. It is often said in the rooms of recovery that "we are as sick as our secrets."

The longer we are in recovery, the more clear the answer becomes: we are the same person wherever we go whether anyone can see us or not.

Most often the things we used to "get away with" hurt us a lot more than they hurt anyone else. We practice being responsible to ourselves because *we* know what *we* are doing. We practice on the little things, like making our bed every morning, whether anyone knows it or not. Why? Because we feel better when we have done our little duties. We practice telling the truth, especially to ourselves, because our addiction wants to make us dishonest.

PRAYER FOR THE DAY
Higher Power, please help me heal and recover,
even in the most secret parts of my life.

TODAY'S ACTION
Have I done anything today that I am keeping secret? Why? When I really take a good look at my secrets, what do I think about them?

Healing in its fullest sense requires looking into our hearts and expanding our awareness of who we are.

— *Mitchell Gaynor*

Our program asks us to look at ourselves very closely and very honestly. A large part of Step work involves taking our inventory and then thinking about what we have found in ourselves. Why? Because this is one of the main ways we heal our wounds.

We learn that most times when something is wrong, we are part of the problem. When there are problems, we think about what our part is and what we can do to correct the situation in a loving way. We ask, "What spiritual principles do I need to put into action to rebalance my life?" If we are willing to do this over and over, we come to know ourselves and love ourselves. This is because we will come to find out just how much of the Divine lives in us.

PRAYER FOR THE DAY
*Higher Power, help me look deep into my heart and soul.
I know that as I do this I will heal. Open my heart
so I can receive the gifts you want to give me.*

TODAY'S ACTION
Today I will write down any problem I am struggling with. I will ask myself, "What is my part? How am I part of the problem?"

*Life shrinks or expands in proportion to one's
courage.*
— Anaïs Nin

When we let our fears rule our decisions, we live our life much the same way every day. We don't try new things. We don't make big changes.

During our active addiction, we were afraid to think about what we wanted in our life. We were afraid to go to friends and family because we did not want them to see who we had become.

In recovery, we learn to face our fears and say, "You are not the boss of me." We make choices that are based on our own values and goals. We learn to act with courage, and we get a lot of practice when we work Step Three, Step Five, and Step Nine. When we work these Steps, we move ahead with action even if we are afraid. When we do these things, we make our world bigger and freer.

PRAYER FOR THE DAY
*Higher Power, help me face my fears today and
remember that I have made a decision in Step Three
that means you—not my fears—are the boss of me.
Give me the courage to do your will for me today.*

TODAY'S ACTION
Today I will make a list of at least ten things I do now in recovery that I used to be afraid to do.

JUNE

*Were entirely ready to have God remove all these
defects of character.*

— *Step Six of Alcoholics Anonymous*

In Step Five, we unloaded the harmful baggage of
shame, guilt, and denial about destructive behavior.
In Step Six, we prepare to live without the defects that
created all that baggage in the first place.

At first, this sounds like a no-brainer to most of us. Sure,
we are willing to give up our problems. But Step Six asks
us to get ready for life without them. That means coming
to terms with how we use our defects to get the things
we want, protect our egos, and make us feel strong. What
will happen if we face the world without them? What if
we became honest, generous, loving, and responsible?
What would we lose? What would we gain? How do we
think these changes might affect our lives?

PRAYER FOR THE DAY
*Higher Power, help me become truly ready
to have you remove my defects of character.
Help me trust that being the person you want me
to be is safe and I can give up all my old defenses.*

TODAY'S ACTION
Today I will make a list of at least ten things I fear will
happen if I give up old behaviors and defenses. I will read
them to my sponsor and talk them out.

Happiness is the sense that one matters.

— *Sarah Trimmer*

Often during our active addiction, we acted as if nothing mattered. We often treated people as if they didn't matter unless they could be of some use to us. We acted as if we didn't need others because we had our alcohol or drugs. Slowly we were choking off happiness. We didn't see that when we acted as if nothing mattered, we were calling ourselves nothing. Void of happiness, filled with doubts, fears, anger, and self-pity, we found our way into recovery.

From the first day we entered, people have been telling us that we matter, to keep coming back. Over time we found ourselves laughing *with* people instead of *at* people. We could see that things mattered and that we mattered. As we did this, we found happiness returning. We smiled more. We laughed more—even at ourselves. We discovered that the world needs us.

PRAYER FOR THE DAY
Higher Power, fill me with happiness. Help me to smile, laugh, and see that I matter. Help me live a life of joy.

TODAY'S ACTION
Today I will try to see if I can make someone who is down smile and realize that he or she matters.

To live is to feel oneself lost.

— *José Ortega y Gasset*

Many times in life we are lost—usually when we are in the middle of a big change in our lives. That simply means we have left a place we know, we're on our way to a place we don't know, and we're not sure of the way.

Being lost is only a problem when we insist that we can find the way by ourselves. When we won't ask for help or listen to the help we are given, we can stay lost for a long time.

When we are in the middle of big changes in our life, it helps to take the role of a passenger and let our Higher Power drive the car. We're going somewhere new—it may be a surprise—and we don't know the way. But everything's fine because our Higher Power is doing the driving. We can trust our Higher Power, sit back, and enjoy the ride. Our Higher Power knows where we are and where we're going, and there's no better place to be than in our Higher Power's loving care.

PRAYER FOR THE DAY
You drive today, Higher Power.
I will watch, learn, and enjoy the scenery.

TODAY'S ACTION
Today I will think of a time in my life when I felt lost. What was going on at that time? How did I find my way? I will write three sentences about the experience. If I could do it over, would I do it differently now? How?

Live your beliefs and you can turn the world around.
— Henry David Thoreau

Having beliefs is one thing, but living them is—well, that's hard.

Living by the Steps is a different type of living. The Steps are a set of beliefs that are spiritual in nature. Living these beliefs will turn a person's world around, from decay and isolation to growth and fellowship. Living by spiritual beliefs releases healing, transformative powers. We just need to hang on! Spiritual adventures are coming our way.

Spiritual adventures occur because our Higher Power believes in us and will continue to place us in situations that demand that we believe more and more in ourselves. With each new adventure, we end up loving ourselves more and more.

PRAYER FOR THE DAY
*Higher Power, help me to live my beliefs so
I can be touched by you. I need your strength
and the adventures you will give to me.*

TODAY'S ACTION
I will write down what my beliefs are. How do I see and allow spiritual beliefs to direct my life?

*As a child, I walked through the world with
wonder and awe. Each day started with a question
and ended with a question. I had the mind of
a beginner.*

— *Anonymous*

Did you ever notice that children ask the best questions?
Why are things the way they are? How do they work?
How did we get here? Who made us? Why?

These are the most important questions in life. Most of
us never really get our questions answered. We just learn
to stop asking people. We act like the things they tell us
answer the questions, but they really don't.

Such questions are questions of the spirit. We can ask
our Higher Power to help us learn the answers. We can
talk with other people who are also interested in these
questions and share our thoughts and ideas. Now that we
are sober we can even read books that explore these questions. The truth is, we may never understand the answers
because we are only human beings. But thinking about
these things is good because it helps us be thankful for
the mystery of life.

PRAYER FOR THE DAY
*Higher Power, I know I'll never understand
everything, but will you please teach me
something interesting today? Thank you.*

TODAY'S ACTION
What have I done lately to learn more about the mystery of
life? What is one thing I can do today?

Discipline, it has been suggested, is the means of human spiritual evolution.
— *M. Scott Peck*

Discipline is not a bad word, though many of us react negatively when we hear it. Discipline is a means to an end. It allows us to channel our energies toward goals. Those goals include living a better life and being of service to others.

Being disciplined has many forms. These forms include turning our will and lives over to a Higher Power, calling a friend in need, writing out a moral inventory, or setting a date to do a Fifth Step. When we make amends for wrongs done, this is a form of discipline.

Discipline always involves action. Often the action is restraint and redirection. Discipline is a beautiful concept that, when put into action, produces beautiful results. It helps bring order to the chaos of our lives.

PRAYER FOR THE DAY
Higher Power, help me live in harmony.
Help direct my energy into a disciplined life.

TODAY'S ACTION
Today I will work to be aware of chaos and how discipline adds order to my life.

It is such a secret place, the land of tears.
— *Antoine de Saint-Exupéry*

There are places in our hearts that words cannot express. One such place is the pain of grief. If we are living fully, if we love others, we will sometimes hurt. That is part of the deal. And tears are part of the healing.

When we're grieving, it helps to reach out to others. It helps to let our Higher Power in. And it helps to remember that our tears honor the people and things we love. Our tears also honor our own heart for being able to love another.

Now that we are in recovery, we never have to be alone with our pain. When we cry, we can have others with us, to hold us in their warmth and safety when we have none of our own. We have true friends.

PRAYER FOR THE DAY
Higher Power, help me love well and learn my lessons easily so that the love can be great and the pain small.

TODAY'S ACTION
Today I will think about the following questions: When was the last time I had a good, hard cry? Have I cried for the pain my addiction has caused me and others? Have I cried for the loss of my booze and my drugs? I might need to. It's okay.

The last of human freedoms—to choose one's attitude in any given set of circumstances, to choose one's own way.
— *Viktor Frankl*

We could feel our self-decay as freedom after freedom was lost to our illness of addiction. Our attitude became more negative as our illness grew. Our negative attitude was a symptom of our decay.

Recovery is as much about attitude as it is about not using chemicals and not acting out. We work to create an attitude of gratitude. We work to replace negative attitudes with actions of hope, service, humility, and love. We know that a positive attitude is an achievement, not a gift. We didn't choose our illness, but we get to choose the attitude we take in dealing with it. So we can go ahead and cop an attitude—as long as it's an attitude of gratitude!

PRAYER FOR THE DAY
Higher Power, today I will have gratitude
about the freedoms that recovery has brought me.
I get to choose because you have given me free will,
and I choose you. Higher Power, do with me as you will.

TODAY'S ACTION
Since getting sober I know a new kind of freedom. I will list the new freedoms recovery has brought to me.

We must develop eyes that look both outward and inward if we are to see clearly.

— *Anonymous*

In Step Four, we decide which of our behaviors are helpful and which are harmful. We learn a great deal about who we are, what we believe, and how we act.

This is work we must do for ourselves, but it is good to get help. That is why we share our findings with another person and our Higher Power in Step Five. We also talk about how we understand ourselves in meetings and with our sponsor and our recovery friends.

We don't do Step Four so that we can feel bad. We do a fearless and searching Step Four so that we can know ourselves very, very well. We do Step Five so that we can get someone else's ideas about what we tell them; this helps us understand ourselves even better. When we do a good Step Four and Step Five, we become persons of true wisdom.

PRAYER FOR THE DAY

Higher Power, help me be wise about myself so that I can have a better life. I want to learn how to be the real me, the best me, and do your will for me. I trust that your will for me is full of care.

TODAY'S ACTION

Where am I with Step Four? If I have done Step Four, I will talk with my sponsor about something important that I learned from it. If I haven't done Step Four yet, I will talk with my sponsor about when I will do it.

Finish each day and be done with it.
— *Ralph Waldo Emerson*

Often we want to carry the worries or the successes of today into tomorrow. As we put our heads on our pillows, we need to let go of today. Each new day needs to begin with a fresh mind. Each new day deserves our full attention. The purpose of the Tenth Step is to allow us to concentrate our energies on the present. Worries, past and future, scatter our energies. Step Ten helps us keep our energies focused and available for today.

Why is this important? It is only in the present that we can truly connect with others and our Higher Power. The present is our gateway to the eternal. Worries and even successes make us less able to step across this gateway into a better relationship with our Higher Power and others. We need to allow ourselves to travel light into tomorrow.

PRAYER FOR THE DAY
Higher Power, help me live in the present. Help me develop more and more willingness to live in the moment.

TODAY'S ACTION
Today I will use the Tenth Step to think about where I am with the world and change the things I can, let go of the things I need to, and recommit to living in the present.

Live in such a way that you would not be ashamed
to sell your parrot to the town gossip.

— Will Rogers

What a relief it is to be free of the cycle of addiction. Our shame was almost too heavy to bear at times—the times when we let ourselves feel it. Then, of course, we used again to forget the shame.

Most people who are not addicted to alcohol or drugs cannot understand this. They probably think we *should* be ashamed. They don't know addiction is a disease that made us powerless and that no amount of shame or willpower could make us quit using. They may never understand.

Addiction is a baffling disease. Many other diseases are baffling, too. But we are lucky that there is a way to live with our disease. We know how to keep our disease in remission: We stay away from that first drink, toke, snort, or dose. We keep going to meetings. We hang out often with people who *do* understand.

PRAYER FOR THE DAY
Higher Power, thank you for my recovery.
Help me walk in recovery today.

TODAY'S ACTION
Perhaps I need to understand that there is shame with other diseases, too. Are there other people I can talk with who have had cancer or diabetes or depression? Can I ask them about whether they have ever felt ashamed?

I really do believe that every human being has serious value. I'm in most people's corner.

— *Elaine Brown*

To look past people's flaws and see them as basically good is rare. There are many days when it is hard to look past our own flaws and see the goodness that lies behind our moods.

But we seem to be able to do just that when we sit in our meetings. We look past the illness of addiction; we look past each other's character defects and keep reminding each other of the good that is part of us all. We cannot afford to let others give up on themselves. Our recovery is based on a collective "we." If one of us does not have faith in themselves, then we allow shame to plant a seed.

There will be times we want to hide in our character defects; we will want to hide in shame. At these times we must remember, if we really believe we are good people, then aren't we *responsible* to be good people? We must always ask ourselves, "Am I refusing to be in my own corner?"

PRAYER FOR THE DAY
Higher Power, you are always in my corner.
Help me to believe in myself and others. Help me
to see past my character defects and to be responsible.

TODAY'S ACTION
Today I will write down three times I thought I wasn't "good enough" so that I could avoid responsibility.

A people that values its privileges above its principles soon loses both.

— *Dwight D. Eisenhower*

What do we see when we look at people? What do we look for? Our society seems to tell us that how people look is the most important thing. If we believe that, we will miss out on their qualities that are really important. These qualities include how they treat people, whether they have a sense of humor, and if they're honest.

We must remember that material things don't have anything to do with friendship or love or trust. They don't offer us support or understanding. They don't teach us how to fill the loneliness in our hearts and offer love to others.

PRAYER FOR THE DAY
Help me be a real human being, Higher Power.
Help me know with my heart what is truly important.

TODAY'S ACTION
Today I will sit down and list my qualities. I will work to be more invested in the spiritual way than in the materialism that surrounds me.

The persistent human cry is, "Hold me tight."
— *Donald Joy*

We need to be loved. We need to be held tight, and we need to hold others tight. Many of us are scared, and for good reasons. During our using years, we held tight to addiction, but this attachment created serious wounds.

In recovery, first we let go of old behaviors, attitudes, and ideas. Then we hold tight to the Steps, our sponsor, the fellowship, and the principles of the program. The tighter we attach to recovery, the quicker its care and love become part of our being. The tighter we hold, the deeper the values of recovery get planted into our minds, hearts, and souls.

It is, then, our job to hold on tight and allow the safety of recovery to hold us tight. We need to go to meetings, call our sponsor, read, pray, and meditate regularly, allowing the care found in the Third Step to grab hold of us and heal our wounds.

PRAYER FOR THE DAY
*Higher Power, I need your love. Please hold me tight,
especially when I'm scared or when I'm angry.
Hold me until I can feel your love.*

TODAY'S ACTION
Today I will meditate on how I can tighten my grip on recovery and how I can let recovery hold me tighter.

Everywhere is walking distance if you have the time.
— Steven Wright

We need to make careful choices about how we spend our time. It's important to ask: Am I happy with the things I spend time on? Do I find meaning in the things I spend time on?

When we are working, do we put our attention into our work? Do we spend enough time taking care of ourselves and our family? Do our friends add quality to our lives?

Addiction has taught us to waste our time on hurting ourselves. And it did become the most important thing in our lives. Taking back our lives, with the help of our Higher Power, means taking back our time to spend on the things that *give*—not *take*—life. One day at a time, one hour at a time, one minute at a time.

PRAYER FOR THE DAY
Higher Power, there are so many dangerous moments in my day when The Addict wants to take me back to using or to using people and places. Please fill my time today with healthy thoughts and help me spend my time on living well, not on the slow death of addiction.

TODAY'S ACTION
Today I will make a list of the things that I need and want to spend my time on in order to be healthy and live a life I like and am proud of. Then I will consider how I can spend more time on these things.

Humans are smarter than people think.
— Eddie Izzard

As addicts, we could be very ingenious at using our wits to create mischief or to manipulate things to our advantage. Now in recovery, we seem to get smarter when we can come together for the greater good, such as being of service to others. Recovery gives us back our brains and also gives us the gift of choice.

Recovery asks that we use our smarts to create miracles. We need to let our minds be guided by spiritual forces and then use them for good. When we do, we will surprise even ourselves at how smart we can be. We must ask ourselves, "Am I using my brain to make the world a better place or for selfish motives?"

PRAYER FOR THE DAY
Higher Power, you have given me back my brain;
this is one of the gifts of recovery. Now help me use it,
not in selfish ways, but for good.

TODAY'S ACTION
Today I will think of three specific ways I can be of service to others.

*The art of being wise is the art of knowing what
to overlook.*
— William James

Our first job in recovery is to become sober. Our second
job is to become smart so we can stay sober. Our third
job is to learn how to make the most of our life.

Becoming sober takes a while. Our ability to think
clearly is impaired for a long time after our last use of
alcohol or drugs. When we can think clearly enough to
look for help, the program is there to help us. All we have
to do is work it.

Wisdom comes in as we learn to quiet the voice of our
addiction and pay attention, instead, to the things in life
that are truly important: our spirituality, our mental and
physical health, and our relationships. We come to understand that we matter, to the people who love us and to our
Higher Power.

PRAYER FOR THE DAY
*The Addict in me wants to make a big deal of all the wrong
things, tempting me to relapse. Higher Power, please help
me quiet the voice of The Addict and pay attention, instead,
to the important thing—living in your care for me today.*

TODAY'S ACTION
What Step am I working on today? This is a good thing to
pay attention to. I will talk with my sponsor about it.

He who requires urging to do a noble act will
never accomplish it.
— *Kahlil Gibran*

The Third Step speaks of willingness. Willingness puts our hearts and souls into the task at hand. Willingness doesn't get rid of the fears, but it helps us find the courage to work through them. Willingness doesn't give us the knowledge to solve the problem, but it may give us the energy to leave our isolation and seek out others with the knowledge. Willingness doesn't do away with ego; it just shows us an alternative to ego. Willingness is the voice of our Higher Power saying, "I believe in you and want you to do the same." Willingness is the seed wanting to break through the soil to see the light of day, to be what it is meant to be.

PRAYER FOR THE DAY
I pray for willingness to do the next right thing.
I seek courage, knowledge, the support of others,
and my Higher Power's guidance.

TODAY'S ACTION
I will work to notice how willingness is behind all actions. I will work today to be a willing participant in my own life, and in my own recovery.

Let us endeavor so to live that when we come to
die even the undertaker will be sorry.

— *Mark Twain*

When we take Step Eight, we think about people we
have harmed and make a list of them. We may have
cheated, lied to, beaten up, or stolen money from these
people. Some are people we asked to love us.

When we love someone, it changes us forever. It
changes how we think about our lives. Loving someone
makes us open and raw and tender and real. It makes us
loyal and attached to one person.

If we asked someone to love us, we must pay attention
to how our disease has affected him or her. Perhaps we
couldn't help it, but this person was probably hurt very
badly. How can we help him or her heal? How can we
help this special individual trust again and love again?

This is one of the hardest problems we face in recovery.
We can get help from professional counselors as well as
our recovery friends when dealing with tough relationship issues.

PRAYER FOR THE DAY
Higher Power, help me face the pain my
disease has caused those who love me.
Help me carefully decide how to make amends.

TODAY'S ACTION
Who are the people in my life that I am attached to? Is it
a good attachment? What can I do about the attachments
that are hurtful?

*The pleasure of criticizing robs us of the pleasure
of being moved by some very fine things.*

— Jean de la Bruyère

Criticizing others is a defense against joy. Addicts
become afraid of joy because this is what our illness
attacks. Just as lung cancer attacks the lungs, addiction
attacks joy and intimacy. Anything important to us will
have to be betrayed or surrendered to our addiction.
Over time, we become afraid to find joy in anything.

When fear overwhelms us and we seek refuge in the
negative, let us remember our program. Recovery shows
us through the Steps how to change bad into good, pain
into joy. Being willing to invest in joy again will make us
vulnerable. And that means we can be hurt again.

But now we don't stand alone. If we lose our joy, we
know where to go to find it or whom to ask to help us
create more. Are we willing to risk again, or do we hide
in negativity because we're afraid to step back into life?

PRAYER FOR THE DAY
*Higher Power, help me turn away from my desire to
be negative. Help me be an example of joy in motion.*

TODAY'S ACTION
Today I will think about the last time I was critical of
something. I will talk to my sponsor about it and try to
find the ways I was using negativity as a defense. How
could I use the program to change this?

The most wasted of all days is one without laughter.
— *e. e. cummings*

One of the true gifts of recovery is that we learn to laugh again. No matter how beat up our spirits have been by our addiction, no matter how heavy or hard our hearts have become, one day we find ourselves laughing. The lightness in our hearts lets us know life is good.

It may happen in a meeting as we suddenly stop taking ourselves so seriously. It may happen as we learn to socialize again and share a joke or score a goal in a group of our new friends. It may happen as we look into the eyes of someone who loves us and our hearts bubble over with joy.

Laughter heals us. It is one of our heart's songs. There is always something to laugh about in our life, somewhere—and we need only look in order to find it.

PRAYER FOR THE DAY
Higher Power, please give me something today that will tickle me with joy or humor. Help me give in to the urge to laugh. I know my laughter is music to your ears.

TODAY'S ACTION
When I notice something to laugh or smile about today, I will share it with others. Humor and joy are meant to be shared.

[She] didn't want her kindness returned. She
wanted it passed on.
— *Karen T. Taha*

One of the most important slogans we have in recovery is "Pass it on." Keep nothing to yourself—especially the joy and happiness you experience. How crazy these types of statements sounded when we first heard them! We may have even said to ourselves, "Cheap little slogans." Now they echo in our minds and offer us comfort during troubled times. Now they are a way of life. Why? Because we're selfish, and love joy and happiness—and working to make others happy about life creates more happiness for us! Recovery taught us that cheap little slogans were, in reality, challenges.

Our slogans teach us to "Keep it simple." When times get tough, "Easy does it" is the way to proceed. When we want to hide in the past or in the future, we hear the challenge "Just for today." When we get afraid and think that a lifetime of recovery will be too hard for us, a cheap little slogan like "One day at a time" will save our lives.

PRAYER FOR THE DAY
Others have given me their joy and kindness when
I had none. Higher Power, help me to "Pass it on."

TODAY'S ACTION
Today I will seek not to receive kindness, but to give it, expecting nothing in return "Just for today."

"The pursuit of happiness" is a most ridiculous phrase; if you pursue happiness, you'll never find it.

— *Charles Percy Snow*

Happiness is a funny thing. We all want it, but we don't quite know what it is or how to get it. Looking for it led us to try alcohol or drugs. But for us, that was a dangerous experiment; it led to our addiction and nearly cost us our lives. We have a deadly disease.

Some people look for happiness in power, some in owning things, some in gambling or sex or danger. None of these paths lead to happiness.

Happiness comes from being who we are meant to be. There is a reason each of us is here. We have things to learn and things to do and people to love. We will discover these things through prayer and meditation, and through listening to people who are happy. That's why we choose a stable and content sponsor.

PRAYER FOR THE DAY
Higher Power, please help me keep my goals straight.
I want happiness—I want to be on my right path.
Help me listen today for your directions.

TODAY'S ACTION
As I pray or meditate today, I will make sure I am clear about who I want directions from—my Higher Power, not my Inner Addict!

We recovered alcoholics are not so much brothers
in virtue as we are brothers in our defects and in
our common striving to overcome them.

— *Bill Wilson*

Our primary purpose in recovery is to help each other
and those who will come after us. What an interesting
task for self-centered people! By helping each other overcome defects of character, we forget about ourselves,
and the voice of our ego grows less intense. The fellowship of recovery works to break down self-centeredness
and to remind us that we cannot do it alone.

We must never forget that it is in the "we" of the program that we find relief from the "me" of addiction. It is
in the "we" that we find the answers to the troubles and
challenges life will give us. Loving relationships ask that
we step outside of ourselves into a larger world. Do we
believe more in the "we" of recovery or in the "me" of
ego?

PRAYER FOR THE DAY
Higher Power, help me overcome my defects of character
by guiding me deeper into the "we" of recovery.

TODAY'S ACTION
Today I will call my sponsor and talk with him or her
about how I can be of better service to others.

All the art of living lies in a fine mingling of letting go and holding on.
— *Havelock Ellis*

Our addiction led us to let go of everything important to us and hold on to our alcohol and drugs. Now that we are sober, we can do it the other way around. We can let go of alcohol and drugs, and the other things that make us sick, and we can hang on to the things that help us get well and stay healthy.

What should we let go of as we learn to live in recovery? Alcohol and drugs. Cravings. Shame. Fear. Being stubborn. Big egos. Having to be in control of outcomes. Having to be in control of other people.

What should we hang on to? Our sponsor. Our Twelve Step group. Our Higher Power. The process of working the Steps. Our values. Our faith. Love. Our dignity and self-esteem. Routines and rituals that keep us healthy.

PRAYER FOR THE DAY
Higher Power, finding the right balance of letting go and holding on isn't easy. Please help me today.

TODAY'S ACTION
Am I a person who has more trouble letting go or more trouble hanging on? I will talk about this with my sponsor.

We have met the enemy, and he is us.

— *Walt Kelly*

We have also met the solution, and *that* is also part of *us.* It is as simple as this: the men and women who choose to face their lostness face their illness. And once we move into the recovery community, our fellow members remind us of what waits for us if we place principles before personalities. Our fellow members also remind us of the Steps and how in working them we find freedom and serenity. But freedom and rebuilding of our lives can only come after we surrender.

When we find ourselves at war with ourselves, as we will, we are to turn to the solution, the fellowship, and the Steps. We need to let the war be over. Surrender needs to be a daily event. It is time to rebuild and recover what we lost to our addiction. We have been our own worst enemy long enough. Now it is time to be a friend to ourselves.

PRAYER FOR THE DAY
Higher Power, fill me with your peace. I surrender
so I can be of service to you and others who still suffer.

TODAY'S ACTION
Today is a good day to surrender. I will write down five problems I am having. I will surrender them to my Higher Power through prayer and meditation. I will surrender them to the program by talking to my sponsor or group about them.

People are what they believe.
— *Anton Chekhov*

What we believe helps us build a framework for our lives. Our most important beliefs, our core beliefs, tell us what kind of person we should be. When we are healthy, our core beliefs are based in love, kindness, courage, and good work.

When we are not healthy, it is hard to live fully and feel good about ourselves. Our disease got us into that situation. We couldn't live fully; we couldn't feel good or act like a good person. Even before our addictions, many of us were told as children that we were not good enough or even that we were no good.

That's why changing what we believe is a big part of recovery. Finding a Higher Power to believe in, seeing ourselves as good people who can do good things in life—these are important core beliefs in recovery. When we believe these things, we become them.

PRAYER FOR THE DAY
Higher Power, help me believe and think in right ways that are helpful to me and to those around me.

TODAY'S ACTION
Today I will list the five things I believe are the most important guides for how to live my life. I will talk with my sponsor about them.

Everything is clearer when you are in love.
— John Lennon

Addiction is an illness in which we betray love. We turned our backs on concern, on the love of others. Even when our Higher Power would whisper words of concern, telling us that we were in trouble, we turned away. Love and care came to feel like an acid on our skin. Love, care, and concern would activate our shame, our fears. We became confused.

Recovery is about love. In the Third Step, we're asked to turn our will and lives over to "care." We, as members of the fellowship, love each other back to health. As we do this—as we surround ourselves with our Higher Power's love and spiritual principles—things become clearer. Addiction is not our purpose. Love and caring for others is our purpose.

PRAYER FOR THE DAY
Higher Power, help me see things clearly. Help me to embrace love even when the challenges of love scare me.

TODAY'S ACTION
Today I will make a list of all the things I lost because of my addiction. I will share this list with recovery friends.

The grand essentials to happiness in this life are
something to do, something to love, and something
to hope for.

— *Joseph Addison*

As we become more comfortable in our new sober life, we get a feeling about what we can do with our time, talents, and skills. We know at a deep level that it is important to work, to care for family members, and to keep the world going. We need to feel like we earn our keep in some way.

We need love, too. Our program teaches us a great deal about love—how it begins with honesty, forgiveness, and acceptance. It grows with gratitude, action, and communication. We learn to share, help others, and love.

We also learn to hope. In Step Two, we came to believe that a Higher Power could restore us to sanity. With this new sanity, we believe our Higher Power has a plan for us that will be better than our own ideas and dreams.

PRAYER FOR THE DAY

Higher Power, you are doing for me what I could not do
for myself. You are giving me health and sanity. Please,
don't stop there! I believe you will give me love, good work,
and a full life. Help me accept these things. Thank you.

TODAY'S ACTION

What did I do today that was worthwhile? Did I act in a caring way toward anyone? Are there mistakes I would like to fix? I will write down my thoughts.

Friendship is always a sweet responsibility, never an opportunity.
— *Kahlil Gibran*

Fellowship and friendship, how nice it is to have found both. But with them comes responsibility. At a meeting, I once heard a woman say that the only reason she was there was to give a friend a ride to help her stay sober. Then she admitted that she cared more about her friend's recovery than she did about her own. She had been planning a drunk in her head because she was tired and angry. However, the two women were going to go out to supper after the meeting and just talk, learning more together on how to stay sober one day at a time.

Often we learn to care for ourselves by caring for others. Our illness taught us to hate ourselves, to hurt ourselves. Recovery—its fellowship, its friendships—gives us the opportunity to love again, to care again, and eventually, to love ourselves again. The miracle of service and friendship to others is the miracle of finding self and purpose again.

PRAYER FOR THE DAY
Higher Power, help me accept the responsibility of friendship, to call my friends to offer support when needed. Help me be part of the miracle.

TODAY'S ACTION
Today I will write down all the responsibilities I believe friendship asks of me. I will share this list with a friend.

JULY

Humbly asked Him to remove our shortcomings.
— *Step Seven of Alcoholics Anonymous*

We learned to be humble—to see clearly who we really are—when we took Step Five. We faced many things about ourselves that we didn't like. We started to realize we'd need a miracle to change all the things about us that need to be changed.

In Step Seven, we ask our Higher Power to work that miracle. We open ourselves to becoming all that we can be, all that our Higher Power wants us to be. We know what we are asking for will mean change—and change is not easy. That's why we need all Twelve Steps.

Step Seven changes our lives. All the Steps before Step Seven get us ready. All the Steps after Step Seven help us repair the damage from our old life and live successfully in our new life.

It's exciting and amazing, isn't it? With our own hard work and a miracle from our Higher Power, we get to live new lives.

PRAYER FOR THE DAY
Higher Power, thank you for giving me a second chance at life. Thank you for the direction and fellowship of recovery, allowing me to live as a new spiritual person.

TODAY'S ACTION
Today I will think about the people at my meetings who have been clearly changed. I will make a phone call to one of those people today and ask about his or her experience with Step Seven.

There must be more to life than having everything!
— *Maurice Sendak*

Greed can cause us to want everything and more. The more we get, the emptier we feel. Then the pain of feeling empty leads us to want more. We think because we hurt, we deserve some kind of reward. Addiction is greed in a very pure form.

Recovery asks that we feed our spirits, not our desires. It asks that we see pleasure as a by-product of deeds done well, not something we are entitled to. It asks that we be of service, that we seek to give instead of just take, that we seek *enough* instead of *more*. The miracle is that when we live a life of sobriety, hope, and service, we have more than we ever dreamed we could have.

PRAYER FOR THE DAY
Higher Power, help me to find balance between wants and needs. Help me be less greedy.

TODAY'S ACTION
Today I will write out five reasons why greed can be dangerous to me and my sobriety.

Fear less, hope more; eat less, chew more; whine less, breathe more; talk less, say more, and all good things will be yours.

— *Swedish Proverb*

The Swedes are practical people. What they are basically saying in the proverb above is this: "Keep it simple. Get out of your own way. Just do the next right thing, and life will go okay."

That is good advice. So often we make things harder than they need to be. We need to work our program every day. When we start out with prayer or meditation, we see the day more clearly. Sometimes we need help or information, so we have to ask for it. That's not as hard as it used to be.

Why? Because the program has given us a great gift— humility. We know we are not better or worse than everyone else. We are who we are, we know what we know, we need help sometimes, and that's all okay. We all need each other.

PRAYER FOR THE DAY
Higher Power, I believe that whatever I need to do you will show me how to do it. I will relax and just do it.

TODAY'S ACTION
Have I ever gotten stuck on little or big things because I didn't ask for the information or help that I needed? I will list three times I have gotten stuck and what I did to get unstuck.

We're all only fragile threads, but what a tapestry we make.
— *Jerry Ellis*

What a wonderful quote to describe the fellowship of recovery! As we meet in our healing circles, we weave together beautiful new lives, beautiful new tapestries. We take bits of wisdom and color from each other and add them to our lives. Together we weave a magical rug on which we journey to new lives and witness grand sunrises and sunsets. Alone we are fragile, but together we are strong and colorful.

PRAYER FOR THE DAY
Higher Power, help me to remember that my strength is not in standing alone, but in standing in the middle of many.

TODAY'S ACTION
Today I will think about the threads that go into my recovery tapestry. Who are the people I most treasure? What are my most valued experiences?

A man is what he thinks about all day long.
— *Ralph Waldo Emerson*

Our disease kept us thinking about alcohol or drugs all day every day until we could think of little else. Finally we became addicts, gobbled up by our all-consuming thoughts and cravings.

Now in recovery, we can be something else. We are becoming free of our addiction, and our minds can think about other things. What do we want to think about? What do we want to be?

It's easy to let the noise around us tell us what to think about. At the end of the day, we can end up feeling out of touch with who we are. We've been giving our minds to whatever is on the radio, television, or the gossip grapevine at work or school. That's why it's good to spend part of each day thinking about things we truly believe are important and worthwhile.

PRAYER FOR THE DAY
Higher Power, help me understand that what I do with my mind and my time is important. What I do with my mind is my inner life. What I do with my time is my outer life. Together they define who I am.

TODAY'S ACTION
I will think about the way I used my mind and my time today. What feels good and fits for me? Is there anything I want to do differently tomorrow?

*Man loves company even if only that of a small
burning candle.*
— *Georg Christoph Lichtenberg*

Our illness kept us alone. As it got worse, we placed
alcohol or drugs ahead of people more and more often.
And we ended up more and more alone. Even people we
care about refused to be around us because of the way
we acted. There were places we were not welcome anymore. Many of us got to a place where we couldn't even
stand our own company.

Being part of the fellowship of recovery means we never
have to be alone again. This can scare those of us who
learned how to survive alone. We pretended we didn't
need others. We now need to allow ourselves to embrace
our new friends and the fellowship of recovery. Within
the fellowship, we will find people to be with. We'll also
find the answers on how to live productive, joyous lives.
The light of each of our candles burning together lights
our way.

PRAYER FOR THE DAY
*Higher Power, you have brought me into recovery
for a purpose. I don't always know the purpose,
but I know I'm to help and nurture the fellowship.
I'm to help others feel not so alone.*

TODAY'S ACTION
Today I will think of ways I may still be keeping myself
alone. I will talk with my sponsor or group about how I
can move deeper into the fellowship.

*In the midst of movement and chaos, keep still-
ness inside of you.*
— Deepak Chopra

Finding the stillness inside ourselves is a lifesaver. If we
think back, we can remember how badly we wanted
peace when the craziness of addiction would get too
awful to bear. We can remember how sometimes we
may have considered ending it all just to find peace.
Nearly all of us have felt that way at times.

But now, in recovery, we have a much better way to
find peace. When the craziness gets big around us, we
can say a prayer, breathe deeply, and take a step back for a
moment. We can see that the craziness is just out there; it
is not in us. It will pass. We are actually okay. All we need
to do is let go of our panic. Trust in our Higher Power.
Breathe. Be ourselves. We know what to do when we go
to that still place inside of us. We know.

PRAYER FOR THE DAY
*Higher Power, help me stay calm inside today.
Help me stay connected to you through all the
day's busy action and activity, even if gets crazy.
With your help, I can stay sane and centered.*

TODAY'S ACTION
Today I will think about the kinds of craziness that sometimes pop up in my day, and I will stop these things from
taking my serenity away. Instead I will focus on two things
I can do to stay centered.

I think I can, I think I can, I think I can.
— *Watty Piper,* The Little Engine That Could

Often in early recovery, we question whether we can be one of the winners. We doubt ourselves, for we had promised ourselves so many times before that we would turn things around, but we did not do it. We were fighting our addiction alone. We thought we were just making bad decisions; we did not know that we suffered from a dangerous and powerful illness.

This time is different, however. We are each other's hope. When we doubt our ability to stay sober, we see others worse than we are working the program. We tell each other, "You help me stay sober today, and I'll help you stay sober tomorrow." Together we know we can do it. The longer we work together for sobriety, the more the doubts fade away. If we ever have doubts, we need only turn to the "we" of recovery and let it nurture us past the doubts.

PRAYER FOR THE DAY
Higher Power, help me to see that doubts are just signs that I need to move closer to you and my recovery friends. Help me run to you with my doubts instead of hiding in them.

TODAY'S ACTION
What doubts am I wrestling with today? I will list these and share them with my Higher Power and another person.

The man who has no inner life is the slave of his surroundings.
                                        — Henri Frédéric Amiel

The culture we live in is not very good for our hearts and souls. If we look carefully at the messages we hear every day about what is important, this is what we hear: It's important to have a sexy smile. It's important to use the right furniture polish, toothpaste, deodorant, hair color. It's important to be rich. It's important to look right. It's important to have a new car. Booze makes us sexy. Cigarettes make us sexy. Being skinny makes us sexy. Sex is better than love. Power is better than sex. Being rich is better than anything.

According to the outside world, we are never good enough. We never have enough things. It's a trap.

How do we get out of the trap? We let go of the messages we hear from outside. We listen to our spirit, our Higher Power, and our spiritual teachers—our sponsor and our friends in recovery. We focus on things that matter and have real meaning.

PRAYER FOR THE DAY
*Higher Power, help me avoid the trap of society's hype
"One day at a time." Help me find out who I am
by listening to you and your messengers. Thank you.*

TODAY'S ACTION
Today I will list the things I do each day that keep me out of society's traps.

*Tell me what company you keep, and I'll tell you
what you are.*
— *Miguel de Cervantes*

Once we were addicted to alcohol or drugs, our prior-
ities changed. Our families wanted our time, but we
gave our time to alcohol or drugs. We found new friends
who used like we did or at least wouldn't ask questions
about how we used.

Recovery asks us to "Stick with the winners." What
do these winners look like? They are women and men
who show up and work to live the spiritual principles of
recovery. These spiritual principles are obvious in the
company they keep. They do the service work; they give
rides to people who need to get to meetings; they make
the coffee; they call people to offer encouragement and
see how they are doing. They are the winners because
of the company they keep.

PRAYER FOR THE DAY
*Higher Power, today I will keep company with you.
I will work to be the person you want me to be.*

TODAY'S ACTION
I will make a list of all the recovery winners I know. I will
connect with at least three of them today.

Aim at nothing and you'll succeed.
— Anonymous

We have an inner need to do something worthwhile. When we have no goals, we are likely to become depressed since there is nothing to live for.

But life does need us. There are things we are here to do—each of us. Our Higher Power will give us the clues we need to find our reasons for being here. All we have to do is keep an open mind. We might be surprised at the path we find for ourselves.

It could just be that our reason for being here is not all about us. We are here to give, to help, to contribute to this group effort we call life.

But what if we don't know our path? Then we suit up and show up and see what needs to be done.

PRAYER FOR THE DAY
*Higher Power, help me pay attention
to where you are leading me.*

TODAY'S ACTION
Today I will write down any secret wishes and goals in my heart that I don't talk about. Then I will write about the reasons I keep them secret. It's okay for today—I don't have to tell anyone.

Service is the rent you pay for room on this earth.
— *Shirley Chisholm*

As active addicts, we became very self-centered, acting as if we were the center of the universe. We demanded free rent. Many of us forgot why we were placed on this earth: we are here to be of service. What does being of service mean? It means being available, and it means doing. It is action, not just thoughts of action. We are to be doers. In our program, we help others get and stay sober. But we also clean coffee pots, answer phones, and attend meetings. We see a need, and we address it.

Outside of our program, we are to help those in need. If we have a friend who is hurt and can't get around, maybe we do some of this person's chores. If we have an elderly neighbor who can't get out, maybe we offer to do his or her shopping. Or maybe it means volunteering at a local agency. Service helps us by freeing ourselves of ego—if we let go. We need to pay our rent, and we need to pay it on time.

PRAYER FOR THE DAY
Higher Power, help me to be of service. I often forget my true purpose in life, which is to be of service to you and others. Help me to remember.

TODAY'S ACTION
I will make a list of four things I can do today to help others. I will do all four things.

What was hard to endure is sweet to recall.
— *French Proverb*

The Big Book says that we should not regret the past, but that we should also not shut the door on it. This is one of the promises of our recovery program. No matter how terrible the times in our lives have been because of our addiction, we will know that they have made our recovery all the sweeter.

It takes a long time and a lot of work to get to that point. The Big Book says that we will get this feeling while we are working Step Nine, making amends to those we have harmed. It's hard to imagine, is it not? The idea that facing the people we hurt will heal us?

Yet that is exactly what happens. As we make our amends, we realize that we are all on this life journey, together or separately. And we all face challenges and tests. We all do the best we can to learn our lessons of faith, love, and hope, and to then live more fully.

PRAYER FOR THE DAY
Higher Power, help me keep my life in perspective.
Help me be happy for where I am today.

TODAY'S ACTION
Today I will list two or three times that were very hard when they happened but in the end had some good come out of them.

*Thou hast only to follow the wall far enough and
there will be a door in it.*

— *Marguerite de Angeli*

Sometimes we are stumped. We want to do the right
thing, but we just don't know what it is. It seems like
there is an invisible wall in front of us, blocking our
vision and holding us back.

If we keep praying and listening, we begin to see the
shape of the wall in front of us, and we can explore that
wall. Sooner or later, we find a way to a door that leads to
the other side.

It's a funny thing, but we seem to always find that door
at just the right time—in our Higher Power's time. Once
we get used to this happening in our recovery, we understand that our Higher Power uses these walls to guide us
sometimes. They are okay. We asked for guidance, and
now we are getting it. We learn to welcome the walls
and to welcome the doors through them.

PRAYER FOR THE DAY
*Higher Power, help me learn to appreciate the
walls as well as the doors. The walls keep me safe
until it's the right time to go through.*

TODAY'S ACTION
Was there a time when I stood face-to-face with a wall I
could not get through? What happened? Today I will write
three lessons I learned from that experience.

The past is never where you think you left it.
— *Katherine Anne Porter*

We often hear that we should "Leave the past behind." Yet our recovery program tells us it's better to face our past and then clean it up.

Why is that? Because all the things that have happened in our life are a part of us, and we'll take them with us into the future whether we want to or not. If we let shame and fear keep us from cleaning up our messes in life, they will pop up and make trouble for us in the future. We might avoid falling in love because we hurt someone we loved once. We might go on a bender when we bump into a using buddy at the grocery store.

Because of our disease, we have these kinds of things in our past. But we don't need to be crippled by them. Instead we can clean up our past as best we can and learn the lessons that are there for us.

PRAYER FOR THE DAY
*Higher Power, help me clean up my past
without shame. Help me keep in mind that I am
accepting my disease and taking responsibility
for my recovery with dignity and respect.*

TODAY'S ACTION
Today I will think about the fact that all kinds of diseases affect people's lives—not just addiction. We are not the only ones who have to change our lives to take responsibility for our recoveries.

The soul is awakened through service.

— *Erica Jong*

Service is one of the cornerstones of recovery. It helps us step outside of our egos and ourselves. The divine in our souls naturally seeks out good and wants to do good deeds. Service is not a duty but a privilege. Service is taking gifts given to us and using them to improve the world and lives of others. It is energy directed toward good. We are designed to be givers and not just takers. When we help another, we can feel our soul smile.

Our illness stole our sense of value, our self-worth. Service helps us to reconnect and see our value and worth. Many say that it was through service work that they first experienced a spiritual awakening. This was their soul smiling, being happy and saying, "Thank you for letting me be involved in life again. Thank you for letting me dance with the souls of others again."

PRAYER FOR THE DAY
Higher Power, show me a need and give me the
power and desire to step out of self and into service.
Help me act from my values and not my shame.

TODAY'S ACTION
Today I will volunteer to do some service work. I will walk through my day looking for suffering that I can help lessen.

If I had been present at creation, I would have given some useful hints.
— Alfonso the Wise

Even with all we have learned about our own limits and how things seem to usually work out when we stop trying to control them, we still think we know best. Our egos never quit, do they? Over and over, we find that when we get what we want, we often end up in trouble. When we get what our Higher Power wants for us, we are happier.

Our recovery program suggests that we pray *only* for knowledge of our Higher Power's will for us and the power to carry that out. Praying in this way takes a great deal of trust. We need to trust that our Higher Power truly does care for us and will lead us through the process of living a good life that fills—not empties—our hearts and souls.

PRAYER FOR THE DAY
Higher Power, I ask only for knowledge of your will for me today and the power to carry that out. I trust that if I do this, I will be living the life that is most fitting for me today.

TODAY'S ACTION
How hard is it to trust my Higher Power? What are the things that have happened in my life that make it hard to trust? Do I think these things were my Higher Power's will? What advice would I have given my Higher Power about these things? I will talk through these questions with my sponsor today.

*Facts do not cease to exist because they are
ignored.*
— Aldous Huxley

This is a hard concept for us addicts to get. We believed
avoidance was a form of self-care. Our illness depended
on our ability to deny its existence. Only when we were
bleeding out of every pore of our body were we willing
to admit that maybe there was a slight problem. We were
afraid of the facts. To face the facts meant dealing with
betraying our illness. It meant admitting we were lost
and in need of help from others.

Recovery, from Step One onward, is about confronting
our issues straight on. We take personal inventory a lot
in order to break through our denial and bond with the
truth. We face, directly when possible, the people we have
hurt because the fact is we have hurt many, and we have a
responsibility to try to help heal these wounds. As we do
these actions, we watch ourselves become stronger. Our
confidence—not arrogance—grows. Do we always like
facing the facts? *No!* But our lives aren't based only on feelings anymore. They are based on doing the next right thing.

PRAYER FOR THE DAY
*Higher Power, with your help and guidance I can break
through my wall of denial. Show me the things I need to face.*

TODAY'S ACTION
Sometime during the day, I will sit down and make a list of
issues I am avoiding. I'll commit to talking with my sponsor about what is on the list.

He that plants trees loves others besides himself.
— *Thomas Fuller*

Trees take many years to become beautiful. They start out small and scrawny, and they need attention and care. Planting them is a lot of work for very little payback in the short term. But over time, trees become big, beautiful, and useful.

When we plant trees, we are doing it for the people who will come after us. We care that this place will be beautiful for them.

Important decisions can be reframed by asking, "What will be the effect of this decision on the children to come after us seven generations from now?"

Seeing ourselves as part of a long cycle of life is truly a gift. We can feel the connections with those before us and those yet to be born. Let's do it with love.

PRAYER FOR THE DAY
Higher Power, help me feel connected to all of life today, and help me to act lovingly with care for the past and the future.

TODAY'S ACTION
What can I do today that will live on into tomorrow? Plant a flower or a tree? Teach a child something new? Send a card to a friend? Today I will do one thing.

It does not do to dwell on dreams and forget to live, remember that.

—*J. K. Rowling*

Recovery, above all else, is about living. We are to exchange our addictive dreams for the tasks of recovery and the challenges of living. Remember that. We are to work the Steps. We are to be of service to others. We are to work not just to live by spiritual principles; we are to *become* those spiritual principles. If we remember these things, we will receive gifts beyond our wildest dreams. It's not magic; it's the miracle of recovery. The more active we are in living a life directed by spiritual principles, the more miracles we will experience.

PRAYER FOR THE DAY

Higher Power, give me the power to do your will, to live life on life's terms. Help me to live by spiritual principles and to be open to the miracles they will create.

TODAY'S ACTION

Today I will consider how comfortable I am with the spiritual principles of recovery. I will ask a friend whom I trust to tell me how he or she sees me doing with my recovery. I will ask this person if there are any ways I could do better.

Most new discoveries are suddenly-seen things
that were always there.
— *Susanne K. Langer*

In recovery we discover new things every day. We discover things about ourselves, about other people, about how life works. Life becomes interesting again.

What a change from the days of our addiction when we were bored with everything except the craving that drove us to get that next high from alcohol or drugs. All our energy went into such a small slice of life that it wasn't even real life anymore. In fact, it led us toward death.

What a great feeling it is to be interested in life again. Now that we are ready to look we will see things that are new to us every single day.

PRAYER FOR THE DAY
Higher Power, help me discover more of your wisdom and your world today. Help me see life as an interesting adventure.

TODAY'S ACTION
Today I will pay attention. I may discover things about other people, about myself, about nature. Would I see these things if I wasn't sober today?

It's not easy to learn to whistle if there's no one to show you how.
— *Janusz Korczak*

How lucky we are for those who have gone before us. They have worked hard to find sobriety and develop it into a program where millions can be touched by it. They developed the Twelve Steps and Twelve Traditions so we have guides in how to get sober and develop lives of dignity and respect.

We also need to see that we are responsible to teach those who need to learn to whistle. We are responsible to serve and reach out to the still-suffering addicts around us. We will teach those we meet to whistle, and they will teach still others to whistle. This is our way. We are to be there for each other and for those who will follow. We pass it on so we can keep it and allow it to get deeper into our hearts and souls.

PRAYER FOR THE DAY
Higher Power, help me to embrace my responsibilities for the still-suffering of the world. Help me use my energy to serve.

TODAY'S ACTION
Today I will reach out to the newest members of my group. I will call them to see how they are doing and to see if they want to go out for coffee. My treat.

The only courage that matters is the kind that gets you from one moment to the next.
— *Mignon McLaughlin*

One of the gifts of recovery is that we become the people we want to be. We want our lives to reflect our new values, like honesty, generosity, caring, and fairness.

Becoming a new person can be tricky, however, because the reality of living out our values means we have to face life in a new way. Being honest means we stop lying. This includes even quick little fibs that don't seem to hurt anyone. Being generous means we give something up—money, time, attention—in order to give to someone else. Being fair means we accept the consequences we have earned.

Living out our new beliefs and values requires courage to face life on life's terms. We stop the slippery behavior we have used in the past to slide past our moments of opportunity. Yes, *opportunity*—to be the person of courage and values that we want to be.

PRAYER FOR THE DAY
Higher Power, please give me courage today to stand up for what I believe and to do your will instead of looking for an easier, softer way.

TODAY'S ACTION
Today I will think about the day that just passed. Were there moments when I chose the easier, softer way instead of standing up for what I believe in? What could I have done instead?

I have lost my favorite teacup. I can have lost my teacup and be miserable. I can have lost my teacup and be all right. Either way the teacup is gone.

— *Chinese Proverb*

It does little good to look back with sadness or shame about the past. One of the promises of recovery is that we will neither regret the past nor wish to shut the door on it. We are to admit and accept. We work to stay in the moment, for in this moment we can work for our future. If we stay sober in this moment, we increase our chances of being sober in the future.

In recovery, we use our energies and attitudes to live in the present. We are to be willing to let the past be the past and just focus on today. Remember this: It is only in this moment that we have choice and influence. It is in this moment where we choose to act to end our isolation or to increase our isolation from family, friends, values, and our Higher Power. And once this moment is gone, we must let it be gone.

PRAYER FOR THE DAY
Higher Power, I can only connect with you in each moment. Help me to have the courage to live in the present and not hide in the past or in the future.

TODAY'S ACTION
Today I will work to develop my skills of living in the moment. I will use awareness and attitude to stay in the present and pull myself back into the moment.

To the person who is afraid, everything rustles.
                                    — *Sophocles*

We addicts know fear. Some of us denied our fear totally, acting strong and tough. Some of us carried real weapons—guns and knives—but most of us used our mouths to scare others away. It worked. They stayed away, and we were alone and scared.

Some of us did not deny our fear. In fact, we drowned in our fear—using alcohol or drugs to soothe ourselves. We looked for someone to take care of us, protect us. But we never trusted. We stayed alone and scared.

In recovery, we learn real courage. We stand in the light of reality. No toughness, no weakness, no weapons, no whining. We learn to face each moment with new tools and a new outlook. How can we make such a huge change? With the help of our friends. In recovery, we are no longer alone.

PRAYER FOR THE DAY
Higher Power, help me remember that you
will give me whatever strength I need
to get through anything that comes my way.

TODAY'S ACTION
Today I will list ten things that I was afraid of during my using days. How do I feel about those fears now? Do I have new fears? I will talk with my sponsor about my experiences with fear and faith.

Heartbreak is life educating us.
— *George Bernard Shaw*

Addicts are children of pain. As our illness progressed, it created more and more pain to let us know we were lost. Pain is a by-product of betrayal, and ours is an illness of betrayal. As we betrayed our values, pain was how our values called to us to return home. Our values were trying to get our attention and educate us about how lost we had become.

Recovery involves listening and learning from our pain or the pain of others. The more we listen, the more we learn. We hear of mistakes made and heartbreak created. We learn that in heartbreak lies the seeds of new beginnings. We learn that our Higher Power enters through the wound of our broken hearts and is always ready to help us transform anger into patience, sadness into serenity, fear into courage. Are we willing to be students of our pain?

PRAYER FOR THE DAY
Higher Power, I bring my trouble,
my problems, and my heartbreaks to you.
Use them to teach me how to grow as a person.

TODAY'S ACTION
Today I will visit or call an old-timer in my group and ask how the recovery process and this person's Higher Power have used heartaches to teach him or her.

And envy and pride, like weeds, kept growing higher and higher in her heart, so that day and night she had no peace.

— Snow White and the Seven Dwarfs,
Grimm's Fairy Tales

Why is it that we constantly compare our lives to those of other people? Like the wicked queen in Snow White, we hate to think that anyone is prettier, smarter, or richer than us. Our envy and our pride can rob us of our peace of mind and can destroy our soul.

Luckily recovery teaches us that our job is to be the best we can be, not to compete with others. Each of us has our own work to do in life, and we have been given the talent and tools to do that work. Our gifts are different from other people's gifts. Our work is simply to be our best selves.

PRAYER FOR THE DAY
Higher Power, help me understand my gifts and my work. Help me see what I can bring to the world that is special. Help me see and claim my special gifts.

TODAY'S ACTION
Today I will make a list of the people I envy. Beside each name, I will write down what it is that he or she has that I want. What can I learn from seeing this list? I will talk it over with someone.

Failure is the opportunity to begin again more intelligently.

— Henry Ford

We tried hard to be good people and good family members, but our illness wouldn't let us. Our addiction works to make us feel ashamed. At some point in our illness, most of us came to see ourselves as failures. We were not. We were opportunities waiting to blossom. We were out gathering information on how to be better people by learning what not to do.

Shame is about failure; guilt is about mistakes. We are guilty of being addicts and alcoholics. Each day that we are sober we have the opportunity to begin again. Hopefully we will take the knowledge we gain from the day now behind us into the actions of the next twenty-four hours.

PRAYER FOR THE DAY

Higher Power, thank you for the gift of getting to begin again. Help me to use the opportunities of the day to help others and to learn. Help me to be open-minded, a learner.

TODAY'S ACTION

Today I will list anything from the past that I still have shame about. I will talk to my sponsor or someone else I respect about how to use the Steps to heal these wounds.

The noblest pleasure is the joy of understanding.
— *Leonardo da Vinci*

Leonardo da Vinci is one of the most famous inventors and artists of the Western world. He painted the *Mona Lisa* and *The Last Supper*. He made scientific inventions. Yet this man said the best kind of joy comes not from *doing* great things, but from *understanding*.

Think about it. When we understand how things work, it can be easier to accept them. Sometimes understanding can even lead to change. We can apply our knowledge of how things work in one area of life to a problem in another area. Understanding helps us begin to know what is possible.

Our recovery is teaching us to understand many things—our addiction, ourselves, our relationships, our spirituality. Now when a new situation comes up in our lives, we have wisdom that can help us.

PRAYER FOR THE DAY
Higher Power, help me understand the lessons you offer me each day. The more I understand, the wiser I become. The wiser I become, the more I want to do your will.

TODAY'S ACTION
Understanding is a gift of my program. I learn to understand myself and others by working the Steps. What am I learning to understand today?

Success is the ability to go from one failure to another with no loss of enthusiasm.
— *Winston Churchill*

Ours is a program of action. Recovery and sobriety require work. We work the Steps. We do service work. We work to make the newcomer feel welcome. Our lives depend upon our success. We can't afford to sit around and wait for recovery to happen. Again, ours is a program of action, and it is action that will create our success.

Recovery from our illness, like other major illnesses, demands that we get involved. Luckily there is much for us to do. There are hospitals we can visit and bring meetings to. There are friends that need our support and words of encouragement. There is always a task that needs us, so let's get busy and help out!

PRAYER FOR THE DAY
Help me to be a person of action. I will do your work. I will place your principles into action, with your help and guidance.

TODAY'S ACTION
What are three things I can do to improve the quality of my recovery today? I will call my sponsor and commit to doing them today.

How can I believe in a Higher Power? I was taught that God is just an idea that weak people use as a crutch.

— *Alcoholics Anonymous Member*

After we admit how serious our addiction is, we have to face our fear and sadness. Without the help of a Higher Power, we are hopeless. That's why we each must find a Higher Power that can give us the help we need.

Some of us don't like Step Two because we think it asks us to believe in somebody else's idea of God. It doesn't. It doesn't even ask us to believe in our own idea of God. The most important thing is to find a Higher Power—not necessarily the Highest Power—to help us stay sober, one that can teach us to succeed in sobriety and one that we trust.

We don't have to understand this Higher Power. We just have to believe that it works.

PRAYER FOR THE DAY
Higher Power, I ask you to come into my life and show me how to trust and understand you.

TODAY'S ACTION
Today I will make a list of three people or things that know more about recovery than I do. I will circle the one I trust the most.

AUGUST

*Made a list of all persons we had harmed, and
became willing to make amends to them all.*
— *Step Eight of Alcoholics Anonymous*

Step Eight scares many of us. But we need to remember
that by the time we get here, we have been changed. We
have everything we need to move ahead into a new life.

There's one thing that holds us back, however—the
damage we did to other people. We carry the guilt and
emotional baggage of knowing we have caused a lot of
hurt. Before we can move freely into our new life, we
need to repair the damage we caused as best we can.
That's the purpose of Steps Eight and Nine.

In Step Eight, we make a list of the persons we harmed
in our past life. Some were hurt by our drinking or drugging, and some were hurt by our Addict personality. It
doesn't matter how or why we hurt them; we just put
their names on a list. We know who they are.

PRAYER FOR THE DAY

*Higher Power, help me remember the people I have harmed.
I need your help to handle my feelings as I make this list.
Help me stay centered and sober as I face this task.*

TODAY'S ACTION

Even if it's not time to do my Eighth Step yet, I will start
by writing down the names of people I've harmed for later
use. I will then talk to my sponsor and make a plan for
doing Step Eight.

There is but one secret to success—never give up.
— *Ben Nighthorse Campbell*

Even if we slip or relapse, we must never give up. Recovery will never give up on us. If we start to feel hopeless, we need only go deeper into our recovery village—to live at the center of the village. We need to surround ourselves with recovery. To get ourselves so busy in recovery and the actions of recovery that we must let go of any feelings of hopelessness. But never give up.

One member said at a meeting, "The only reason I have thirty years of sobriety is because recovery never gave up on me. Even after repeated relapses, they kept a chair open for me." Remember this: the recovery community needs us, and there is always a chair open for us.

PRAYER FOR THE DAY
Higher Power, when I have a moment of wanting to fail, help me to be a success. Get me to a meeting. Have me call my sponsor or a friend. Give me service work to do. Thank you for never giving up on me even when I gave up on myself.

TODAY'S ACTION
Today I will write down a plan of what I will do if I ever feel like giving up. Whom will I call? What are my favorite readings that bring me hope? Where are my places of sanctuary?

Get busy living, or get busy dying.
— The Shawshank Redemption

In order to really be in sobriety, we have learned to surrender to the fact that we have a disease. In Step One, we get our ego out of the way and admit that our disease has control. In Step Two, we find something or someone we believe can lead us back to sanity.

By the time we get to Step Three, we make the big decision: "Get busy living, or get busy dying." We choose. That is true freedom.

If we choose to get busy living—to work a recovery program—we need to take a big step into the program. Right now. We're in or we're not. If we step into recovery, we stay free. We have all the help we need to stay sober and get well. If we don't step in, we're on our own—and we know where that got us.

Change is always scary, but it's worth a try. So we step into recovery. If we don't like sanity, health, and serenity, we can back out and have our old life again.

PRAYER FOR THE DAY
Higher Power, I am stepping into recovery for today.
Please help me get busy living.

TODAY'S ACTION
Today I will find a place to be alone for a few minutes. I will stand tall, feet slightly apart, hands held open, and chest high. I will say the prayer for the day. Then I will listen.

There is more to life than increasing its speed.
— *Mohandas Gandhi*

We live in a fast-paced world. It will not be slowing down. And as addicts, we often enjoyed the intensity and drama that living a fast-paced life creates. The rhythm of addiction is fast and chaotic.

Recovery has a different rhythm, a different pace. We need to go at a pace that allows us to stay connected. Connected to others, connected to our Higher Power, connected to our values. In recovery, we reduce our speed. We meditate. We sit in meetings and adjust ourselves to the pace of the meeting. In slowing down, we start to see the details of life; it is in the details that we find meaning, answers, solutions, and the beauty of life. We need to resist the pace of the world around us and embrace the pace of the spirit.

PRAYER FOR THE DAY
Higher Power, help me slow down to your pace.
Yours is a steady, sure pace like the sun moving
across the sky, slow and steady. Help me resist the
temptations of this world, one of them being speed.

TODAY'S ACTION
Today I will work to be conscious of the pace I move at. I will ask this question throughout my day: "Am I moving at a pace that allows me to stay connected to my Higher Power and to recovery?"

I've looked inside both good and bad, evil and
righteousness, and have seen hope and felt fear.
— *Erik Johnson*

A friend in recovery, taken from us before his time, wrote
this quotation. His heart gave out, some say because it
had grown too big for his body. But he died sober, living
his dream. In the time he had been sober, he gave much
to those he loved. He knew life was paradoxical. He
knew that each of us has two sides, and life demands
that we choose and be responsible for our choices.

We need to choose love and choose hope. In doing so,
we will always be turning our will and lives over to the
care of our Higher Power. These were Erik's choices.

PRAYER FOR THE DAY
Higher Power, help me live life with respect and
dignity. Help me honor those of us who have gone before.
Watch over all of us, and help me to not just find hope
and love, but to be living examples of hope and love.

TODAY'S ACTION
Today I will call someone who is important to me and tell
that person how important he or she is to me and why.

The strongest principle of growth lies in that of human choice.
— *George Eliot*

Recovery's biggest gift to us is the gift of choice. We are given back free will; we are free as long as we stay sober. Our illness, our dependency on alcohol or drugs took away our ability to choose. We didn't choose to be an addict, however. Our illness made that choice for us. We lost the ability to say no. In our hearts we wanted to say no, but our addiction wouldn't allow it.

Now that we have the gift of choice back, we have to ask, "How am I using this gift? Are my choices mainly self-indulgent, self-centered choices? Or do I work to be of service to others and my Higher Power?" Growth means choosing to place principles and others ahead of oneself.

PRAYER FOR THE DAY
Higher Power, I choose you. Please help me to put this choice into action. Show me the tasks that you want me to do. Give me the power and will to do them. Help me to not be self-centered.

TODAY'S ACTION
Today I will make a list of all the ways I was a taker during my active addiction. Then I will ask myself, "Am I still acting in these ways? Can I make better choices?"

Be willing to have it so. Acceptance of what has happened is the first step to overcoming the consequences of any misfortune.
— William James

We addicts are not known for being willing to accept the truth. For years we pretended there was no problem. Some of us, even in recovery, pretend that our problem was less than it was. The Serenity Prayer asks us to "accept the things we cannot change." We hear people say at meetings, "I think I finally accepted the First Step." Why so much talk about acceptance? The function of acceptance is energy conservation. We addicts waste a huge amount of time and energy struggling to make things happen that will never happen. In recovery, we work to practice acceptance because we need the energy to build a sober life.

PRAYER FOR THE DAY
Higher Power, today help me know the difference between the things I am able to change and the things I cannot change.

TODAY'S ACTION
Today I will reflect on this question, "What are the things I'm not willing to surrender over to my Higher Power?" I will then write out my answer.

Every great mistake has a halfway moment, a
split second when it can be recalled and perhaps
remedied.
— *Pearl S. Buck*

During our active addiction, we may have had some
moments of insight where we saw that alcohol or drugs
were starting to own our lives. But we got scared and
ran deeper into the forest we were already lost in. Why?
Because facing the truth would mean admitting we were
lost addicts who needed others and a Higher Power.

Recovery teaches us to stop and reflect. We develop
these skills by daily prayer and meditation, by doing the
Fourth and Fifth Steps, by doing the Eighth and Ninth
Steps, and by taking a daily inventory. The better we
learn to stop and reflect, the better we can protect against
relapse. By learning to slow down, we start to see those
split seconds where mistakes can be made or be avoided.
We see those split seconds when we can reach out to
others and our Higher Power, and let them help guide our
decisions. Have we learned to slow down?

PRAYER FOR THE DAY
Higher Power, help me slow down and spend
time talking with you and my friends.

TODAY'S ACTION
Today I will take time out to sit and reflect on how my
impulsiveness has gotten me in trouble. I will work to
walk slower through my day.

The problem is not that there are problems. The
problem is expecting otherwise and thinking that
having problems is a problem.

— *Theodore Rubin*

As long as we live and breathe, we'll have problems. They are simply a part of life. We need to get used to that fact and stop getting upset about every problem that comes along.

We can use the same process to solve our problems as we use to stay sober. First we take a good look at the issue and decide how big it really is. Then we decide whether it is something we can handle by ourselves. If we need help, we get it. Then we think through all the parts of the problem and decide how to fix it. We can talk it over with someone else for feedback.

Next we take action. Sometimes fixing a problem takes time, and we have to have patience. Sometimes it can't be fixed, and we need to learn to live with it.

Remember, having problems is just part of life, and overall, life is a lot better than it used to be.

PRAYER FOR THE DAY
Higher Power, help me pay attention and do what
I need to do about my problems and then let go.

TODAY'S ACTION
Today I will make a list of my problems. I will decide if I am doing the right things to work on them today. Then I will relax and do something fun.

We are all travelers in the wilderness of this world, and the best that we can find in our travels is an honest friend.
— *Robert Louis Stevenson*

Addiction destroyed many of our relationships. It took away our ability to get close to others. The above quotation reminds us that real friends are more important than the people we hung around with while using alcohol or drugs.

Recovery is all about bettering our relationships. Our lives depend upon this. We find honest friends in recovery. We are not alone anymore. We are honest with each other about character defects and work to help each other have better, ever-closer relationships. Our lives also depend upon this. We work to help each other find a way out of the wilderness or at times just survive in the wilderness. Over time, we see that, even though people can be a pain at times, friendships and relationships are the best things in life.

PRAYER FOR THE DAY
Higher Power, teach me how to be a good, honest friend. Comfort me as I travel in the wilderness of life.

TODAY'S ACTION
Today I will think about what makes a good friend. Then I will do an honest inventory of what type of friend I am. Am I there for others in the bad times as well as the good times?

*The things we take with us when we die will nearly
all be small things.*
— Storm Jameson

When we die, we will pick up our spirit and go. What does this mean? What will we take with us?

Smiles. Memories of hugs and laughter and looking into the eyes of our loved ones. The warm feeling of holding our lover, of a child on our lap, of the hand of another addict joined in ours at a meeting.

Courage. We have taken many leaps of faith in our life. Getting sober and turning our life and will over to our Higher Power was the biggest leap of faith. It took courage. When we die, we will take another leap of faith.

Curiosity and hope. The love and goodness we have found in life is enough. But they are only a drop in the bucket of the love and goodness that exists in the realm of our Higher Power.

PRAYER FOR THE DAY
*Higher Power, let me live each day so that I have many
wonderful small things to take with me when I die.*

TODAY'S ACTION
Today I will make a list of the people and experiences I cherish. Do I need to be more nurturing of these people and experiences on a daily basis?

Waste no more time arguing what a good man should be. Be one.
— *Marcus Aurelius*

Oh the ways we would work during our active addiction to convince others that we were good. When family members, friends, and employers would confront us, the words and attitude would start to fly. How dare they question us! How dare they ask more of us!

But as it turns out, recovery is mainly about action. Recovery teaches us that actions are where the rubber meets the road. Though we talk about and study the Steps, we must learn to work the Steps.

An important cornerstone of recovery is that our program is one of attraction versus promotion. We are wonderful promoters, but it is our actions that will attract others to the program. Do we offer our friends a hand or a shoulder to cry on? Do we apologize when we are wrong and then change our behaviors? Do we greet the new person at our meetings? Action! Action! Action!

PRAYER FOR THE DAY
Higher Power, help me to hear my lies. Help me to always do the next right thing, especially when I don't want to.

TODAY'S ACTION
Today I will do three actions to help someone else's day go better. I will do them in secret to make sure I'm not doing them to feed my ego.

Hitch your wagon to a star.
— *Ralph Waldo Emerson*

When we are new to recovery, there is a lot we don't know. We learn it, a little bit at a time. One of the best ways to learn more about how to work a recovery program is to work with a sponsor. Even after we have been in recovery for a long time, sponsors are very important.

Sponsors are our personal guides to living in recovery. We should choose someone who we admire, works a good program, and seems like he or she might understand us. We never have to be afraid to ask someone to be our sponsor. This person will feel good that we asked and will say yes or no depending on whether he or she can do it.

Some sponsors ask their "sponsees" or "pigeons"—that would be us—to call them every day to check in. Other sponsors might prefer to talk with us less often. They help us learn how the program applies to our daily life and relationships.

PRAYER FOR THE DAY
Higher Power, I need your help for sure, but I also need a real live guiding star to talk with—a sponsor. Help me reach out to someone who would be a good sponsor for me.

TODAY'S ACTION
If I already have a sponsor, I will talk with this person today and thank him or her for working with me. If I don't have a sponsor, I will make a decision to ask someone to sponsor me.

The emptiness inside was like an explosion.
                                        — *Eleanor Clark*

Many of us addicts have had moments during our illness when all of our denial and excuses stopped working and the hell of this illness hit us directly in our face. The emptiness of our life became too much to bear.

We did not know that we had an illness that was keeping us from being the person we wanted to be. We did not know there were people in recovery circles ready and waiting to help us be that person. They were to be our guides. They laughed about their mistakes and learned from them instead of repeating them. They made room for the pain of others instead of running from it. They were the answer to our emptiness, filling it with joy, spiritual principles, and genuine relationships.

PRAYER FOR THE DAY
*Higher Power, bless and watch over my family and friends.
Thank you for giving me these crazy, wonderful
people who make up my recovery network.*

TODAY'S ACTION
Today I will take time to thank the people in recovery who now live in my heart. If I have no such people in my heart and the emptiness still lives inside of me, I will think about whom I could invite into my heart.

It is the paradox of life that the way to miss plea-
sure is to seek it first.
— *Hugh Black*

The desire for pleasure is one of our most basic human drives. We need pleasure to be healthy physically, emotionally, mentally, and spiritually.

Pursuing pleasure, however, can be difficult to manage. We found that out with our addiction. Chasing the high gradually led to never being able to get high enough or stay high long enough. We can do that with other pleasures, too, if we are not careful to stay balanced.

So how can we have healthy pleasure? By understanding that pleasure is not the goal of life. Rather, pleasure is a result of doing our life well. When we do relationships well, they give us pleasure. When we work hard, relaxing becomes a pleasure. When we've been in meetings or dealing with customers or kids all day, our favorite music is a pleasure to listen to. After a healthy meal, dessert is a pleasure. Why? Because these things are not the main thing; they are special.

PRAYER FOR THE DAY

Higher Power, help me take care of the important things in my life today. And now and then during the day, help me feel some pleasure as a reward for keepin' on keepin' on.

TODAY'S ACTION

I will think of the moments of pleasure I've had over the past twenty-four hours and make a list. How did they happen?

Safety is all well and good; I prefer freedom.
— E. B. White

Addiction seduced us into believing we were safe. We had problems, and we ran to the bottle or our pills. We calmed down and felt safe, at least at first. It was only later into our illness that we learned we were trapped. We had exchanged our freedom for dependence. Addiction is the loss of freedom. Addicts can't say no. This is the nature of our illness.

Recovery is about freedom. But all freedom comes at a price. We must work to create freedom for ourselves and to help others get free. With freedom comes choice, and with choice comes responsibility. Until confronted, we often don't realize that we're avoiding responsibility with excuses and blame. And we're not alone. Dependent people don't like responsibility. We want others—our families, our friends—to take care of us. To keep from slipping into old behaviors, we need to confront ourselves and avoid retreating into old, "safe" habits.

PRAYER FOR THE DAY
*Higher Power, you gave me free will, and I
exchanged it for dependence. Help me to accept
your gift and all the responsibilities that come
with it. Give me the power to do your will.*

TODAY'S ACTION
Today I will list the different ways I've avoided responsibilities. Then I will ask myself, "Am I still avoiding becoming a responsible person?"

Talk is cheap because supply exceeds demand.
— *Unknown*

"Walking the walk" is the real test of whether we are changing. "Talking the talk" is just, well, talk.

During our active addiction most of us talked often about changing. We swore we would get our act together, we would never make the same mistake again, or we wouldn't do it all again. Sometimes we actually meant it when we promised to change, but we were surprised we could not do it. We were powerless as long as we were using alcohol or drugs.

Now we know we have a disease, so we finally see the need to live differently. We have surrendered to a life without alcohol and drugs. Now we are "Walking the walk."

PRAYER FOR THE DAY
*Higher Power, please help me be the honest
and trustworthy person I have promised to become.
I know I need to stay sober in order to make this happen.*

TODAY'S ACTION
Is there anything I said I would do that I have not done? What is it? What is my plan to take responsibility for this? I will talk with my sponsor about it.

Resourceful and energetic as a street dog.
— James Mills

Not all of the things we learned during our addictive years need to be gotten rid of. We learned to be clever and resourceful. We learned determination. Just ask anyone who stood in our way of getting high.

In recovery, we take these qualities and let them be guided by spiritual principles. We now use our determination to heal old hurts and build new relationships. The mistakes we made during those years now become our teachers and guides.

As the program teaches us, we will not wish to shut the door on our past—for in our past are many diamonds covered in mud. We need to find these diamonds and use the program to shape and polish them into a new story of hope and gratitude.

PRAYER FOR THE DAY
Higher Power, direct my "street dog" energy into
doing good. Help me to stay close to the principles
of the program and their healing powers.

TODAY'S ACTION
Today I will list the parts of my using days that I can use to build a new life. I will recover that which is useable and let go of the rest.

There's nothing enlightened about shrinking so other people won't feel insecure around you. We were born to manifest the glory of God within us. It's not just in some of us; it's in everyone.

— *Marianne Williamson*

Our Higher Power asks for us to be our best and help each other. But most of us act like, "Who, me? Little old me? I can't."

The truth is, we *won't*. We go around acting as if we aren't enough—not good enough or smart enough or strong enough to do our Higher Power's work. So we all sit around being afraid or lazy, and our Higher Power's work doesn't get done.

Are we ready and willing to be smart, talented, and strong? Are we ready to like ourselves and the spirit within us? We need to just do it. We need to remind our friends to do it, too.

PRAYER FOR THE DAY
Higher Power, help me turn on my spiritual headset today so I can hear what you are asking me to do. Help me just do it.

TODAY'S ACTION
Today I will look at how I practice Step Eleven. I will talk with my sponsor about tuning in to my Higher Power's will for me through Step Eleven.

*The greatest of faults, I should say, is to be
conscious of none.*
— Thomas Carlyle

Many of us may have resisted the self-examination of
recovery. We didn't wrong anyone; we were the victims!
We acted like the world owed us something. But the
reason that the program is so heavy on taking inventory
is because it helps us build awareness. It helps us break
through the denial that is part of our illness.

Constant self-examination for character defects is a
wonderful way to build awareness and conscience. Prayer
and meditation help us create conscience and awareness.
But we must be sure not to beat ourselves up over our
character defects. This is just another form of avoidance.
As active addicts, we would often hide in the forest of
shame instead of seeking help. Let us not make that same
mistake in recovery. Conscience needs to have compassion wrapped around it.

PRAYER FOR THE DAY

*Higher Power, help me uncover my character defects and
change them. I offer up these defects to you, for it is only
with your help that I can change them into growth.*

TODAY'S ACTION

Today I will call my sponsor and ask him or her to help me
develop a daily inventory sheet of my character defects. If
I don't have a sponsor, I will get one.

Progress, not perfection.
— *Alcoholics Anonymous Slogan*

We don't expect our lives to be perfect. We don't expect ourselves to be perfect. We just want to stop the insanity of addiction and begin to live lives that make sense.

We don't expect to be perfect, but most of us do want to be good. We can actually live up to that goal now that we are sober. It takes a lot of work, and we are always seeing new ways to improve. Working the Steps helps us learn a great deal about how we can be better people. Having the love and support of our recovery friends and the guidance of our sponsor gives us the strength and help we need.

In fact, the work of being a good person brings many rewards. We invite spiritual teachers into our lives, we make true friends, we gain respect for ourselves, and we find that others respect us, too.

PRAYER FOR THE DAY
Higher Power, help me see today how I can pitch in to make things better in some way at work, at home, or for someone who needs a bit of kindness.

TODAY'S ACTION
What's one small thing I am willing to do in the next twenty-four hours to bring a bit of goodness to a situation? Call a friend who needs support? Bring flowers to work to brighten the day? Take time to really visit with a child? I will make a decision to do one special thing—and do it!

Prayer may not change things for you, but it sure changes you for things.
— Samuel Shoemaker

Prayer, that personal talk between our Higher Power and us, is very important. Each time we pray, we deepen our relationship with our Higher Power. Our Higher Power will not appear before us and change the things we want changed. But each time we pray, our Higher Power will put before us the spiritual principles that fit our situation.

The actions of prayer are surrender and preparation. In prayer we open ourselves up to our Higher Power and get ready for the changes that will come, sometimes quickly but most often slowly. The miracle of prayer is how we change. Our views change, our attitudes change, and just maybe, we find ourselves accepting what we couldn't accept before.

PRAYER FOR THE DAY
Higher Power, change me. Make me into the person you know I can be. When I resist your desires for me, whisper how much you love me and that it will be okay. Help me walk past my fears.

TODAY'S ACTION
I will take time throughout the day to pray, even if it's just a simple pray of gratitude such as, "Thank you, Higher Power, for today."

Friendship with oneself is very important because
without it one cannot be friends with anyone else
in the world.
— Eleanor Roosevelt

What do we need from a friend? Let's think about that for a moment and see if it applies to how we treat ourselves.

Let's start with the basics: a friend is *for* us, not *against* us. That means a friend won't do anything to harm us if he or she can possibly help it. A friend is there for us when we need understanding, tells us the truth, and does the things he or she promises to do. A friend likes to be around us, thinks we are a good person, and believes we are honest. A friend shares what is going on in his or her life and cares about what is going on in ours. A friend does things to help us feel happy. A friend forgives us when we ask for forgiveness.

We do these things for our friends. And we do a much better job of them now that we are sober. But do we do them for ourselves? It's a question worth thinking about: am I a good friend to myself?

PRAYER FOR THE DAY
Higher Power, help me pay attention to myself
the way I pay attention to my friends.

TODAY'S ACTION
I will have a little friend-to-friend visit with myself right now. How am I doing? What's going on with me? Want to go for a walk and talk, catch up on things? How about going to the new exhibit at the art museum this weekend?

*The human mind treats a new idea the way the
body treats a strange protein; it rejects it.*

— P. B. Medawar

All of us are guilty of rejecting what seems foreign to us.
As active addicts we heard, "You should get sober," and
we rejected the idea. We rejected any idea that got in the
way of our using. As our illness progressed, we became
close-minded and rigid. The primitive parts of our brain
controlled our lives.

Recovery pushes us to be open-minded—to put ideas
before instincts, to place principles before personalities.
We are to stop and think about what will happen if we
start using again. We call it thinking through the high.
One of the most beautiful gifts of recovery is that we get
our mind back. Whether we choose to use it or not is up
to us.

PRAYER FOR THE DAY
*Higher Power, you gave me a wonderful gift: my mind.
Help me to use it to better my life and the lives of others.
Help me to not be rigid and close-minded.*

TODAY'S ACTION
Today I will list the ways I became rigid and close-minded.
Because fear most often creates rigidity, I will ask myself
what I may be afraid of.

Colors fade, temples crumble, empires fall, but wise words endure.
— *Edward Thorndike*

When we were in our active addiction, our focus was very narrow. We felt that things outside our own life were very distant and didn't matter. No one had any words of wisdom for us, no one understood us.

We were surprised to find in treatment and the rooms of recovery that other addicts do understand us, more than we ever thought possible. Now we have another surprise waiting: we are not so different from all people through the ages.

To connect with people across time and distance, we can read about how others see things. There have been great books that are still important after hundreds of years.

With books around, there's never a reason to get stuck in our thinking. We can share in the experience, strength, and hope of wise people through the ages.

PRAYER FOR THE DAY
*Higher Power, help me learn to enjoy reading
as a way to tap into the wisdom of the ages.*

TODAY'S ACTION
Today I will find a book that looks interesting. Then I will find a comfortable chair and try reading for five to fifteen minutes.

God gave you a gift of 86,400 seconds today.
Have you used one to say "thank you"?
— *William Arthur Ward*

Ours is an illness of negativity. As our illness progressed, our lives decayed. This is normal. Over time, we became comfortable in being negative and cynical. When someone was happy around us, we'd find ways to diminish that person's joy, or we'd make fun of him or her.

In recovery, you hear people talk about the importance of having an "attitude of gratitude." A common motto is, "If you're sober today, you've had a good day." Why so much about gratitude? Is it just because we're not living a life of hell anymore? No, for life in sobriety can be hell at times, too. It's because gratitude and negativity can't be experienced at the same time. If we are practicing gratitude, then we are working to free ourselves from the negativity of addiction.

Remember, our Higher Power is about care and love, not about being negative. We need to ask ourselves, "Am I practicing an attitude of gratitude?"

PRAYER FOR THE DAY
Higher Power, thank you for this day.
Thank you for the struggles and the gifts of today.
Teach me to find and believe in joy again.

TODAY'S ACTION
Throughout the day, I will find ways to say thank you to others and my Higher Power. In the past, how did I use negativity as a defense?

Cruelty cannot stop the earth's heart from beating.
— *Evelyn Coleman*

Sometimes it seems like all the things we talk about in recovery make life sound wonderful and perfect after we stop using alcohol or drugs. Of course, that is not true. Everything will never be perfect, at least not anytime soon.

There will always be plenty of bad things happening. Sometimes they happen by accident, sometimes through addiction, sometimes because some people choose to act for their own power or pleasure at any cost.

We can't control all those things. We can only decide whether we want to be part of the problem or part of the solution. We can become part of the life energy of the earth's beating heart. We do this by stepping into our Higher Power's will for us, the life energy that is there for us every minute, every day.

PRAYER FOR THE DAY
Higher Power, please help me be part of life's good energy today. Thank you.

TODAY'S ACTION
Today I will look to see what kinds of cruelty are going on around me and will put this into a list. What am I doing so that I will not be part of the problem?

Let the beauty we love be what we do.

— *Rumi*

It is up to us to search for happiness and joy in our recovery, to search for the beauty and love that fill the recovery rooms. Why? Because we are needed! At times, all of us feel as if the world would not miss us if we were not around. But what about the new person who may see us as having what he or she wants? What about this person's family members who are seeing him or her sober, maybe for the first time in years? We are needed. Our stories of transformation are needed.

We just need to look around our meeting room. If these people were not here, would we be here? We keep ourselves accountable by being accountable for and to others.

We don't dare pretend that we have no importance. We must put any self-pity or self-hate aside and get busy being of service. We are here to help ourselves by helping others. This is what we do.

PRAYER FOR THE DAY
Higher Power, help me see the value that I hold.
Help me be of value to you, the world,
and the still-suffering addicts.

TODAY'S ACTION
I will list all my qualities that can be used to make this world a better place. I will make at least two other people smile today.

*Trust yourself. You know more than you think
you do.*
                                    — *Benjamin Spock, MD*

Our addiction put us in a downward spiral of bad behavior and bad feelings. With all that negativity in our life history, how can we trust ourselves?

That's where the fellowship of recovery comes in. We learn to trust ourselves by opening up our thoughts and feelings to others and listening to their feedback. With their help, we sort through the beliefs and attitudes we have picked up over the years. We keep some, fix some, and throw some away.

We need to trust ourselves. As we dig deeper into what we really know, believe, and want—what gives us purpose—we will find that we are good people, and we know more than we think we do.

PRAYER FOR THE DAY
*Higher Power, help me remember that sometimes bad
things happen to good people, and that at times good
people make bad decisions—but that is part of life's
journey and not a judgment on who we are. Help me
trust that I am a good person, and that I have value.*

TODAY'S ACTION
Today I will write down ten good things I know about myself. Then I will put my hand over my heart and read these ten things to myself, out loud.

What man was ever content with one crime?
— *Juvenal*

What alcoholic has ever been content with one drink? What addict has ever been content with one pill or one shot? One is not in our nature. We are the people of more. Ours is an illness of more.

We can also think of our illness as a criminal. We can think of all the things it worked hard to steal from us. Did it not steal our self-esteem, dignity, and integrity? Did it not steal our family, career, and health?

Recovery works to protect us from this thief. Like a homeowner who installs a security system, we install spiritual principles into our lives. We also bring other recovering people into our lives to help protect us from relapse. Many make the mistake of believing they can protect themselves, but we cannot. We need to let others help and guard us. In turn, we must help others guard against this thief called addiction.

PRAYER FOR THE DAY
*Higher Power, you are my greatest protection
from the thief of addiction. Help me accept
your help through the actions of others.*

TODAY'S ACTION
Today I will list the things my addiction has stolen from me. If I have friends or family members whom I have lost to this illness, I will place them at the top of the list.

You have to stop when you're lonely and listen.
— *Charlotte Zolotow*

Every one of us gets lonely sometimes. It's part of being human. We seem to be made so that we hunger for love and understanding from others.

When we were into our addiction, we turned to alcohol and drugs to fill that lonely, empty feeling. They can't. Substances and things can't fill our emotional needs.

Now that we are in recovery, we know that loneliness will often visit us and try to move in. When it does, we know where to go—to people who understand and love us. To our sponsor and our recovery friends. To our family. To our Higher Power.

PRAYER FOR THE DAY
*Higher Power, please come into my heart
and fill any emptiness that I may feel today.
Ease my loneliness with your gentle peace.*

TODAY'S ACTION
Today I will listen to the voices of others. I will listen to the voices of nature. I am not alone. I will listen.

SEPTEMBER

Made direct amends to such people wherever possible, except when to do so would injure them or others.
— *Step Nine of Alcoholics Anonymous*

There's a good reason Step Nine comes after we have worked the first eight Steps of our recovery program. By the time we get to Step Nine, we have a clear picture of who we have been and what we have done. We have trust in our sponsor and other recovery friends. We have a spiritual advisor with whom we took Step Five. We now have a whole team of people to help us carefully repair our past damage.

We use our support team to help us decide how to best make amends to the people on our Step Eight list. We must make amends with care, or we may do more harm than good.

What do we get out of it? As we fulfill our responsibility to repair past damage, we become free to move into our new life, a life beyond our wildest dreams.

PRAYER FOR THE DAY
Higher Power, please give me good judgment and courage to make true amends to those I have harmed. Help me have good understanding, the right timing, and the help of my recovery support team to keep me sane and sober.

TODAY'S ACTION
Today I will think about the last time I made an amends to someone I harmed. Did it take courage? What happened? I will write down two things I learned from that experience.

I take it as a man's duty to retrain himself.
— Lois McMaster Bujold

All of us have an instinctual side to our being. It is a wonderful, energetic part of who we are. It seeks out fun and pleasure, and works to avoid pain. It is ready to fight or flee if scared. There is nothing wrong with this side of us unless we let it run our life as it did during our addictive years.

This side of our being needs to be disciplined and guided. This is where spiritual principles come in handy. They are like the reins on a horse, directing our energies and spirit toward a goal. We need to retrain old impulses that could get us to use again. This retraining is sometimes called growing up. Some of us just do it later than others. And some people never grow up. These people stay trapped in denial and remain slaves to their impulses. But we're growing up, and it feels right.

PRAYER FOR THE DAY
Higher Power, you gave me instincts for a reason.
Help me to use the energies and spirit of them
to have a joyous life and to do your work.

TODAY'S ACTION
Today I will list all the ways I still need to grow up. I will ask my sponsor to talk with me about how to use the Steps to help in this process.

Tenderness and kindness are not signs of weakness and despair but manifestations of strength and resolution.
— *Kahlil Gibran*

We seem to think that the mean people are strong. We give power to people who are rude or cruel.

Many of us used to play by those rules. We were afraid, so we acted mean, rude, tough, or cool to keep people away from us. We tried to make other people more scared of us than we were of them.

Now in recovery, we are learning kindness is strength. It's not easy to be kind when others are mean or when we are in pain or afraid. It's not easy to think about others instead of ourselves when we are tired or frustrated with problems of our own. But we are learning to do these things, and we are becoming strong enough to do them. We are not ruled by our feelings anymore. We can choose to be kind and tender.

PRAYER FOR THE DAY
*Higher Power, help me remember that all
true strength and power come from you.
Give me grace today to be strong, kind, and tender.*

TODAY'S ACTION
Today I will think about the tugs of frustration, anger, and fear I've felt over the past twenty-four hours. I will talk with my sponsor about how to "Let go and let God."

The purpose of education is to replace an empty
mind with an open one.
— Malcolm Forbes

All of us need to be educated. All of us are close-minded
in some way. If we step back and examine close-minded-
ness, we see that it is really fear. Fear shuts a mind down
quicker than anything. We should be mindful that messages of fear are not always true. Remember when fear
told us that sobriety was dangerous and that we should
continue living our old lives? Fear would have us retreat
into more fear.

It is hard to keep an open mind, especially when fear
is shouting its messages. This is why we go to meetings
on a regular basis; we go to keep our minds open, even
when fear wants them shut down. Meetings have a way
of lessening fears.

Meetings are like going to school. We re-educate ourselves in how to live life. Addiction educated us in the
ways of fear; recovery educates us in human and spiritual ways. We study spiritual principles, but we also study
each other's lives, seeing miracles emerge. So we ask ourselves, "Am I willing to re-educate my mind?"

PRAYER FOR THE DAY
Higher Power, when fear comes, as it will,
help me to seek out you and others who love me.

TODAY'S ACTION
Today I will list my fears. How do I become close-minded?
I will work to turn these fears over to my Higher Power.

Courage is resistance to fear, mastery of fear—
not absence of fear.
— *Mark Twain*

Which of the Twelve Steps teach us how to handle our fear? The Steps that scare us the most! For many of us, that would be Step Three, Step Five, and Step Nine. These Steps ask us to move from one place in our life to a new place.

Step Three asks us to let go of the life we are leading and to step into a new life. We have faith that it is okay to do so because we have come to believe in a Higher Power that will restore us to balance and sanity.

Step Five asks us to move from a secret life to a life of openness. We have to leave our hiding place, take off our masks, and let someone else see us as we really are.

In Step Nine, we take responsibility for our past actions. We face the people we have hurt, and we do what we can to repair the damage we caused.

Each of these Steps teaches us courage.

PRAYER FOR THE DAY
Higher Power, give me courage to move into
the new life you have made open to me.
All I need to do is take the Steps to get there.

TODAY'S ACTION
Today I will think about my courage in my recovery.

Love is life; and if you miss love, you miss life.
— Leo Buscaglia

Our love for alcohol and drugs got in our way of loving ourselves and others. When loved ones asked us to change or get help, we turned away from their love. As the pain of our addiction increased, we just drank or used more. We missed a lot of life and love because of our illness.

As we start to heal from our illness, we are asked to step back into life. We must be willing to become vulnerable again. This is why love takes courage. Love demands that we put ego aside and put loved ones first. Before we know it, we're stepping out into life. As addicts, we often preferred the sidelines. Recovery pushes us to go to meetings, to do service work, and to get counseling when we need it. Recovery keeps pushing us to be better people, to move back into love and life.

PRAYER FOR THE DAY
Higher Power, push me back into life, especially when I want to sit on the sidelines. Teach me the skills of love so I can better serve the world.

TODAY'S ACTION
Today I will list the primary parts of life I avoided because of my alcohol or drug use. What would my life look like if I acted more from love?

*Even though a number of people have tried, no
one has yet found a way to drink for a living.*

— *Jean Kerr*

Some of us may have dreamed about working at a winery
or a brewery so we could taste the product all day. A true
addict's dream! "Making a living" means making money
to support ourselves and our family. Because we have a
disease, we cannot afford to drink or use drugs because
our addiction gets in the way of our larger lives.

Even if someone else pays the bills and feeds and clothes
us, all of us need to "make a life" for ourselves. Making a
life is not just about money. It is about the other things
that are important to us: family, a sense of purpose, love,
fun, good health—everything that makes life enjoyable.
We can't do a good job of making a life by drinking or
using drugs either.

What good are drugs and alcohol? No good for us. They
cost us just about everything in life that matters.

PRAYER FOR THE DAY
*Higher Power, help me see how rich my life can be
as I live sober in recovery. Help me want the truly good
things in life: love, friendship, healthy fun, and purpose.*

TODAY'S ACTION
Today I will make some time to sit and list all the things I
would lose if I returned to my addiction. I will also make a
second list of things I need to do today to create a good day
for myself and others.

The best way to cheer yourself up is to try to cheer somebody else up.
— *Mark Twain*

Our program warns us about ego and how our illness is mainly one of self-centeredness. During our active addiction we yelled at our families; we got arrested; we passed out on the living room floor. Let's face it: addiction is not a cheerful way to walk through life. Addiction is all about getting loaded.

Now that we are in recovery, we are beings who need to step out into the world. Our spirits need to interact with other spirits. As spiritual beings, we need to help others and see others being touched by our care and love. A woman starting a job in a treatment facility was asked, "Do you know what your job is here?" She replied, "To fix people?" He replied, "No, they get to decide that. Your job is to make one person smile each day." After that day, the woman said she started helping people.

PRAYER FOR THE DAY
Higher Power, help me walk cheerfully through my day. I know it is easier to be negative, but I need to turn my life over to care and love. Help me make others smile today.

TODAY'S ACTION
I will work to bring cheer and smiles to others. Today the smiles of others are more important than my ego.

Half of the harm that is done in this world is due to people who want to feel important.

— *T. S. Eliot*

Humility is a wonderful gift for us addicts. We tend to think we are better or worse than everyone else. We are not. Humility is simply knowing that we have a right to be alive and breathing as much as anyone else and no more.

Of course, we are different in some ways. We have different talents and gifts. We each have a great deal to offer, and that is good because there are a lot of needs in the world. Our job is to pitch in and make the work lighter for everyone.

Humility means taking on the role of showing up for life and doing our best. We don't expect others to do all the work for us. We don't stand outside the group feeling that we are not good enough to join in. We show up, suit up, and get to work.

PRAYER FOR THE DAY
Higher Power, thanks for helping me enjoy being part of the human race, for showing me that I'm a person who has gifts and talents that I need to share.

TODAY'S ACTION
Today I will list the talents and gifts I bring to people. Then I will ask two people, "When you see me coming, what do you expect me to bring to whatever is going on?" I will write down what they say.

When one door of happiness closes, another opens;
but often we look so long at the closed door that we
do not see the one which has opened for us.

— Helen Keller

Helen Keller, whose sight and hearing was impaired at an early age due to illness, became angry and frustrated in her suddenly silent, dark world. Her teacher, however, knew there had to be another way. This teacher taught Helen how to read, write, and communicate, which transformed Helen. She then used her vision to help people and became a symbol of hope.

We are a lot like Helen Keller, and our sponsors are a lot like her teacher. We were trapped in a dark world. Surrendering to a Higher Power, help arrived for us. Like Helen, our help also came in the form of a relationship. Those who have gone before us were ready to help us. We had to be willing to let the addictive door close and see that another was opening for us. We had to risk by letting go of one way of life and creating a new one. We should ask ourselves, "Have I closed the door to the addictive world, or do I keep it open ever so slightly?"

PRAYER FOR THE DAY
Higher Power, when I want to reopen the door
to addiction, please stand between it and me.

TODAY'S ACTION
I will think about where I am in my sobriety and what I can do today to deepen my commitment to recovery.

Life was suddenly too sad. And yet it was too beautiful. The beauty was dimmed when the sadness welled up. And the beauty would be there again when the sadness went. So the beauty and the sadness went together somehow.

— William Steig

Now we know that we can expect sadness in our lives. It goes along with the beauty. Everything that is born will one day die. Every person we love will one day die. Does that mean we should not love? Of course not! We enjoy the beauty, and we survive the sadness when it comes, with the help of our Higher Power and our friends. When we love others, we are open to sadness. It's true, and it's part of life's larger picture.

PRAYER FOR THE DAY
Higher Power, help me accept the fact that life holds sadness as well as beauty and joy. Light to dark, summer to winter, joy to pain. These are the rhythms of living. Your love helps me handle them gracefully.

TODAY'S ACTION
How can I plan to survive losses that will come in my future so I can stay sober? I will talk with my sponsor or a recovery friend today about love and loss, sadness and beauty in recovery.

Act as if what you do makes a difference. It does.
— *William James*

As active addicts, we walked through life as if we were disposable. Shame kept telling us we had no value, and over time we acted as if we had no value. We acted as if how we conducted ourselves didn't matter—but it did. A fellow addict used to say that it wouldn't matter if he dropped dead tomorrow. When he died of his addiction, there were many tears at his funeral, especially by his children.

We must go out into our life and make a difference. With each new day that we stay sober and live by spiritual values, we get rid of a bit more shame. Over time the shame goes away, and we start to see the happiness that our new way of being brings. We see that just being at home, playing with our children or spouse, makes a difference. We see that just being a good employee makes a difference. We see that just being a good citizen makes a difference. We see our value, and it makes us happy.

PRAYER FOR THE DAY
Higher Power, when I am not able to see my own value, help me to see that I make a difference. Take away my shame.

TODAY'S ACTION
Today I will practice walking through my day as if I make a difference. I will work to be helpful to others and to conduct myself with dignity.

Prayer is not overcoming God's reluctance, but laying hold of God's willingness.

— *Martin Luther*

We don't have to talk our Higher Power into helping us heal from our addiction and regain our life. Our Higher Power is ready to help—has been all along. We talk to our Higher Power to let our Power know that we are ready or that we want to be ready, and we would like some help.

We need to remember that our Higher Power is used to getting shut out or ignored by us, so we need to *invite* divine help. That's why we pray.

PRAYER FOR THE DAY

Higher Power, thanks for being patient and waiting for me. I need and want your help today, and I am ready to accept it. Thanks for helping me know your will for me today and giving me the power to carry it out.

TODAY'S ACTION

Today I will try to think of some times when I did not want my Higher Power's help. Then I will list a few of those times. Why didn't I want help? What has changed?

Most of us can, as we choose, make of this world
either a palace or a prison.
— *Sir John Lubbock*

Oh, really? If we could choose to live our life in a palace
or a prison, we'd all be living in palaces, right? Wrong.
Perhaps we would all wish to live in palaces, but would
we do the work it takes to make that choice?

Making a choice means deciding where to spend our
time and energy. Making a choice means we choose a
goal and do the work to get to our goal.

We can't stay sober today by wishing for sobriety. But
we can stay sober by choosing sobriety today—or even by
choosing sobriety this hour or this minute, one moment
at a time. When we choose sobriety, we put our time and
energy toward things that will keep us sober. And the
things that will keep us sober—caring for others, being
honest, doing our work well, eating and exercising to stay
healthy—take up our time and energy.

PRAYER FOR THE DAY
Higher Power, help me realize today that the way I spend
each moment is how I choose what my life will be. Thanks
for helping me get sober so I can make good choices.

TODAY'S ACTION
Today I will make a list of the things I wish for. Are they
worth the work? Will I choose to live my minutes, hours,
and days to get them?

*Friends are quiet angels who lift us to our feet
when our wings have trouble remembering how
to fly.*
— *Anonymous*

It's great to have friends, isn't it? When we were drinking and using drugs, the disease that stole our life also
stole the quality of our friendships. Even our best friends
could not get through to us about what we were doing to
ourselves. And our worst friends thought we were doing
just fine; they were just as bad off as we were.

Now that we are in recovery, we are able to be a good
friend to our friends again. We're making new friends,
too. We are free of the blinding self-centeredness of our
need for alcohol and drugs. We are clear of the fog that
kept us from seeing what was going on with the people
around us—how *they* were feeling and what was going on
in *their* lives. We can actually listen to our friends without the preoccupation, defenses, and denial that used to
block out whatever they were saying to us.

We're sober now. We're available for friendship again.
This is a true blessing.

PRAYER FOR THE DAY
*Higher Power, thanks for all the people in my life
who care about me and choose to be connected
to me as we go through life. Friends teach me a
lot about how much you care about me, too.*

TODAY'S ACTION
Today I will thank my friends for being in my life.

You lose a lot of time hating people.
— Marian Anderson

Many of us wrapped ourselves in a blanket of anger and hatred. We believed it would protect us. We used anger as a way to try to get some distance from the powerlessness of our illness. At least when we were angry, we didn't feel the powerlessness that was surrounding us. Remember, anger was primarily a defense. The more we sought refuge in anger, the more our fears grew. Eventually anger and hatred pushed us deeper into our addiction.

Recovery asks that we seek refuge in the fellowship and in spiritual principles. The energy we used to waste in anger and hatred is needed to build our new lives. Anger is a secondary emotion. What is under the anger—fear, sadness, or a sense of powerlessness? We work the Steps to get at these underlying emotions.

PRAYER FOR THE DAY
Higher Power, help me question my anger and to give up my hatred. I can't afford to be angry. I need the energy to build my new life and better relationships.

TODAY'S ACTION
Today I'll list five times when I used anger to put distance between me and others. I will ask, "What was under the anger? Was it fear, sadness, or a sense of powerlessness?"

Faith is, above all, openness; an act of trust in the unknown.

— Alan Watts

Many addicts struggle with finding or connecting with the idea of a Higher Power in which to have faith. Many people do not believe in God or Buddha or The Great Spirit, and so they cannot believe in a Higher Power.

Other addicts know what they believe in, and have strong beliefs about exactly who or what a Higher Power is for them.

So which group does better with its recovery? Neither—or both. It does not seem to matter specifically what these persons *believe or don't believe* about a Higher Power. What seems to matter is how people *act*. A lack of belief does not have to prevent anyone from asking for help. We just need to ask for help.

It's kind of like turning on the lights. It doesn't matter whether we understand electricity or even whether we believe in it. If we take the action to flick the light switch, it works. On the other hand, we can believe all we want, but if we don't take the action to flick the switch, there will be no light.

PRAYER FOR THE DAY
Higher Power, I know believing in you is not enough. Please give me the courage and trust I need to ask for your help, which is an action of faith.

TODAY'S ACTION
Am I taking actions of faith today? Why or why not?

It is our choices . . . that show what we truly are,
far more than our abilities.
                                              — J. K. Rowling

Many people with great abilities make bad choices. We just need to look around the rooms at meetings and we will see it. As addicts, we regularly chose alcohol or drugs over our family, Higher Power, and community. Our choices also affected our abilities. Then, at some point, we lost our choices, and our illness made our choices for us. This is what addiction is—the loss of choice.

Recovery gives back our sense of choice. Today we make different choices. We choose to go to meetings, even when we don't want to. We choose to do service work. We learn a new way to walk through the world, a more human way. People see that we are making new choices, and over time they come to trust us again. This is another gift of recovery.

PRAYER FOR THE DAY
Higher Power, I choose to turn my life and will over to you.
Please give me the wisdom to make good choices.

TODAY'S ACTION
Today I will make a list of the everyday bad choices I made during my using years. Then I will ask myself, "Am I making the same choices today?"

We may not always be happy, but we can always
be hopeful. And there's no hope without faith.
— *Terry Mark*

During our active addiction, we were used to feeding our cravings whenever they showed up. We kept a hidden bottle or stash, or kept our dealer's phone number handy.

One benefit of recovery is that it's easier to get what we need anytime we need it. All we have to do is ask for help and then accept it.

Recovery emergencies require action. The most important thing for us to remember is this: don't use. The next most important thing is: get help and support. We can pray or meditate, call our sponsor, or wake up our roommate.

The emergencies will fade the longer we stay sober and work with our group and the Steps. Each time we get through an emergency, we gain trust that we can really do this. We can have a good life.

PRAYER FOR THE DAY
Higher Power, please give me the grace to
turn to you immediately when I feel a recovery
emergency coming on. Guide me to use my program
to get through it sober and stronger. Thank you.

TODAY'S ACTION
Today I will write down the things I do each day to make recovery my way of life. The more recovery behaviors I practice each day, the more likely I will use them.

*I've learned that you can't have everything and
do everything at the same time.*

— Oprah Winfrey

We wanted it all. We wanted to feel good all the time.
We wanted to be right and have everyone see how right
we were. We wanted to always be at the center of all
the action. We wanted life to adjust to us, instead of
us adjusting to life. What a house of cards. Often we
wanted so much because we felt so empty inside.

If we try and do it all and have it all, we will fail. Life
has limits, so we have to make choices. As we go through
life, we pick and choose. We put together a good or poor
life. In recovery, we learn that we are to pick people over
things, principles over ego, and values over sensations. All
of this involves stopping and thinking. We need to reflect
on what our Higher Power wants for us. Instead of trying
to do everything, we just concentrate on doing the next
right thing. Over time we stop wanting everything and
start to see we are enough, and we have enough.

PRAYER FOR THE DAY
*Higher Power, help me to see that with you, my friends,
and my family, I am enough. When I feel empty, direct me
toward that which feeds my spirit instead of my desires.*

TODAY'S ACTION
Today I will sit, reflect, and make a list of how my desire
to have everything got me in trouble. I will then share this
information with a friend.

*Every man has to learn the points of the compass
again as often as he awakes, whether from sleep
or any abstraction.*
— Henry David Thoreau

The secret, for us, is to never let our recovery wander
away from us. We keep a good compass by working
the Steps. Working the Steps tells us what we need to
be doing and where we need to go in our recovery. Our
sponsor helps us with this and helps us stay on course.

We also need the energy behind us to keep us from getting stalled out. We keep this energy—this "tailwind"—
by making our program a way of life. The more we put
ourselves in its path, the more the recovery wind keeps
us moving. We stay in the path of this wind by going to
meetings at least once a week and by using recovery tools
as a matter of habit every day.

PRAYER FOR THE DAY
*Higher Power, help me remember that my spirituality
has a lot to do with the way I use my life energy.*

TODAY'S ACTION
Are there days when I'd like to skip my reading, my prayer,
my meetings, my conscious contact with my Higher
Power? I will talk with my sponsor about a plan to get
through this kind of day next time it comes up.

People grow through experience if they meet life honestly and courageously. This is how character is built.

— *Eleanor Roosevelt*

As active addicts, we had many experiences. But as the quote says, honesty and courage are also needed if we are to grow. What the quote doesn't say is what happens if we don't meet life with honesty and courage. If we meet life with denial and fear instead, we withdraw and start to decay from the inside out. We lose our character and dignity.

The Twelve Steps are all about character development. The First Step demands that we embrace honesty. The Fourth Step asks that we embrace courage. If we work the Twelve Steps, we will develop and grow into good people with character. We go from being characters into people with character. This is the type of growth we are seeking.

PRAYER FOR THE DAY
Today I pray for your help to meet my day with honesty and courage. Help me walk through fear instead of hiding.

TODAY'S ACTION
Today I will ask myself, "Am I being dishonest about anything? Am I hiding and allowing my fears to control me?" If the answer is yes, I will call my sponsor and talk about how I am hurting my character development.

If you go around thinking you are being cheated,
life becomes very unpleasant.
— *Felix Salten*

Sometimes we feel cheated that we have been given this darn disease to cope with. Why us? Why can't we just be like normal people? Why did we have to get into so much trouble and pain as a result of a disease that hit us and skipped over other people?

Another way to look at it is: "Hey, I'm really lucky. I have a killer disease, and I'm beating the odds. I'm sober and getting healthier every day. I got my life back."

Another way to look at it is: "At least I have a disease that I can recover from. Better this than some other disease that would have killed me outright, left me limited mentally or physically, or made life really difficult in some other way."

Feelings of self-pity disappear by the time we are working Step Nine. We may even be grateful for the path that led us to recovery. Do we believe it? There's one way to find out: we need to try it.

PRAYER FOR THE DAY
Higher Power, help me to remember that there are
a lot worse things in life than being in recovery.

TODAY'S ACTION
What are five good things that I have gotten from recovery? Ten? I will write these down and refer to them when I'm tempted to feel sorry for myself.

When all hope is lost, then it is time to surrender
to begin a new life.
— *Anonymous*

Surrender is a wonderful thing. The act of admitting we
are lost allows us to seek help—if we can keep our pride
at bay. Many of us have been taught that surrender is
a bad thing. We are never, ever to give up. How many
brothers and sisters in the program have we lost because
of this? Recovery teaches us that only by surrendering can we start to reach out to others and our Higher
Power. Without surrender, we never work the program.
At best, we just attend meetings. It's like going to the
movie theater and just staying in the lobby; we never get
to see the show.

As we get better at surrendering our issues to our
Higher Power, group, and sponsor, we learn we don't have
to wait until all hope is lost. We get better and quicker at
the skill of surrendering. Why? Because we are basically
greedy; we want the relief and solutions that lie on the
other side.

PRAYER FOR THE DAY
Higher Power, when I get afraid to surrender
my will and life over to you, please give me a
gentle reminder of how you love me and will be
there for me. Help me to remember I'm not alone.

TODAY'S ACTION
Today I will list five times I refused to surrender during my
active addiction. How did this get me in trouble?

Arrogance will always seek its own destruction.

— *Anonymous*

This saying may remind us of a little kid learning to ride a bicycle. About the time she gets it all put together—steering, balance, pedaling—she looks up to yell, "Look at me!" Then crash, down she goes.

It's important that we always stay as alert as a beginner about our recovery. We can enjoy our recovery and be happy about it, but we can't afford to think we've got it all down cold.

Other people sometimes encourage us to slack up on working our program by appealing to our pride. An old buddy might call and try to tempt us into our old habits—drinking and using. That's exactly when we need to keep our focus.

We must never forget that there are things we need to do to stay sober. "First things first"—keep pedaling.

PRAYER FOR THE DAY
Higher Power, I know it's the process of recovery,
not my pride, that keeps me sober. Please
help me keep working that recovery process.

TODAY'S ACTION
Today I will think about the times I've wanted to take my recovery for granted, and slip and slide a little in the way I work my program. How was pride involved?

When tomorrow comes, I hope that I can look back at today with pride and happiness.

— *Anonymous*

We in recovery programs are told over and over to live "One day at a time." We hear "Work to stay sober—just for today." We don't find out until later that this is how people build a future. We are creatures of habit. Even though our addictions created chaos, they also had a structure and stability to them. Over time, one lousy day became like the next lousy day. But on the other hand, if we live by our values to the best of our abilities today, we increase our chances of doing the same tomorrow.

So we should practice living our principles to the best of our abilities today. Tomorrow we may need the skills we learned today. Concentrate on today. Concentrate on being sober, happy, and free today. We deserve it, and others need us—"Just for today."

PRAYER FOR THE DAY
*Today I pray that I will have the strength
and power to live a life of values.*

TODAY'S ACTION
Today when I find myself living in the past or the future, I will gently bring myself back to the moment. I will practice living a day at a time. Practice makes better.

*The very first condition of lasting happiness is
that a life should be full of purpose, aiming at
something outside self.*

— *Hugh Black*

When we were children, we began to ask a very important question: "Why?" We probably drove our parents a
little nuts with our constant questioning. "Why it the
stove hot?" "Why is it Saturday?" "Why have a baby-
sitter?" "Why does a dog bark?"

Even as children, we humans want to know the purpose of things. At some point, we come face-to-face with
a very personal question: "Why am I here?"

We want to know that there is a purpose for our lives.
This is a core spiritual question. We find the answers we
are seeking through spiritual awakening.

Our recovery program states that we will have a spiritual awakening if we work the Twelve Steps to the best
of our ability. When we do, we will understand why we
are here.

PRAYER FOR THE DAY
*Higher Power, I may not know the purpose of
my life yet, but I know enough to turn over my life
and will to you today. Please help me know what
to do today and give me the power to do it. Thanks.*

TODAY'S ACTION
Today I will think about why I am here and what my purpose in life might be. I will write down these ideas.

A fool sees not the same tree that a wise man sees.
— *William Blake*

We do not see alcohol and drugs the way many others do. Research shows that as addicts, we have a different experience than nonaddicts when we drink or use. We can't stop after one drink or hit, and we become the fool. We give up things in order to keep using. We give up dignity, family, friends, and values. Many of us give up our lives.

When we enter recovery, we get introduced to a base of wisdom. We get to see the world the way it is, not the way we want it to be. We learn practical useful wisdom that cuts through our denial and inflated egos. It brings hope to the hopeless and humility to the arrogant. As soon as we leave our meetings, we start losing this wisdom. We always need to return for more.

PRAYER FOR THE DAY
Higher Power, I pray for wisdom and insight
into your will and vision for me. Help me to see the
world as it is, not just the way I want to see it.

TODAY'S ACTION
Today I will list five pieces of practical wisdom I have gained from my recovery program.

When I am alone, I feel like a day-old glass of water.
— *Diane Wakoski*

Being alone can be like water without bubbles. It's a little flat. It's a little boring. If we're staying away from people to avoid conflicts, then we need to be especially careful. We can easily develop a bad case of "Stinking thinking" if we sit by ourselves too long.

That's why we don't go it alone for more than a day. It's good to touch base with other people for at least a few minutes every day. Human contact keeps the waters of life moving, fresh and sparkling. When we share what we are thinking and talk it over with others, it's like refilling with fresh water.

PRAYER FOR THE DAY
*Higher Power, keep me fresh by giving me
an active life filled with good people.*

TODAY'S ACTION
Today I will think of one new idea I got by talking with someone else over the past twenty-four hours. I will keep my mind fresh today by listening and talking with others.

Our hearts harden when we close out grief and hurt, and our hard hearts bring us more loneliness. It's a cycle we need to break in recovery.

— Anonymous

The life of an addict is a life of a wounded heart. The grief of slowly losing relationships, self-esteem, and dignity takes a toll on us. When we walk into our homes and our family walks away instead of smiling at us, our hearts hurt.

Our hearts know what is right and what is wrong. But addiction slowly corrodes our concern for family and friends. Our spiritual values decay as well. Despite how we neglect others, we end up feeling like victims. And in a sense, we are being victimized—not by others, but by our illness. If we surrender our lives over to recovery, we slowly begin to heal and see that our illness hurt others and us. We see what we need to do to recover and do it willingly.

PRAYER FOR THE DAY
Higher Power, my addiction blinded me from your wishes. Thank you for never leaving me. Help me to see the next right thing and do it.

TODAY'S ACTION
Today I will make a list of all the different ways I became blinded by my addiction. I will share my list with a recovery friend.

OCTOBER

Continued to take personal inventory and when we were wrong promptly admitted it.
— *Step Ten of Alcoholics Anonymous*

The first nine Steps of the program help us put our past to rest so we can focus on living a new life. Step Ten teaches us to keep our lives clean by meeting life as it comes. We can continue to take personal inventory in several ways: by watching ourselves through the day as things come up, by reflecting on the day's issues each evening, and by taking "mini" Fifth Steps once in a while.

In this way, we keep our emotional baggage light. We refuse to carry anger, guilt, resentments, and fears. We take care of issues, and then we let them go. When we have trouble doing this, we call our sponsor for advice and pray for our Higher Power's help. What do we get in return? Serenity, happiness, wisdom, relief from fear, friends, and a true sense of belonging.

PRAYER FOR THE DAY
Higher Power, help me take responsibility for meeting issues head on so I can keep my emotional baggage light.

TODAY'S ACTION
Today I will look at how I continue to take my personal inventory. Does this method work, or am I carrying anger, fear, resentments, or shame? I will talk with my sponsor and decide whether I should try something new.

Whenever a human being becomes a battleground
for the instincts, there can be no peace.
— Twelve Steps and Twelve Traditions

As addicts, we lived a life of feeding our desires and appetites. We were self-centered and blamed others for our problems. As addicts, we didn't know the meaning of the word *enough*. We became like animals always on the hunt, looking for more chemicals.

Recovery asks that we become disciplined and place principles before personality. We're asked to do what's right rather than feed our desires. There will be times when we can't do this. This is why we need the fellowship. Sometimes we keep ourselves sober, and sometimes (most of the time in the beginning) the fellowship keeps us sober. As we get better at surrendering to the principles of the program, the battle ends, and we come to know peace of mind and peace of heart.

PRAYER FOR THE DAY
Higher Power, I surrender my will and life over to you.
Let me understand your will, not mine.

TODAY'S ACTION
Today I will list five examples of how I placed instinct and desires ahead of principles. What was the cost?

Friendship is certainly the finest balm for the pangs of disappointed love.
— Jane Austen

Many of us live with the pain of ruined love relationships. Active addiction made it impossible to love ourselves well, so we couldn't love others well either. Sometimes our relationships, if they were once healthy, can be slowly restored as we recover from the symptoms of addiction. That may happen only if both persons heal from the damage and hurts. But other times, we need to let go of failed love relationships.

At these times in our lives, we need to rely on the love of friends. Our recovery friends especially understand what it is like to lose our dreams of love.

We all hunger for love. The good news is this: we can make it on the love of friends and family.

PRAYER FOR THE DAY
Higher Power, remind me not to take the love of my friends and family for granted. Help me remember that you love me and there is plenty of love in my life to keep me going and growing.

TODAY'S ACTION
Today I will make a list of the people who love me. I must think carefully; some of the people who love me might be angry right now, but they still love me. I will read the list to my sponsor.

Courage is like love; it must have hope to nourish it.
— *Napoleon*

Hope was something we couldn't afford to have during our active addiction. Hope makes us vulnerable. Hope has us invest in life, others, and our values. Hope has us look toward the future with joy and excitement. When we were active addicts, the future meant more of the same—pain, anger, and more problems. We used all our courage just to face the day instead of facing challenges. Love of life and others shifted to love of drugs and alcohol. All hope was lost.

In recovery, we are given hope back if we are willing to embrace it. Hope holds the energy of excitement and joy. It is a belief that the world and the future hold adventures and gifts for us. It is a belief that we have gifts to give to the world. However, hope will make us vulnerable again, so we need courage to let down our defenses and let hope in.

PRAYER FOR THE DAY
*Higher Power, please help me embrace hope
so I can nourish and grow my courage.*

TODAY'S ACTION
Today I will think of my recovery friends who have the most hope and joy. I will ask them to teach me how hope has nourished their courage, their love.

*Keep love in your heart. A life without it is like a
sunless garden when the flowers are dead.*

— *Oscar Wilde*

We have heard it over and over in many different ways:
"Be happy. It's good for you." Sure. But how?

1. Our program tells us how.
2. Work the Steps. Drop the rock.
3. Live and let live.
4. Let go and let God.
5. Think before you act.
6. Be grateful every day.

If we do these things every day, our hearts will fill
with gratitude, love, and happiness. We will have some
sadness, too, because that is part of life. Still, we have to
work for the things we most want in life. The more we
work the program, the closer we are to full hearts. Soon
we will be people with joyful hearts who sometimes feel
sad instead of people with sad hearts who get drunk or
high to kill the pain.

PRAYER FOR THE DAY
*Higher Power, help me have a grateful,
loving, happy heart. Thank you.*

TODAY'S ACTION
Today I will list five things in my life that make my heart
full of happiness and love. When did I last enjoy each of
these things?

We cannot become what we want by remaining what we are.

— Max De Pree

We need to let ourselves change. To try new things. To have exciting adventures. We shouldn't stay closed to recovery, its principles, and the fellowship but should instead jump in! Nothing grows by staying the same. We are meant to develop and help others develop into the best they can be. This is opposite of addiction where we helped others and ourselves develop into the worst we could be.

Addiction made us rigid and afraid of change. Now we embrace change. With each new day, we should challenge ourselves to try a new adventure. But we need to make sure the new adventures fit within our values, support our sobriety, and honor our Higher Power.

PRAYER FOR THE DAY
Higher Power, help me overcome fear, anger, and resentment. Help me to embrace change and become the person you want me to be.

TODAY'S ACTION
I will commit to trying one new thing today, something that honors my values, my sobriety, and my Higher Power.

*Selfishness—self-centeredness! That, we think, is
the root of our troubles.*
— Alcoholics Anonymous

Every addict has to cope with a voice inside that constantly begs for attention. "Feed me!" it demands. "Feed
me alcohol!" or "Feed me drugs!"

In recovery we learn that we *have* enough. We learn
that we *are* enough. We can be good human beings. We
can reach out to others. We can share the work and joys
and sadness of life with our family and friends. We can do
our share and be a part of the human community.

PRAYER FOR THE DAY
*Higher Power, thank you for giving me life to
share with others in my community. Even if
all I can do today is smile or hold open a door,
help me remember to do something for others.*

TODAY'S ACTION
Today I will remember what I have done and thought
about over the past twenty-four hours. I will make a list
of the things that have taken my time and attention, and
then circle the things on the list that are about myself. I
will put a star in front of each thing that is about other
people or something outside myself. How many circles do
I have? How many stars? Is this a good balance? Do I want
to make changes?

Out of difficulties grow miracles.

— Jean de la Bruyère

We in recovery know a lot about miracles. We go to meetings and sit among the miracles of our fellow recovering addicts. A meeting is a miracle in progress. Next time we go to a meeting, we should take time to study the miracles around us. Where were these people before they received the miracle of sobriety?

We in recovery know the elements that make up a good miracle: willingness, honesty, openness to change, spiritual principles, laughter, tears, Higher Power, fellowship, and a large amounts of action. When we throw these elements at our difficulties, miracles happen—sometimes slowly, sometimes quickly. We then are to give thanks for these miracles. Miracles are our Higher Power and others doing for us what we couldn't do for ourselves. Miracles are gifts given and received. We should ask ourselves, "Am I willing to give up my difficulties—my old ways—and allow myself to be changed into a miracle?"

PRAYER FOR THE DAY
Higher Power, take my problems, issues,
and bad attitudes, and use them to make a miracle.
Today I will work with you and not against you.

TODAY'S ACTION
When I go to my next meeting, I will listen to the miracles that surround me and give thanks for the miracle of these changed people.

And as we let our own light shine, we unconsciously
give other people permission to do the same.
— *Marianne Williamson*

Like it or not, people are social animals. We want to fit
in. We want to be liked. We want to be a little different from others, but just a little. Mostly we want to be
like other people in the important ways. We are afraid
to step out and be really different, really special, really
smart or talented or helpful.

But what if one of us started? And then two? What
if we all decided to enjoy our differences? What if we
thought it was neat to be really true to ourselves and the
jobs our Higher Power is giving us instead of trying to be
like everyone else?

Letting our light shine means we put out energy—
energy that shines on other people. Another word for
energy is *power*. There are plenty of things in life we have
no power over—including our addictions. But the kind of
power we use when we let our lights shine is not power
over anything. It is power to live and act in good ways.
Power that makes us all free.

PRAYER FOR THE DAY
Higher Power, let your spirit move through me today,
making me free and good for myself and others.

TODAY'S ACTION
I will invite some other people to feel good about themselves today. I will tell three people something good I see
in them.

Isolation is like a tomb.
— Ian Kennedy Martin

The end road of addiction is isolation. As our illness surrounded our hearts and souls, we lost the ability to truly connect with others. We became trapped in a tomb with someone we couldn't stand, our Addict. The voice of our Addict kept haunting us with what we had become. The faces of those we had chased away also haunted us. As our illness created more pain, we used more chemicals.

The Twelve Steps and the fellowship of the program offer a passage out of our tomb. We may be scared at times because we don't always know where the Steps will lead. But they are the way out. We need to follow them, to keep walking until we see the light of our Higher Power and the smiles of the fellowship. We need never be trapped in the tomb of isolation again.

PRAYER FOR THE DAY
Higher Power, thank you for your guiding light.
Help me use it and follow it. Thank you for the
new friends I can turn to when I feel alone.

TODAY'S ACTION
Today I will connect with others and give thanks to my Higher Power. I will remind myself that if I feel alone, it is now by choice, and I can make different choices.

We are each gifted in a unique and important way. It is our privilege and our adventure to discover our own special light.
— *Mary Dunbar Hewlett*

Many of us have no clear idea of what our special light is. We feel as if we are no good at all, and nothing we do is worth much. Yet somewhere, deep inside, we can also feel the smallest belief that there is something we can do very well—something that is our special gift.

The longer we are sober, the more clues we will get to help us find our special light. People who know us will tell us things they see in us. We will learn through experience what kinds of service activities we enjoy. Our own inner voice will become clearer, and we can find our Higher Power's messages to us.

In order to find our special light, we need to be open. Perhaps our gift is something we already want and know, but it may come as a surprise.

PRAYER FOR THE DAY
Higher Power, what special light, what important gift have you given to me so that I can share it with others? Please help me find it.

TODAY'S ACTION
Today I will make a list of things I know about myself and things people say about me. Then I will look for clues in this list that might point to my special light.

God dwells wherever man lets Him in.

— *Jewish Saying*

Addiction is an illness where the only things we let into our hearts are the things that support our addiction. When our Higher Power, working through others, tried to enter, we blocked the way. Through it all, our Higher Power kept speaking to us, using our pain to get our attention. Our Higher Power wanted us to return to lives of good principles and joy. But as practicing addicts, we turned away. We turned to alcohol and drugs.

But now we can open the doors wide and invite our Higher Power into our lives. How? By inviting others back into our lives. We need to find the good people who are happy and have a good sense of purpose, and invite them into our lives. We need to find the winners and stick with them. We need to let their gifts become our gifts.

PRAYER FOR THE DAY
Higher Power, I invite you into my life.
Thank you for staying with me during the hard
times. I ask that my heart be your home.

TODAY'S ACTION
If I better my relationship with family, friends, and people in recovery, I will better my relationship with my Higher Power. Today I will do three things to get closer to others.

*I learned of my value not through books or talking
with people, but by helping people.*
— Pete P.

Doing things for others is a good way to get to know ourselves. We hear a great deal about finding our souls through prayer and meditation. But we hear much less about finding our souls through *action*—good old hard work.

When we do service work for other people, for our Twelve Step group, or for any cause, we live our values.

Service can be doing small things such as making the coffee at a meeting or helping to set up the chairs. It can be shoveling the snow, mowing the lawn, or running an errand for an elderly neighbor. Service simply means helping others.

When we were using alcohol and drugs, our actions could serve only our addiction. If we use even just a little bit of our time and energy now to work for the good of others, we will see how much our souls will grow.

PRAYER FOR THE DAY
*Higher Power, please help me see
a chance to do service today.*

TODAY'S ACTION
Today, when I see a chance to help someone, I will ask myself, "Am I able to do this? Do I have the time and the ability to be of service in this moment?" If I can do it, I will do it. If not, there will be another chance for service. I will keep watching.

It is greed to do all the talking and not to want to listen at all.

— Democritus

Sometimes at meetings, we see people who are in love with their own voice. They smile as they quote sayings and pages. We see them being happy at how clever and smart they are. This is life. This is ego, and as the above quote says, it is greed. They may be taking time away from the newcomer who needs to speak and whom we need to hear.

Ours is more of a program of listening than talking. We always need to be listening to the newly sober. It is their stories, pain, and fears that need to be heard. Their speaking helps them heal and reminds older members to be grateful and not greedy. We can't afford to become smug and self-righteous. All of us are just one drink or pill away from relapse. We should ask ourselves, "Am I someone who enjoys listening to the newcomers or just someone who enjoys listening to my own voice?"

PRAYER FOR THE DAY
Higher Power, open my ears and my heart, especially to the newcomer. Help me to be of service to others, sometimes just by listening.

TODAY'S ACTION
Today I will go to my meeting and ask the newest member to tell me his or her story. Then I will listen and learn.

I have been over into the future, and it works.
— *Lincoln Steffens*

Sometimes we worry about the future. Can we find a way to live and stay sober, to make a life that is good and happy? The answer is "Yes!," if we work the Steps. We will not worry about money. Our courage will be greater. We will have an understanding of life, and we will know what to do when we have a problem. We will know a feeling of peace and serenity.

How do we know this will happen for us? Look around at the people in your meetings who have been working a good program. Ask them if their lives are better in recovery.

Recovery cannot change every hard thing in life. People we love will still grow old and die. We must still make wise choices with our money. Storms could still come and blow down our house. So how can we be happy? Because, when we are sober, we have clear consciences, better decision-making skills, and the love and support of good friends. What could be better?

PRAYER FOR THE DAY
*Higher Power, help me live in today and do
today's work, which will make tomorrow better.*

TODAY'S ACTION
I will talk with three people today who have been in recovery longer than I have. I will ask them, "Is life better today than it used to be? How?"

Envy is like a fly that passes all a body's sounder parts and dwells upon the sores.

— *George Chapman*

As our illness progressed, we created more and more sores. Often envy and self-pity became a sick way for us to try to feel better. We wanted what others had and thought we deserved their blessings over them. We felt bad when things didn't go our way and life wasn't fair. We felt entitled and acted that way, too.

With recovery and spiritual principles, we heal these sores. We learn to exchange envy for gratitude. Gratitude is the action of being thankful for what we have, even our sores. We come to know that if we are open and work hard, they will be transformed into gifts. We now know that we have no need for envy, for we have been given a new life, a second chance.

PRAYER FOR THE DAY
Higher Power, help me to be forever grateful for the new life you and recovery have given me. Help me see envy as a character defect that can be removed.

TODAY'S ACTION
Today I will make a list of anyone or anything I envy and a list of things I have to be grateful for.

*We all live with the aim of being happy; our lives
are all different and yet all the same.*

— Anne Frank

All normal people want to be happy. It is a natural craving. People all over the world understand what a smile means.

There is one thing addicts want more than happiness. When we were in our active addiction, we gave up happiness for our alcohol and drugs. We started to use them because we thought drinking or getting high would make us happy—and it did in the beginning. But the cost became heavy. Addiction took our happiness away, yet still we wanted it more than happiness.

The program teaches us that we are born to be happy, and we can find our way to happiness by doing the work of the Steps and living responsibly. We will know pain at times, of course. We will know fear, and life will not be perfect every minute. But in the center of it all, we can be happy.

PRAYER FOR THE DAY
*Higher Power, help me recognize that there
are happy moments in every day. Help me learn
to live life in a way that brings more happy moments
and brings me help in times of fear and sadness.*

TODAY'S ACTION
Today I will list five good things I gave up so I could drink or use drugs. What will I do about these things now that I am sober? I will talk with my sponsor about this.

*Piglet was so excited at the idea of being useful
that he forgot to be frightened anymore.*
— A. Milne, Winnie-the-Pooh

Recovery is about action, and finding and creating our
place in the world, whereas addiction is about pretending. Recovery pushes us to do service work because in
service work we see that we have value and that the
world needs us. Our active addiction was a life of fear,
which we often changed into anger or grandiosity. We
acted as if we had purpose when secretly we believed
we had none.

So we need to get involved, to get busy. In fact, we
should get so busy that we forget we have fear. We will
start to see fear as a signal for us to get busy. We must
remember that recovery is a program of action. It is not
a spectator sport. We should ask ourselves, "Am I into
action or into fear?"

PRAYER FOR THE DAY
*Higher Power, you gave me fear for a reason.
I now see it is a sign for me to get busy.
Help me be a person of action and purpose.*

TODAY'S ACTION
Today I will list any fears that are getting in the way of my
recovery. I will talk with my sponsor about what action is
needed.

Living well and beautifully and justly are all one thing.
— *Socrates*

It is not complicated to live a good life. It is not hard, most times, to know what is the right thing to do. We can ask ourselves, "Is this the fair thing? Will it hurt anyone? Would it be okay if others do this, too?" Doing the right thing reflects good values such as justice, love, peace, and happiness.

We know how to ask ourselves these questions, and we know how to answer them honestly. The Addict inside our heads does not want us to face these questions. The Addict wants us to do the wrong thing so that perhaps our shame will lead us back to our addiction.

Luckily our friends in recovery help us ask the right questions—as long as we are open with them and share all the things that go on in our lives. Our sponsor and our recovery friends help us live well, beautifully, and justly.

PRAYER FOR THE DAY
Higher Power, thank you for the gift of friends who help me live my new sober life in a good way. Help me be a good friend to others, too, and help them live well.

TODAY'S ACTION
Today I will list three times I have talked with recovery friends about a choice I faced. Did they help me choose an action that fit with beauty and justice? When have I helped others think about the choices they face in their own lives? Was this helpful to me, too?

It hath been often said that it is not death, but dying, which is terrible.

— *Henry Fielding*

At some point during our active addiction, many of us started looking forward to death. The pain of feeling ourselves dying a little bit more each day and the anguish of being a phony became too much to bear. We were dying and we knew it. The hopeless often seek refuge in the endless night of death.

Recovery asks that we stop assaulting our bodies and minds with powerful poisons. It asks that we seek out life and join the party, not the wake. We embrace life-giving spiritual principles. We embrace a purpose-filled life and feel more alive. We start to smile and laugh again. We help others by being of service, and in so doing, we feel vital and alive. The only things that can stop us now are fear and bad choices. So we stay close to others and seek their advice to make good choices and walk past our fears.

PRAYER FOR THE DAY

I have been given a second life. Higher Power, help me live a life of principles and purpose so when death does come, I can meet it with dignity and honor.

TODAY'S ACTION

Today I will list five ways I was dying during my active addiction. I will then list five ways I am now more alive in recovery.

Cunning is a sort of shortsightedness.
— Joseph Addison

Addiction makes us cunning. It is one of the symptoms of our disease. We become very good at figuring out short-term solutions. How can we get what we want? How can we keep fooling people? How can we get out of this jam? We think we're pretty smart.

We learned to solve these problems to protect our addiction. We told lies, stole money, blamed other people for our mistakes—all those crazy behaviors called defense mechanisms. But all the time we were being so smart, we were actually digging a deep hole for ourselves. We spend the early time in our recovery trying to get out of that hole with our oh-so-smart Addict personality in charge.

Now we have no need for cunning. These days we're into wisdom. It's a whole new way to think!

PRAYER FOR THE DAY
Higher Power, please grant me the wisdom to
know the difference between what I can change
and what I can't. Please also teach me the difference
between short-term cunning and long-term wisdom.

TODAY'S ACTION
Today I will think about the problems I solved yesterday. Did I use cunning or did I use wisdom to solve my problems? I will then talk with my sponsor about this.

They can because they think they can.

— *Virgil*

These words describe the fellowship of our program. We gather together to see each other as sober and free. Alone we can't imagine a life without alcohol and drugs. Together we see and create a life free of alcohol and drugs. We borrow each other's minds in order to have new thoughts, ideas, and visions. We work to think of new ways to help each other stay sober and grow as spiritual beings. We exchange addictive logic for spiritual logic. We work to do the next right thing. Together we chase away doubts. Together we do for each other what we couldn't do for ourselves. We should ask ourselves, "Am I willing to stay close to the 'we' of the program?"

PRAYER FOR THE DAY
Higher Power, I pray that my thinking will include the voice of the fellowship and your voice. Help me to chase away doubt. Help me stay close to the "we" of recovery.

TODAY'S ACTION
Today I will think about how the "we" of recovery has helped change my thinking.

*Not only is there a right to be happy, there is a
duty to be happy. So much sadness exists in the
world that we are under obligation to contribute
as much joy as lies within our powers.*

— *John Bonnell*

Our recovery program is a program of "Attraction, not
promotion." Many of us may have heard this before.
It means that we are supposed to be happy. How else
would we ever attract new members into recovery?

Some of us are feeling more happiness in our lives
already. We have faced our guilt and made our amends,
and we are ready to face the world without guilt and
shame.

Once we have cleaned up the mess from our past, we
can keep our lives clean by working the Steps in our lives.
Joy now comes from what we add to the world instead of
what we can get from the world.

PRAYER FOR THE DAY
*Higher Power, help me accept the happiness in
my life. I must do my part by living well and by
seeing the gifts of life when they come to me.*

TODAY'S ACTION
I will list ten things in my life that I am happy about today.
If it is hard, I will ask for help from my recovery friends.

An ounce of loyalty is worth a pound of cleverness.
— *Elbert Hubbard*

During our using days we prided ourselves on being so
clever. We often were very proud of all the things we
were getting away with. However, it is time that we put
cleverness aside and become loyal to our spiritual principles and the fellowship. Loyalty involves caring about
something other than oneself. Being loyal to recovery
involves sacrificing at times. For example, maybe we
want to spend the evening at home, but a member in
need calls. Loyalty means we answer the call.

As we deepen our loyalty to our recovery, we heal
deeper wounds. We become more skillful in how to be
a friend, a partner, and a member of a community. We
give up trying to be clever and just work at being better
people.

PRAYER FOR THE DAY
Higher Power, my cleverness got me in trouble.
Help me turn my desires to be clever into
deeper loyalties to you and your wisdom.

TODAY'S ACTION
Today I will list five ways my cleverness has backfired on
me.

Shirking responsibilities is the curse of our modern life—the secret of all the unrest and discontent that is seething in the world.

— *L. M. Montgomery*

Believe it or not, responsibilities are wonderful things. We only have to think back to our childhood when we *wanted* responsibilities. We wanted to help the big people do things, to prove that we were big, too. Being a big person—and having responsibilities—was good because we believed that big people had power and freedom.

We were right back then. Being responsible means that we do a good job taking care of the business of life. Being responsible means growing up.

When we do Step Four, we find in ourselves the character defects that keep us from growing up: mostly laziness or fear.

In Step Six, we become ready to give up the fear and the laziness that keep us from growing up. We become willing to take action and do our own work.

PRAYER FOR THE DAY
Higher Power, today please help me understand the benefits of truly "adulting," so that I can start to live like a grown-up.

TODAY'S ACTION
I will think of one thing I did today that was a responsible, new behavior. I will be proud of it.

The difference between genius and stupidity is that genius has its limits.
— *Unknown*

We have the ability to take the most stupid of ideas and turn them into a plan. In the old days, we often got resentful or pitied ourselves if others didn't see the genius in our plans. Then we used our hurt feelings as an excuse to get loaded. Or maybe we fell into "big-shotism" and wasted huge amounts of time developing crazy plans of how we'd show the world. Just because we're sober doesn't mean that we can't come up with some pretty crazy ideas.

This is why we continue to work a program, to tell our sponsors of our resentments, self-pity, and grand plans. We share what is going on in our minds so that someone can stop our stupidity. Remember, our best thinking got us to these meetings. So we need to be willing to exchange personal stupidity for the wisdom of many. We should always be ready to let go and to laugh.

PRAYER FOR THE DAY
Higher Power, protect me from my stupidity. I pray for conscious contact. I pray that when I'm thinking or acting poorly you will whisper or yell, "Stop it!" in my ear.

TODAY'S ACTION
I need to do a daily inventory of my thinking so I don't take goofy ideas and turn them into plans. I will do a good Tenth Step today.

Courage is the price that life exacts for granting peace.
— Amelia Earhart

A peaceful life does not mean a life free of problems. We need courage to find peace in our lives. To find peace, we need to work the Twelve Steps, and that takes courage. It takes courage to face our disease. It takes courage to face our Higher Power and the other people in our lives. It takes courage to give up trying to run our own show and surrender to our Higher Power's plan for us.

Why does it take courage? Because when we live by our values and principles, we are doing life differently than many of the people around us. We stop going along with others.

We also need courage to trust that following our Higher Power's direction in our life will work out for us. This involves that scary old Step Three, the one that changes our lives.

PRAYER FOR THE DAY
*Higher Power, please give me the courage to do
your will for me, just for today. Help me remember
that the life you create for me offers the peace
I can't find when I let my own ego take control.*

TODAY'S ACTION
Today I will think about two times I felt confused and stressed out about a decision or choice I had to make. What about my thinking process could have contributed to the conflict? What did I learn?

What is a friend? A single soul dwelling in two bodies.

—Aristotle

In the fellowship of recovery, we are to take the principles of the program and put them into our hearts, into our souls. We work not just to live by these principles—honesty, willingness, courage—but to become them. Hundreds of thousands of recovering addicts are doing this. We see that we have thousands of friends all over the world, all with a single purpose of recovery and helping others to recover. This is the anonymous part of recovery; we give up being one to become many.

PRAYER FOR THE DAY
Higher Power, when I feel alone, remind me
of my friends and help me to reach out to them.
Help all of us as we go about our purpose of
getting sober and helping others get sober.

TODAY'S ACTION
Today I will reflect on what it means to be a friend and what it means to be anonymous.

It's not that some people have willpower and some don't. It's that some people are ready to change and others are not.
— James Gordon

What does it take to be ready to change? Some people say that no one changes until the pain is so great they have to change. But as we listen to the stories of the people around us, we know that answer is too simple.

Being ready to change is not just about having huge amounts of pain. It is also about believing that we don't have to have this pain, that there is a good way out. Next we have to love ourselves enough to do what it takes to get out of the pain of addiction.

We are a lot like people with other chronic diseases: we can choose to try to get well, or we can choose to let our disease kill us. If we love ourselves and we know that recovery works for many people, the choice is a no-brainer.

PRAYER FOR THE DAY
Higher Power, help me love myself enough to live in recovery today. I know sometimes love takes work, and I'm ready to do it. Will you please help me?

TODAY'S ACTION
For the next twenty-four hours, I will watch the way I treat myself. I am sober, yes, but do I take good care of my health, safety, and happiness? I will pay attention to my eating, driving, and exercise. I will look at my social contact. I will do the things that will help me be healthy, safe, and happy.

*To every disadvantage, there is a corresponding
advantage.*

— *W. Clement Stone*

We often hear people who have been in recovery for a
few years say that they are glad that they are an addict.
They have transformed the disadvantage of this illness
into an advantage. The advantage that they now have is
the program and its fellowship. They are not just trying
to make it through another day; they now have purpose.
They have found answers to the questions that before
haunted them: "What am I doing?" "Why is this happening to me?" "When do I get to have a good life?"

The emotional isolation that was so much a part of
active addiction is gone, replaced with laughter and fellowship. Recovery is all about transforming negative
into positive, disadvantages into advantages. We get rid
of what doesn't work and replace it with what does. We
work to find our character defects and transform them
into integrity.

PRAYER FOR THE DAY
*Higher Power, you are my advantage.
Your principles and your power will continue
to make me a better person. Thank you.*

TODAY'S ACTION
Today I will think about what my present disadvantages
and character defects are that need to be transformed into
advantages and assets.

Each small task of everyday life is part of the total harmony of the universe.

— *Saint Thérèse of Lisieux*

When we stop to think about it, it becomes clear that we are a tiny part of our Higher Power's creation. Consider the growing seasons of plants, the daily rising and setting of the sun, the miracles of birth and death. The cycles go on, creating a rhythm, an order in nature.

We can choose to be part of nature's order. We can eat healthy, exercise, and sleep enough to care for our health. We can keep our living space clean and neat. We can join in the work of life and be part of the human community. We can make it easy by developing good habits.

In order to go with nature's flow, we need to pay attention. That's what we do in our daily prayer and meditation. We work on conscious contact with our Higher Power and practice being part of the harmony of nature.

PRAYER FOR THE DAY
*Higher Power, please help me calm down and go
with your flow. Help me contribute well to your world.*

TODAY'S ACTION
Today I will think about my basic living tasks. Do I do them well, making a good base for my life?

NOVEMBER

Sought through prayer and meditation to improve our conscious contact with God as we understood Him, *praying only for knowledge of His will for us and the power to carry that out.*

— Step Eleven of Alcoholics Anonymous

Beneath all the chatter in our heads, beyond our desires for the perfect marriage or a shiny new car, we all have one basic wish: we wish we knew why we are here. "What," we wonder, "is the purpose of my life? What am I supposed to be doing while I am here on this earth?"

We find our answers to these questions as we work Step Eleven. We ask our Higher Power to help us get in line with what we are supposed to be doing. We meditate to hear the guidance of our Higher Power.

What do we want in our heart of hearts? To be doing our Higher Power's work—bringing peace, love, forgiveness, harmony, truth, hope, and joy to others. When we get our own will—our own plan—out of the way, our Higher Power will show us our purpose and give us the energy to accomplish it.

PRAYER FOR THE DAY
Higher Power, please help me get my will out of the way. Help me make your will my goal.

TODAY'S ACTION
Today I will try to think of some times I gave up my own will to do what I knew was the right thing. What happened? I will talk about these experiences with my sponsor.

*We are made wise not by the recollection of our
past, but by the responsibility for our future.*
— *George Bernard Shaw*

Our recovery program promises that we will know a
new wisdom and a new happiness. How do we get this
new wisdom? By learning from our past and applying
the knowledge to the way we step into our future. As
we work Steps One, Four, Eight, and Ten, we look at our
past. We examine our behavior and the choices we have
made, and we take a clear look at the consequences of
our actions. Doing these things gives us information
about what has or has not worked well in our past.

We become wise as we learn to apply this information
to the choices we make today, tomorrow, and each new
day. We do this "One day at a time."

PRAYER FOR THE DAY
*Higher Power, please make me wise. Help me
use my knowledge to live well today.*

TODAY'S ACTION
Today I will think about the most important lessons I have
learned about living in ways that will improve my future. I
will then make a list of at least five lessons I want to apply
in my life.

Fear grows out of the things we think; it lives in our minds. Compassion grows out of the things we are, and lives in our hearts.

— *Barbara Garrison*

We have been trained to be afraid. We are afraid of other people; we are afraid of failure; we are afraid of the unknown. We are even afraid of little things such as being late for the bus or wearing the wrong kind of clothes to a gathering. This is the way of addiction; it likes us to be afraid. As addicts, we have often eased our fears with alcohol or drugs.

Our sober self is much braver. We are less self-centered. We focus more on what is in our hearts. We pay attention to other people, not just to ourselves. And we actually care about others for a change!

PRAYER FOR THE DAY
Higher Power, help me stay in the safety of caring about others today. When I think about myself too much, I get in trouble.

TODAY'S ACTION
Today I will ask myself the following question: "When I need to do some serious thinking about myself, whom do I trust to help me?" I will make sure I go to this person for input and guidance, and to avoid the fear that will develop if I isolate myself in my own thoughts.

Love doesn't just sit there like a stone; it has to be made, like bread, remade all the time, made new.
— *Ursula K. Le Guin*

Everyone could use a new batch of love every day. Way too often, we forget to make a new batch. Then we end up eating hard, old, crumbly stuff that doesn't even taste good. We forget to talk with the people we love. We tell ourselves that they should "know" we love them, even if we haven't called to connect with them for a long time. So we expect them to live off hard, old, dry crumbs, too!

But baking a fresh batch of love is a lot easier than baking bread. All we have to do is make a phone call, write a letter or an e-mail, send a text, or stop by our mom's house. We need to deliver the message that the people we love are important. What could be easier or more rewarding?

PRAYER FOR THE DAY
Higher Power, help me remember that love is a verb—something I do, not something that can be given once and stored forever. Help me be active in loving the important people in my life.

TODAY'S ACTION
I will make it a point to make a fresh batch of love today and deliver it—in person or in a call, e-mail, letter, or text.

Fortune favors the brave.

— Ennius

Many of us had some strange ideas about bravery. We thought alcohol or drugs could give us courage. Now we know that what we got was not bravery; all we got was a way to deny our fear. We didn't know what to do with our fear, so we blotted it out by getting high. That did not make us brave; it made us act like fools.

Fear serves a good purpose. It warns us to take care. It helps us realize that some things are bigger than we are and that we need help to face them. Turning to alcohol or drugs was the old way. The new way in recovery is to ask for help from someone whom we can trust.

When we ask for help from our Higher Power, a sponsor, a friend, a teacher, or a boss, we get real help. When we trust this help, that's what makes us brave. If we are going to live a full life, we will take risks every day. We will need to be brave every day. And that's no problem when we have help that is available and trustworthy.

PRAYER FOR THE DAY
Higher Power, help me face the risks I need to take today. I trust that things will turn out for the best when I do this because you are helping me.

TODAY'S ACTION
Today I will list my fears from the last twenty-four hours. What did I do to deal with my fears? What can I do to deal with my fears in the next twenty-four hours?

Never mistake motion for action.

— *Ernest Hemingway*

We are always in motion. Even while we sleep, our bodies are moving—blood pumping, lungs breathing, cells dying and being born.

One of the goals of recovery is that we learn to use this energy to do things we actually want to do. When we take hold of our energy and use it to accomplish something, we act. Action means we think before we move, and we direct our movement in ways to accomplish something.

The more we become aware of ourselves as responsible people with values and principles, the more prepared we are to act. The more we find our own skills and talents, the more prepared we are to act. The more we listen to direction from our Higher Power, the more prepared we are to act.

PRAYER FOR THE DAY
*Higher Power, help me use more of my energy
to do your work through action.*

TODAY'S ACTION
I will choose one thing that I do every day, such as brushing my teeth or eating a meal, and will make a decision to do it with my full attention today. I will think about why I am doing it and what I am accomplishing. It will seem different to do it this way because I'm changing it from a movement to an action.

Every man loves what he is good at.
— *Thomas Shadwell*

Some people are very clear about what they are good at. They use their skills and talents well, and they find joy in doing this. Many of us aren't so lucky. We need to find our special gift.

In our first years of recovery, we learn how to look closely at ourselves, our behaviors, and what we want to fix. We also ask other people to tell us how they see us. This helps with our healing.

These same skills will help us find lifelong growth and our special talents. To find out what these talents are, we need to look at two main things. First, we pay attention to what makes us feel happy. Second, we ask other people for feedback on what we do well. We then need to sort through these answers. Somewhere in there, we will find our special gift, the one that makes us happy when we use it.

PRAYER FOR THE DAY
Higher Power, I know you made me with a purpose.
Help me find it so I can finally feel like I have a purpose.

TODAY'S ACTION
Today I will pay attention to what gives me joy. Playing with children? Solving problems? Cooking? Building something? I will write down the moments of my day that bring me happiness. Then I will call my sponsor and ask, "What is one thing that I do really well?"

*First say to yourself what you would be; and then
do what you have to do.*

— *Epictetus*

Each of us is becoming many things in our lives—a
spiritual person, a friend, a family member, a worker,
a member of groups, a citizen, a person with a partic-
ular hobby. In each of these areas, it helps to have an
idea what kind of person we want to be: What kind of
spouse? What kind of sponsor? What kind of artist or
hunter or parent or friend?

Often wc form these personal goals by watching other
people. We want to be as good a sponsor as our own
sponsor. We want to be as good a relative as our favorite
aunt or uncle. We want to be as good at our job as our
respected mentor.

One of the gifts of our program is that it teaches us how
to do what we need to do to reach our goals. We set the
goal, we take a good look at our own skills, we learn about
how to do it, and we ask for the help and support of people
who can teach us. Then we practice!

PRAYER FOR THE DAY
*Higher Power, help me set good goals,
and help me do what I need to do to get there.*

TODAY'S ACTION
Today I will list ten things I want to be in my lifetime. Next
to each item, I will write the name of someone I can ask
for help or information. I will then share my list with my
sponsor and three other people who are important to me.

Trust only movement. Life happens at the level of events, not of words. Trust movement.
— *Alfred Adler*

The wise long-timers in our recovery groups remind us often that recovery is about "Walking the walk"—not about "Talking the talk." It's easy to get caught up in listening to what people say instead of watching what they do. That's why we sometimes are surprised when one of the members that "talks a good recovery" disappears from the meeting rooms and picks up alcohol or drugs again.

Action, not talk, is what makes our recovery real. Talking is important because it helps us think through our actions. But action is the goal. Action is the test. Action is reality.

PRAYER FOR THE DAY
Higher Power, help me always look past the words to see the reality in action.

TODAY'S ACTION
Today I will think about whether my talk matches my actions. I will list three times I have had to make an excuse because I said one thing but did something different. I will then talk with my sponsor about "Walking the walk."

I long to accomplish a great and noble task, but it is my chief duty to accomplish humble tasks as though they were great and noble.

— Helen Keller

In early recovery, our lives are filled with drama. We have very difficult work to do—detoxifying our bodies, coming to grips with the facts of our disease, finding a Higher Power who can rescue us from the death spiral we are in. Then we face the mess we made of our lives and our relationships, and we learn everything we can from all this experience.

Then we move on to the humble tasks of daily living, of managing our disease every day and living a good, healthy life. We live by our principles and values. We experience less drama but more sanity, more peace, more love. It's a good, noble trade-off.

PRAYER FOR THE DAY
Higher Power, help me let go of my attraction to drama and crisis. Help me enjoy the fruits of healthy living.

TODAY'S ACTION
Today I will ask myself, "Do I miss the excitement and drama of my using days? What makes me feel alive now?"

*Let us not worry about the future. Those who do
what is right are always rewarded.*
— Beatrice Schenk de Regniers

Our program tells us "One day at a time." "First things
first." "Do the next right thing." If we do these things, we
are told, the future will take care of itself.

It works. We don't always get the results we had in
mind, but in the big picture of life, it always works out for
the best when we pay attention to doing the right things
today.

What a relief. We don't have to figure out what the
future holds, as if we could anyway.

PRAYER FOR THE DAY
*Higher Power, please guide my actions today. I will put
my energy into listening to you and following directions.
I don't need to know what tomorrow will bring. I trust you.*

TODAY'S ACTION
Today I will think about the last time my Higher Power's
influence sneaked up on me and how I surprised myself
with my own actions. Did I speak up to stop someone who
was gossiping or speaking hate? Did I help someone open
a door or pick up something he or she had dropped? It's
these new actions—one at a time—that will turn me into
a new person.

Turn your wounds into wisdom.
— *Oprah Winfrey*

We've all been hurt. We all carry scars from the healing of wounds—big ones and small ones. In early recovery, we think about those wounds and how we got them and what we might have done differently if we could do it all over. We gather information and we think and we learn about what happened.

When we learn about the nature of our wounds, we can turn them into wisdom. Wisdom means we use what we have learned from the past, and we make our future choices based on what we have learned by experience.

Wisdom is a gift. Does that mean our wounds are gifts, too? No. But the ability to learn from our wounds and to live differently in the future *is* a gift.

PRAYER FOR THE DAY
Higher Power, please help me learn from the wounds and hurts I have experienced in life. Then help me use what I have learned to guide me today and every day.

TODAY'S ACTION
I will list five things that I will do today that are a big change from the way I used to do things during my using days.

People pay for what they do and even more for
what they allow themselves to become, and they
pay with the very lives they lead.

— *James Baldwin*

We have learned in our recovery that we paid dearly for
our active addiction. Now we are taking our lives back
from our addiction.

As we live our lives in recovery, we will face many
choices. Our sober choices will affect our lives in important ways, so we must try to make wise choices. Our
choices about food and exercise will affect our health.
Our choices about education will affect our jobs and the
way we spend many hours every day of our lives. Our
choices about relationships are equally important.

We should be careful about how we spend the time
in our lives so that the things we do with our minutes,
hours, days, and years bring us the experiences we want
and value. We are sober. We can now live with care for
ourselves and for others.

PRAYER FOR THE DAY
Higher Power, help me be aware today that the
choices I make affect my life. My time is important.

TODAY'S ACTION
Many of the choices that I make are not about "good" or
"bad." They are about what is right for me, to bring the
things into my life that will make me whole and happy.
What is one choice like this that I will face in the next
year? I will talk with my sponsor about it.

We cannot think first and act afterward. From the moment of birth we are immersed in action, and can only fitfully guide it by taking thought.
— Alfred North Whitehead

There's a good reason that one of the slogans we use most often in recovery is direct and to the point. It is because this one slogan can guide everything we do. We caution each other to always do one thing: "Think." We are always moving, always doing things that have an effect on others and on ourselves—and if we don't think, we are dangerous! When we don't think, we are an accident waiting to happen.

Thinking is how we take responsibility for the things we do. Thinking is how we are careful or gentle or strong when we need to be. Thinking is how we make good use of our time and energy. Thinking is how we make our actions loving toward others and ourselves. Most important, thinking is how we remember to do the things every day that help us stay sober.

PRAYER FOR THE DAY
Higher Power, sometimes I get moving so fast through my day that I forget to stop and think. Please help me think today so that my actions will be useful.

TODAY'S ACTION
Today I will consider how I could spend a bit more time thinking through my day's plans in order to make my actions more effective. I will then try making a to-do list for today and see whether it helps.

Safeguard the health of both body and soul.

— *Cleobulus*

We have stopped hurting our body with alcohol and drugs. That is a very big deal. When we were using, nasty things were happening to our brain, heart, liver, and other organs. We damaged our immune system, and as a result of some of our previous choices and actions we may be living with chronic conditions such as HIV or hepatitis C. Some of us may not have been to a dentist in years.

Now that we are sober, it's time to take a look at how we treat our bodies. We need to drop the denial. Remember, our bodies are our vehicles for living. The quality of our new sober life—our ability to move, love, work, play—all depend on our body doing its part. We need to take care of ourselves today so we can live better every day. If we have health concerns, we should take action and see a doctor.

PRAYER FOR THE DAY
*Higher Power, please guide me today to take
better care of my body by making a change
or two as I choose my food and exercise.*

TODAY'S ACTION
Today I will list the foods I've eaten during the last twenty-four hours and any exercise that I did. Have I made healthy choices? What change could I make today to improve the care I give my body?

Reason is our soul's left hand, faith her right.
—John Donne

Our soul is the life energy, the spirit inside us that makes us alive and connects us to other living things and to our Higher Power. Our soul has spiritual energy and mental energy. If we are going to be on track in our lives, we need both of these to work together.

Mentally we need to be careful that we do our thinking with our mind—not with our instincts. Thinking with our mind—with reason and wisdom—keeps our Inner Addict's instincts from warping our soul and our life.

Spiritually we need to get our energy from our faith, our connection with our Higher Power. The more we develop a conscious contact with our Higher Power, the more energy and direction we have in our lives.

During our active addiction, our Addict's instincts beat out our reason and our faith every time. Now that we are in recovery, we can live the life we were born for—the life our soul knows!

PRAYER FOR THE DAY
Higher Power, my Addict was in charge of my thinking, my energy, and my beliefs for a long time. Please help me put my soul back in the driver's seat of my life.

TODAY'S ACTION
Today I will consider the difference between the way my Addict wants to run my life and the way my soul wants to run my life. I will talk with my sponsor about this today.

Fear is a question: what are you afraid of, and why? . . . Your fears are a treasure-house of self-knowledge if you explore them.

— *Marilyn Ferguson*

Our recovery program teaches us to take a close look at our fears, our pains, our joys, our dreams. We look at all the important questions, and we learn so much about ourselves as we find the answers.

Not only do we find the answers, but we also talk about what we learn with other people. An amazing thing happens when we do this. We learn that we are a lot like other people. They have fears, too. When we share the knowledge we learn about ourselves in recovery, we begin to see how we fit next to other people. We join with others in crying and laughing about our problems and issues. Suddenly our problems seem a lot smaller.

PRAYER FOR THE DAY
Higher Power, help me remember that I was not born alone on a desert island. I am supposed to be with people. I belong. All I have to do is open up.

TODAY'S ACTION
Today I will consider the things about myself that I hide from other people. Why do I keep these things hidden? What would happen if I told my sponsor about them? I will do a test today. I will call my sponsor and talk about one thing that I am afraid to share. I will write down what happens.

How I loved my shadow, this dark side of me that loved all the things no one else could see.

—*Amy Tan*

The Addict seduces us to feel unique, mysterious, and alone. Alone except for alcohol or drugs, with their promise of comfort, relief, and understanding. The Addict lures us with false promises that will ease our pain.

Our Addict is no friend to us. Our Addict can't even love—us or anyone else. There's only one promise it keeps: it doesn't leave us. The Addict inside waits for the chance to seduce us once more.

The way we stay in recovery is to open up to others, stop thinking we need secrets, and experience real love, friendship, and intimacy. We start by facing and making friends with ourselves. Then we share openly and make friends of others. We don't need darkness. We don't need secrets. We need to be real!

PRAYER FOR THE DAY

Higher Power, thanks for helping me be real. Real feels good, honest, open, and simple. Real leads me to form relationships with other real people, not with an object!

TODAY'S ACTION

Today I will list ten lies my addiction told me. Then I will write the truth about these things that I now see in recovery.

When the character of a person is not clear to you, look at their friends.
— *Japanese Proverb*

We have learned in recovery that there are persons, places, and things that we need to avoid to stay sober. More and more we find ourselves avoiding our old drinking and using companions, especially if they are still living the same old way.

We have also learned to stick with the winners, the sober people in the program who live the kind of life that we want for ourselves. At our meetings, how can we tell the real winners from those that just "talk the talk," the ones who sound healthier than they actually are? We need to take a look at the bigger picture of their lives. What are they doing outside meetings? Who are their friends?

The biggest talkers in our meetings may not be the real winners. We need to choose our sponsor and our friends carefully.

PRAYER FOR THE DAY
Higher Power, I know that I can be fooled. Help me keep my eyes and heart open so I can stick with the real winners.

TODAY'S ACTION
Today I will list three of my closest friends in recovery. I will then take a good hard look at what they stand for by looking at their behavior. Do they stand for good values, or do they continue old behavior that is unkind, unsafe, or dishonest? Can I safely trust these people to support my recovery?

The first rule is to keep an untroubled spirit. The second is to look things in the face and know them for what they are.
— *Marcus Aurelius*

We keep an untroubled spirit by searching out a Higher Power that we trust to make us sane and by staying connected to this Higher Power no matter what happens. This is how we can get the serenity we see in the long-timers in our recovery meetings.

These same long-timers have a lot of common sense, too. That's because the Twelve Steps teach us to look things in the face and know them for what they are. Once we see clearly and call things as they are, life becomes so much simpler.

When we have a Higher Power to direct us and we see clearly what we are dealing with, it's pretty simple to know how to do the next right thing. No confusion. No excuses. Just serenity and common sense.

PRAYER FOR THE DAY
Higher Power, today I trust you to lead me to the next right thing. I'll keep my eyes open and look life in the face to do my part and make your job easier!

TODAY'S ACTION
Today I will think about whether there is anything troubling my spirit. If so, I will write about it. I will then call my sponsor and ask for help to figure out whether the problem is caused by lack of faith, by failing to see things clearly, or by something else. I will figure it out!

People show their characters in nothing more clearly than in what they think laughable.

— Joan Didion

Humor is the best medicine. We've heard it a thousand times. It does feel good to laugh. A chuckle over a funny joke or comment lightens the day. When we share humor, we are connected with other people in a nice way. A real belly laugh, well, that's a treasure. We can just feel the stress roll away when we laugh so hard our stomach hurts.

But we all know that humor can be used as a cover for behavior that is cruel and nasty. Some people use the cover of humor to spread their anger, racism, sexism, or just plain meanness. Jokes and comments made under the excuse of "just kidding" can do a lot of damage. Even when the victim of the joke is not around to hear it, someone hears it, and the poison spreads.

Our recovery teaches us to find the humor in ourselves and in the events of our lives. The more we pay attention, the more humor we find. Let's just make sure it's funny humor, delivered with love.

PRAYER FOR THE DAY
Higher Power, bless me with the gift to see the funny things that happen every day. Remind me to share these stories with others in love and healing.

TODAY'S ACTION
What can I do today to bring a healthy laugh to someone? If I do it, I will consider myself a healer "Just for today."

Life is a long lesson in humility.
— James M. Barrie

Being humble simply means we know who we are, what we bring and have to give, and we do our part. We are the right size. We're not too big for our britches. We let out the hot air when we got sober, and now we're solid; you can count on what we say. We're not trying to fit into anyone else's shoes either. We're happy with our own feet. We wear the right size shoes—not too small because that would cripple us, and not too big because that would trip us. We wear the right size so we can walk and run and dance through life without worrying about our feet.

In terms of our egos, we understand that we are part of a bigger picture—a picture we are responsible for helping to create. There's a lot of work that goes into keeping our families, communities, and society working. We do our part. We don't expect a free ride. But we don't try to do it all. We do what we have the gifts to do. That's humility.

PRAYER FOR THE DAY
Higher Power, teach me—gently, please—
what gifts and talents I have to give.
What part of your work has my name on it?

TODAY'S ACTION
Today I will watch the big picture of what is going on around me. I will step in to help with the work that makes the world go round. Then I will call my sponsor to talk about service.

Creativity is ... seeing something that doesn't exist already. You need to find out how you can bring it into being and that way be a playmate with God.

— *Michelle Shea*

When we take Step Three, we make a decision to take a leap into something that doesn't exist yet: our new, sober life. Once we've decided to do it, the program teaches us how. First we have to sort out the baggage of our old life in Step Four. Then we show the baggage to someone in Step Five, getting advice about what to take with us into our new life and what to let go. In Steps Six and Seven, we repack our bags for our life. In Steps Eight and Nine we clean up our old life.

As we work Steps Ten, Eleven, and Twelve, we get our Higher Power's direction to create a new life.

PRAYER FOR THE DAY
Higher Power, help me with each stage of creating my new life. Remind me that I need to repack my bags every so often. When I leave a place behind, teach me to leave it better than I found it. And above all, point me in the direction you want me to go.

TODAY'S ACTION
Do I need to make a decision? Did I forget to ask for direction? If I'm feeling bogged down today by any issues, I will talk with my sponsor.

*I have not failed. I've just found ten thousand
ways that won't work.*
— *Thomas Edison*

How many ways have we tried to control our relationship with alcohol or drugs? How many ways have we
tried to fix the problems caused by our use? Before
coming into recovery, most of us tried many things. We
switched around, trying different kinds of alcohol or
drugs. We tried using only at certain times or on certain days. We tried to cut down the amount we drank
or used. We found friends who didn't get upset about
our use. We left family members who nagged us about
our alcohol or drug use (if they didn't leave us first).

No matter what we tried, we just couldn't control our
alcohol or drug use for very long. We couldn't stop the
problems it caused in our lives. We finally found that the
only thing that made sense was to cut our losses and walk
away—into sobriety.

PRAYER FOR THE DAY
*Higher Power, I have found many, many ways to have
a relationship with alcohol or drugs that didn't work
for me. Help me accept the fact that I need to stay away
from them. Help me to do that "One day at a time."*

TODAY'S ACTION
Today I will make a list of problems caused by my alcohol
or drug use. Next to each problem, I'll list the ways I tried
to fix it. I will then talk with my sponsor about these problems and what effect walking into recovery had on them.

Holding on to anger, resentment, and hurt only gives you tense muscles, a headache, and a sore jaw from clenching your teeth. Forgiveness gives you back the laughter and the lightness in your life.
— Joan Lunden

We have a lot of history in our lives that brings up anger, resentment, and hurt. For some of us, it seems as if life gave us a raw deal from day one. We were born to parents who were not able to do a good job of raising us. We felt bad at home and school. One thing led to another; we became addicts, and the bad stuff just kept piling up. We were hurt, we hurt other people, and we just could not find love, trust, or happiness. We may feel that we have a right to be angry. But we can't dwell on this because we have a new chance to change things. The huge and wonderful gift is this: we can walk right into a new way of living. We need to focus on learning this new way of walking in life—and to do that, we need to leave the old ways behind.

PRAYER FOR THE DAY
Higher Power, please help me let go of my anger, hurt, and resentment even though I have a "right" to them. Teach me to free myself from their grip.

TODAY'S ACTION
Today I will focus on the good stuff that happened to me. Instead of stewing on the negative, I'll think about the positive in my day.

Humor is the affectionate communication of insight.
— *Leo Rosten*

Humor is a wonderful gift. Some of us have it naturally, but some of us take everything much too seriously. As we try to become more joyful and see the lightness we can enjoy in our lives, we like to share it with others. When we do this in a spirit of love, we make our relationships and our lives more fun and interesting.

Let's take a moment and think about the humor and laughter we hear at many Twelve Step meetings. What are people laughing at? Usually we laugh when we remember the way we used to act or think. As healthy, sober people, we can look at the bumbling behavior of addicts—ourselves and others—with gentle insight and humor. We understand the insanity of active addiction and can soften the pain of remembering with our gentle humor.

PRAYER FOR THE DAY
Higher Power, I know the humor of recovery is a healing thing. Help me really know and understand the insanity of my addiction by working the Steps—especially Steps Four through Nine—and then help me let it go with gentle laughter.

TODAY'S ACTION
Today I will consider Steps Four through Nine—understanding the nature of my wrongs, making amends, and moving on with gentle acceptance and humor. If I haven't done these Steps yet, I will talk with my sponsor about how to proceed.

> *Human beings, by changing the inner attitudes*
> *of their minds, can change the outer aspects of*
> *their lives.*
> — William James

How do we see our life today? Are we feeling lucky because we are sober? Or maybe we feel angry because we don't want to be sober? Do we feel sorry for ourselves because we are sober—or because we are in relapse? Do we feel rich because we have enough food to eat or poor because we can't afford the sports car or home we really want? Do we feel sad because a person we love is ill or happy because our friend's illness is mild?

We get to choose our feelings about life. Our feelings are connected to the ways we think about life. We can change our thinking by talking things over with other people and getting a new way to see things. When we do, we change our lives.

PRAYER FOR THE DAY
Higher Power, please help me be happy about the
good things in my life. Help me focus on my attitude.
My real life is in my spirit, not in the material things
I own or the head games people play with each other.

TODAY'S ACTION
Today I will list ten things I can be happy about. I will focus on them. I will call my sponsor and chat about this question: what difference does my attitude make in my life?

*Dreams are renewable. No matter what our age
or condition, there are still untapped possibilities
within us and new beauty waiting to be born.*

— Dale Turner

When we were kids, we had big dreams of what we
would do when we grew up. Some of us feel sad when we
compare the big plans we used to have to the real place
we find ourselves in today. In some ways, our dreams
got smaller and smaller through the months and years
of our active addiction.

The good news is this: it's never too late to dream bigger
dreams, just like it's never too late to get sober. If we are
willing to do the work we need to do to get sober and the
work we need to do to stay sober, we have what it takes
to make new dreams come true.

PRAYER FOR THE DAY
*Higher Power, feed my dreams by showing me your
will for me. You gave me talents and a purpose in life.
Put them in my dreams and help me get there.*

TODAY'S ACTION
Today I will make a list of all the dreams I have had about
my future ever since I was small. What parts of those
dreams are still possible? Do I need a new dream?

The world is . . . simply throbbing with rich trea-
sures, beautiful souls, and interesting people.
Forget yourself.
— Henry Miller

Many of us found that during our active addiction, our lives seemed to get smaller. We put our time and energy into our alcohol or drugs, and hung around the people, places, and things that supported our addiction.

Early in our recovery, we put most of our time and energy into learning to stay sober. We need to practice putting the basics of recovery to work in our lives. Once we get the hang of living sober, we can develop other interests, too. That's the great thing about being in recovery. It means we can put some of our energy into enjoying hobbies and new experiences.

We need only look at the old-timers in our recovery groups. They have fun. Some love music or skiing or motorcycles. Others write stories, act, or design stage sets in community theaters. The world opens up to us when we are sober. Let's enjoy it!

PRAYER FOR THE DAY
Higher Power, help me stretch and try new things.
Help me discover the things that bring me joy,
and help me get moving and do them.

TODAY'S ACTION
Today I will list ten things I like to do and circle the ones I have not done in the last six months; then I will list ten new things I want to try.

Soul appears when we make room for it.

— *Thomas Moore*

When we work our recovery program, we make room for our soul. It appears first in our pain. The pain of the soul comes out as fear, hurt, grief, and guilt over the things that have happened during our active addiction. That's the bad news.

The good news is this: no matter how bad our lives got during our active addiction, our soul lives. Once we get into recovery, our soul begins to heal. We heal by working the Steps, by joining with others in a community of recovery, and through prayer and meditation.

Healing takes time, but every bit of it makes life better and more worth living. Every bit of our healing leads us closer to the life we really want.

PRAYER FOR THE DAY
Higher Power, thank you for preserving my soul. Guide me through the healing I need to do, even when it hurts.

TODAY'S ACTION
Today I will make a list of the reasons I believe that there is a life spirit inside of me. I will call someone from my recovery group and ask that person for his or her thoughts on this issue. What did he or she say?

DECEMBER

Having had a spiritual awakening as the result
of these steps, we tried to carry this message to
alcoholics, and to practice these principles in all
our affairs.

— *Step Twelve of Alcoholics Anonymous*

There is a promise hidden in Step Twelve: If we work the
other Steps, we will have a spiritual awakening. We will
be able to cut through the confusion of everyday chatter
and be real with ourselves, with our Higher Power, and
with other people. We will be able to love and be loved
at a deep level. This is what we mean by true intimacy.
When we have found our own spiritual core, we can
share and connect with others at that level.

We will want to live our lives guided by that deep love
and truth. We will learn to apply this spiritual approach
in our work ethic, our family life, our friendships, and
our role as a citizen. Oh the power of that kind of love! It
can change the world.

PRAYER FOR THE DAY
Higher Power, thank you for the new spiritual
life I am finding in this program. Help me stay
spiritually awake everywhere I go today.

TODAY'S ACTION
Today I will think about what the words *spiritual awaken-*
ing in Step Twelve mean to me. Am I waking up spiritually? I will call my sponsor and find out how he or she has
experienced a spiritual awakening in recovery and what
it was like.

*I always keep a supply of stimulant handy in case
I see a snake—which I also keep handy.*
— *W. C. Fields*

W. C. Fields, the famous comic who often played the role of a drunk, joked that he kept his excuse for drinking handy at all times.

Many of us have our own snake—our own favorite excuse for drinking or using—that we have carried around with us for years. We pulled it out as often as we wanted to, acted as if the fear or pain were brand new and way too much to bear, and then we drank or drugged with "good" reason.

Our program helps us empty the snakes—the reasons for drinking and drugging—out of our pockets, briefcases, purses, and lunch boxes.

PRAYER FOR THE DAY
Higher Power, help me identify all the excuses and reasons I used to drink or use drugs. Help me face them and let them go.

TODAY'S ACTION
Today I will think about my "snakes," the old hurts and fears that I used to get drunk or high over. I will list them and talk with my sponsor about how to empty them out of my pockets.

It is confidence in our bodies, minds, and spirits
that allows us to keep looking for new adventures,
new directions to grow in, and new lessons to
learn—which is what life is all about.

— Oprah Winfrey

This sounds good, but how do we get that kind of confidence in our bodies, minds, and spirits? Well, we're already working on it. We have done our bodies, minds, and spirits one big favor by getting sober. Now we nurture these things each day as part of our recovery lifestyle.

Our bodies are getting stronger if we eat better now and get some exercise a few times a week. We are reading and discussing ideas with others in our meetings, so our minds are getting stronger, too. Our spirits heal more each day with the help of a little bit of prayer and meditation.

Now that we are sober, we are getting to know all aspects of ourselves. When we know ourselves, we know what we can do. We trust ourselves. That's called confidence.

PRAYER FOR THE DAY
Higher Power, help me do the things that make my body,
mind, and spirit healthy and strong. Help me learn to
use my new health and strength to live more fully.

TODAY'S ACTION
Today I will ask myself, "How am I doing at self-care in these three areas: body, mind, and spirit?" I will then talk with a recovery friend about self-care.

*You are a child of the universe, no less than the
moon and the stars. You have a right to be here.*
— *Max Ehrmann*

Like everything in nature, we have a place and a purpose
for being here. The first thing we need to do is accept
that. No matter how beat up we are by our addiction,
no matter what bad things we have done—we are right
where we are supposed to be.

We have a job to do. Like the moon and stars, we have
our own special light to bring to the world. If we don't do
it, no one else will; in fact, no one else can—because it is
our special light. When we do our part, we help make the
world a more beautiful place. We do it with help from all
the other stars out there. We are part of a sky full of other
shining stars. Each day we live in recovery, our stars shine
a little brighter.

PRAYER FOR THE DAY
*Higher Power, my disease has gotten in the way of your plan
for me. Help me recover today so I can do my part in the world.*

TODAY'S ACTION
Today I will write down three times I have touched someone with my light. What happened? Did I feel the power of
my gift of recovery coming through?

*We all have big changes in our lives that are more
or less a second chance.*
— Harrison Ford

Change is such an important thing in our lives, yet we understand it so little. It seems like we run into a lot of changes we just aren't ready for. Sometimes we understand with our head, yet we have pain in our heart when we meet with changes. For example, a favorite elder in our life dies; we know these things happen, yet our heart feels like it will break.

Other times our heart seems to say, "Do this! It's really important to take this path!" But our head says, "You're nuts! Stay right where you are and don't change a thing. Don't rock the boat!"

One of the great gifts of recovery is that we meet many successful people who can help us through the changes we face. They teach us and support us through the big change of getting sober and starting over in life. They will also help us with daily problems.

PRAYER FOR THE DAY
*Higher Power, today I want to invite you into both my
heart and my head. Help me accept change with my
heart and use my head to understand and learn from it.*

TODAY'S ACTION
Today I will make a list of ten changes that have come into my life in the last year. Which changes have I struggled with? Which changes have been easier for me to accept? I will talk with my sponsor about these changes.

Life's greatest happiness is to be convinced we are loved.

— *Victor Hugo*

Do we know that we are loved? For some of us, it's very hard to let that idea sink into our minds and hearts. Love, we think, is for other people. Yet in our hearts, we know we do need love.

How can we start to let the feeling sink in? We need to slow down. Spend time with good people we care about. Share our ideas and joys. Talk out our fears and problems. Work together. Play together. Be part of something with others. After a while, we realize that we are not alone anymore. We are loved and accepted by people we love and accept.

After a good start in recovery—a year or more—we may be ready to develop an even closer love with a life partner. When we add this kind of love to our lives, it is more important than ever that we stay connected to our recovery and the support of people who love us.

PRAYER FOR THE DAY
Higher Power, I'm afraid to lose love, and I'm afraid to have love. Help me to relax and let love in.

TODAY'S ACTION
I will spend time talking about the day's events with someone I care about, and I'll tell that person they are important to me.

*To see what is right and not to do it is want of
courage.*
— Confucius

We have all been guilty of failing to do what we know
is right at some times in our lives. Why did we fail at
those times? Usually out of fear. We were afraid that
doing the right thing would make us uncomfortable in
some way. Perhaps it would cost us money. Or maybe
it would mean our friends might reject us. Perhaps we
could have been fired from a job. For whatever reason,
we were afraid.

Being afraid is a very human thing. Courage, on the
other hand, is a very spiritual thing. Courage means to act
with heart, to act from our beliefs and values.

Our recovery program asks us to work at learning courage. We practice courage in Steps One through Nine. By
Steps Ten, Eleven, and Twelve, we find it comes more naturally as long as we keep practicing it every day.

We live our new values, and this practice makes us courageous, spiritual people. It's a miracle. We are miracles.

PRAYER FOR THE DAY
*Higher Power, wherever I am in my recovery
today, please help me see what I need to do
and have the courage to do it. Thank you.*

TODAY'S ACTION
Today I will think about the courage I show in my recovery
and will talk with my sponsor about it and be proud of
myself.

A drinker has a hole under his nose that all his money runs into.
— *Thomas Fuller*

Whether we took our drugs in liquid, powder, pill, smoke, or aerosol form, we poured our money into feeding our addiction. We poured our time and attention into feeding our addiction, too. There wasn't much of us left over to give to others.

What a difference recovery makes. Yes, it takes time and attention, but not all of it. We have some left over to give others. It takes money, yes, but at least we see it before it flies up our nose or down our throat. We make choices now with our money.

We now have time, a clear mind, and maybe money we didn't have before. We have something to give now.

PRAYER FOR THE DAY
Higher Power, help me extend myself to others.
Thanks for helping me be a giver, not only a taker.

TODAY'S ACTION
Today I will think about how I will give of myself this week. Will I give some attention to greeting a lonely person at work or in my neighborhood? Will I do volunteer work at a food shelf, lead a scout troop, or help with a political campaign? Will I sponsor newcomers to recovery? I will talk with my sponsor about ways I can give.

One reason that I don't drink is that I want to know when I am having a good time.

— *Nancy Astor*

The holiday season can be dangerous times for us addicts. We gather more often with family and friends, and in some of these groups, people drink alcohol or use drugs. They offer us drugs or alcohol. They look as if they are having such a good time; it's tempting to join in. However, it's time to remember why we *don't* drink or use.

We stay sober, even on holidays, unless we want back all the things that went with our drinking or using. What were those things again? Ah, yes—embarrassing scenes, apologies the next day, waking up in strange places, losing the car again, hangovers, arguments.

Now we can actually enjoy the holidays and use them as a chance to connect with people we care about. We can create meaningful rituals and celebrations that add joy to our holidays and create good memories.

PRAYER FOR THE DAY
Higher Power, help me enjoy the holidays as a special spiritual time to enjoy my own relationship with you, with myself, and with the special people in my life.

TODAY'S ACTION
Today I will make a list of things to do to celebrate the season. I will stay in touch with my sponsor because this time of year isn't easy.

Learning teaches more in one year than experi-
ence in twenty.
                                        — *Roger Ascham*

Some of have taken pride in learning by experience. We
have tried many things, been through many hard times,
and perhaps have had a lot of fun—and a lot of pain—
along the way.

The problem with this style of learning is that sometimes we just have the experience. We don't learn the
most helpful things from it.

But we never learned about recovery this way. We had
to first ask for help, listen, read, learn—and *then* experience recovery. Now we learn a little every day by reading
and talking with our sponsor between meetings. It's a
great shortcut to learning about good recovery. *Then* we
experience recovery for ourselves "One day at a time."

PRAYER FOR THE DAY
Higher Power, help me learn today how to live a
healthier, more spiritual life in recovery. Help me learn
my lessons the easy way—by listening and reading—
not the hard way of painful experience.

TODAY'S ACTION
Today I will think for a few minutes about my recent experiences. What are three things I have learned through
experience in the last few days? I will write them down.

Little things have big results sometimes.

— *Margaret Moore*

Every day we do little things. We make choices each day about our actions and behavior. We offer a smile, make an amend, or do our daily prayer and meditation.

When we were trapped in the crazy thinking of active addiction, these seemed like big things. But in the scope of life, they are small. When we get our ego out of the way, we see that what we are learning to do now is to simply act like good human beings. We act with care. We clean up our messes. We ask our Higher Power to guide us. It's what we do; it's how we live now. No big deal.

The results? Our lives are sane. We are good people. We have good friends. We are blessed.

PRAYER FOR THE DAY
Higher Power, help me do the little things
today in the way you want me to.

TODAY'S ACTION
What little things have I done lately that had big results? Today I will list five, then I will call a recovery friend and talk about what a difference those little actions made.

True friends never owe each other anything.
— *William Pène du Bois*

We cannot begin to keep score with our friends. We owe each other nothing—and everything. Without our friends, we would not know ourselves very well at all. Without our friends, we would drown in life's difficult times. Without our friends, we would have no one with whom to celebrate our joys.

With our friends, we can live through anything. We honor our friends by using their support to make our lives good. With our friends, we simply face what life brings for all of us and make the very best of it.

PRAYER FOR THE DAY
Higher Power, thank you for the gift of friends.
Through them, I feel a bit of the warmth of your love for me.

TODAY'S ACTION
Today I will think about what recovery has taught me. How has it made me a better friend to others?

Talking about oneself may be a way of hiding oneself.

— Friedrich Nietzsche

We all know someone in our recovery rooms who talks too much. This person is often a great help to newcomers and seems to really get the program.

But sometimes talking too much, especially about ourselves, is a way of controlling how we see ourselves. We want to control the way others see us, but we also end up fooling ourselves. Why? Because we don't listen. To really know ourselves, we have to be quiet and listen.

PRAYER FOR THE DAY
Higher Power, help me be open to learning through listening to you, to other people, and to my own heart.

TODAY'S ACTION
Today I will list three times I have tried to control a situation by talking too much. What was I trying to do? What was I afraid of? Was talking too much a way of hiding my real self?

Clarity of mind means clarity of passion, too; this is why a great and clear mind loves ardently and sees distinctly what it loves.
— *Blaise Pascal*

Love is our Higher Power's greatest gift. Love takes many forms. There is the love of our Higher Power that offers us care and guidance. There is the love between parents and children. There is the love of one friend for another. And there is the love between spouses and life partners.

We were not able to love well when we were sick with our active addiction. Even early in our recovery, we needed time for the healing of the program to take effect in us. After about a year, our heads and hearts become clear enough for us to make good choices and love well. In recovery, we focus first on learning to love our Higher Power, friends, family, and ourselves better. Then we are ready to develop our love for our life partner, taking love to a new level of honesty, openness, and intimacy.

PRAYER FOR THE DAY
Higher Power, help me to learn to love well in all my relationships. Help me have patience with my healing so that when you show me my life partner, I am ready to love clearly and passionately.

TODAY'S ACTION
I will talk with my sponsor today about my progress in loving clearly. What does this mean? Which relationships am I ready for in my life at this point?

The farther behind I leave the past, the closer I am to forging my own character.

— *Isabelle Eberhardt*

How can we leave the past of our active addiction behind us? By walking through the door to recovery and continuing to walk into our new life!

The path of recovery leads us to forge our own character. We may take the same Steps as others in our Twelve Step program, but the way we do them and the things we learn are personal for each of us. We each forge our own character. We each develop into the person we are meant to be.

To see this in action, we just need to look at the variety of people in our meetings. Even better, we could go to a new meeting—across town or across the world. We'll see how unique we all are even though we share a great deal as recovering addicts.

PRAYER FOR THE DAY
Higher Power, you made me to be someone special. Help me realize your goals for me.

TODAY'S ACTION
Today I will think about what I have learned about my own nature as I work the Steps. What natural gifts do I have that can help me build my own character? I will write these out and look at the list every day for a week.

When you haven't forgiven those who've hurt you, you turn your back against your future. When you do forgive, you start walking forward.
— Tyler Perry

Being angry takes a lot of energy. It keeps us focused on the past. It keeps us stuck to the person we are angry at. It holds us back from making the most of today and tomorrow.

We forgive another person simply by letting go of our anger. Forgiveness doesn't change the other person at all— but neither does our anger at him or her. Other people come under the category of "things we cannot change."

Accepting others the way they are does not mean we have to like them. We can make a decision to stay away from people who have hurt us if that is the only safe thing to do.

When we forgive, we accept. We unhook the anger that ties us to that person and the pain he or she caused. When we forgive, we are free.

PRAYER FOR THE DAY
*Higher Power, help me forgive those who
have hurt me, whether they deserve it or not.
I am tired of being tied to old hurts.*

TODAY'S ACTION
Are there people I am angry at? I will write down their names. I will think about how my anger keeps me bonded to these people. I will then ask myself, "When will I be ready to leave this behind and move on?"

Drunkenness is the ruin of reason. It is premature
old age. It is temporary death.

— Saint Basil

How many holiday seasons did we spend drifting in and
out of the fog of alcohol or drugs? Who were the people
we spent these times with? Do we remember? Did they
matter to us?

How did our addicted behavior hurt other people
during these special times? Did we miss special family
events? Did we show up late? Were we drunk or high
when we arrived? Did we make a scene? Did our behavior
scare the people we love or make them sad?

In our recovery, every holiday is an opportunity to
make good memories for ourselves and the people around
us. We can choose healthy ways to celebrate, bring our
good humor and loving attention to others, and think
more deeply about the reasons we are celebrating. What
a gift.

PRAYER FOR THE DAY
Higher Power, thanks for helping me join the people I
love in celebrating special times. Thanks for the gift of
recovery—which is the gift of clarity, purpose, and love.

TODAY'S ACTION
Today I will think about the next holiday coming up in my
life. What does it mean to me? How would I like to celebrate this year? I will start making plans and talk them
over with my sponsor.

I lie to myself all the time. But I never believe me.
— S. E. Hinton

Remember those days and years when we used to lie to ourselves all the time? At first we had to, to protect our addiction. Then lying became a habit. We just lied any time it seemed easier than telling the truth.

Many problems result from lying. One of the biggest problems is that we chip away at our integrity. The stories we tell are not the only things that are full of holes—so is our character. We simply are not who we pretend to be.

Now that we are sober and working a recovery program, we change our habit of lying. First we face the truth about our addiction. Then we start facing the truth about all the other problems in our lives.

What happens? We get back our integrity. We stop lying. People can count on us. Even more important, we can count on ourselves.

PRAYER FOR THE DAY
*Higher Power, help me face the truth and
tell the truth. The idea often scares me,
but I want to be an honest and open person.*

TODAY'S ACTION
Today is a good day to look at my progress in becoming honest. I will list five lies I told to protect my using. I will then list five lies I have told that had nothing to do with my using. When was the last time I told a lie? Why? I will call my sponsor and talk about honesty.

Laughter is the closest distance between two people.

— *Victor Borge*

Real laughter makes our stomach jiggle and opens us up to other people's energy. When we laugh with another person, we connect with that person for a brief moment in time.

Little kids connect with others through laughter everywhere they go—at the grocery store, in church, at the park. They don't worry about whether they are cool. They just wave and make faces and laugh with anyone willing to play with them. Why do they do it? Because they are little human beings who love to connect with others.

We are big human beings who also love to connect with others. Yet so often, we don't. Why not?

PRAYER FOR THE DAY
Higher Power, thank you for the gift of laughter. Help me loosen up, open up my energy to connect with others, and laugh.

TODAY'S ACTION
When was the last time I had a good laugh? Was it over a joke? A funny mistake? Something cute? How can I let more laughter into my life? Today I will call someone I laughed with recently and remind him or her of the joy of that moment.

Don't mistake pleasures for happiness. They are a
different breed of dog.
— Josh Billings

Pleasure results from activities that fill our senses: eating good food, walking in the sunshine, taking a warm bath. Using alcohol or drugs, in the beginning, gave us pleasure, too. But eventually addiction took over, and these substances no longer gave us pleasure. All we wanted was more and more of the addictive substance. We were never satisfied.

Pleasure can be good or bad, that is, healthy or destructive. Pleasure is a good thing when it helps us feel renewed, loved, and ready for action. It can be bad when it leads us to destroy the values and beliefs that we hold as important.

Pleasure is different from happiness. We feel happy when we are living in peace with our beliefs and values. We need to find pleasures that support our happiness.

PRAYER FOR THE DAY
Higher Power, help me find healthy pleasures in
my day. Help me enjoy a beautiful sight, a good laugh,
or a back rub. Thanks for the gift of pleasure.

TODAY'S ACTION
I will list ten healthy things I like to do that make me feel good. I will do at least one today.

Let your light shine. Shine within you so that it can shine on someone else. Let your light shine.
— *Oprah Winfrey*

The Twelve Steps take us through a process of finding our own inner light and letting it shine. In Steps Four and Five, we take a good look at what's inside us—good and bad. First we put our energy into dealing with the bad stuff. But we also need to take out the good stuff and shine it up, use it, and share it with others.

Step Seven asks us to be humble in giving up our shortcomings. We sometimes forget to be humble in the other way—to offer our skills and gifts to our Higher Power, too. Our Higher Power can use our skills and gifts—our light—to get spiritual work done in the world.

We are the ones who can do our Higher Power's work, using our light. We need to bring it on out. To let it shine.

PRAYER FOR THE DAY
Higher Power, thanks for the gifts and talents you have given me. Help me use them well to do your will.

TODAY'S ACTION
Today I will list ten things I am good at. I will talk with my sponsor about how I can use these talents—my light—to help others.

Having given all he had, he was then very rich indeed.

— *Lao Tzu*

Being rich can mean owning a lot of expensive things or having a lot of money. Another meaning of rich is having a good supply of qualities that are highly valued. For example, we can be rich in serenity, faith, or good health. Recovery helps us become rich in freedom, friendship, hope, and better health. We'll come to value these qualities over possessions and money.

The Promises of the Twelve Step program tell us that economic insecurity will leave us as we work the Steps. That doesn't mean we will suddenly get a lot of possessions and money. Instead we will discover that our fears over money and other daily problems will begin to subside. We start to believe that we have enough. We start to feel rich in other ways, in ways that feed our spirit as we work the Steps.

PRAYER FOR THE DAY
Higher Power, thank you for the riches in my life today. Thanks for changing my thinking so that I pay attention to what's important.

TODAY'S ACTION
Today I will think about my time and energy as the most important things I spend in my life. What do I invest my time and energy in? What do I get back? How does investing time and energy compare with investing money? I will write a few sentences about this and talk with my sponsor about it.

Forgiving those who hurt us is the key to personal peace.
— *G. Weatherly*

Many of us in recovery from addiction have been terribly hurt. For many of us, it was someone in our family who hurt us so deeply. Now we become sad at times when we see other families enjoying good times together. "Why," we think, "couldn't I have grown up in a family like that?"

There seems to be no answer to that question. The important thing now is that we have the choice to forgive our family and move on. Sometimes we can have a relationship with those who hurt us—if they have changed. Other times, we need to let go of them, gently, and find new people to form a sort of family.

Let's try to remember to be grateful that we have choices now. We are able to find ourselves good friends, a loving "family" in recovery. We feel sorry for those who hurt us; their own fear, pain, and damaged souls need healing. But we are the lucky ones; we have found that healing.

PRAYER FOR THE DAY
Higher Power, help me forgive those who have hurt me and to let them go if they have not changed.

TODAY'S ACTION
Today I will list those times of the year that are more difficult for me to stay positive. I will talk with my sponsor about my list and make a plan about how I will get through the next hard time.

It is only with the heart that one can see rightly;
what is essential is invisible to the eye.
— *Antoine de Saint-Exupéry*

The world distracts and entertains us with so many material objects. It's tempting to favor people who appear wealthy or powerful. We may even disregard quiet or modest people. But we need to look beyond the surface to what is really important. We need to spend time with people who care about us and give us courage to meet each day.

Sometimes the visible picture of wealth hides a poverty of spirit. Sometimes a visible picture of modesty hides a wealth of love, courage, and loyalty.

The Steps of our program teach us to look beyond the obvious. We learn to do this by looking at ourselves, our invisible character traits, our behavior and motives, and the condition of our heart and soul.

PRAYER FOR THE DAY
Higher Power, teach me to see the world through
spiritual eyes. Help me to see through the world of
things, into the world of love, faith, and values.

TODAY'S ACTION
How is my life richer today than it was a year ago? I will list three ways my life has gotten better in essential ways. I will talk about this with my sponsor or a recovery friend today.

To him it was not the gift that mattered, but the giver.
— *Walter de la Mare*

In our material world today, we often get off track. We forget that what we really need in our lives is love and close friendships. It's too easy to take our relationships for granted. It's also too easy to take our sobriety for granted—the big gift of another chance at life.

For Christians, today marks the birth of Jesus, the child who came to bring love and forgiveness to all. Whether we are Christian or not, as recovering people, we know that love and forgiveness do open the gates to new life. When we live in the light of our Higher Power—whether we call that power Jesus, Yahweh, Muhammad, Buddha, or Creator—we find ourselves living that new life.

Let each of us, in the name of our own Higher Power, spend this day to celebrate the new life we have been given.

PRAYER FOR THE DAY

Higher Power, thanks for delivering new light into my life and giving me another chance. Teach me to live in the light of love and forgiveness. What a gift.

TODAY'S ACTION

What gifts of love and forgiveness can I deliver to others today? What can I give from my heart that will bring someone light and joy? A smile and a hug? A phone call? An afternoon of conversation and play? I will remember to contact my sponsor today.

It is not the level of prosperity that makes for happiness but the kinship of heart to heart and the way we look at the world.

— *Aleksandr Solzhenitsyn*

The values of society often seem to leave us feeling hungry for more things, more status, more power. The pressure can be strong to have the "right" friends, clothes, or house.

There is, of course, a catch. This whole way of thinking is a lie. The real way to happiness is by opening our hearts and joining with other people. Real joy can be found in having real friends with whom we share our deepest thoughts and feelings, and with whom we have fun and solve problems. We can be happy, and it is not about money and things. It is about bringing heart-to-heart acceptance into the world.

PRAYER FOR THE DAY
Higher Power, help me focus on the riches in my life: friends, faith, and the health I am regaining in sobriety. Help me remember that no amount of wealth can buy these things.

TODAY'S ACTION
How do I look at the world? Today I will make a list of the five things I believe are most important in life. I will read them to my sponsor and talk about how I am doing at building these things in my life.

You saved me once, and what is given is always
returned. We are in this life to help one another.
— Carlo Collodi, The Adventures of Pinocchio

As the end of this year approaches, we think about endings and beginnings. This past year brought us both difficulties and happiness, both pain and healing. It has been a year of growth because we are sober.

Let's think about the year that is ending and be thankful for its gifts. We need to take time to rest before the next year begins. We shouldn't worry about what the next year will bring. We can simply know that next year will bring us the chance to help other addicts who still suffer. We have been saved. We are living a new life. Let's be grateful, and let's plan to reach out next year to share the wealth of sobriety. After all, we are in this world to help one another.

PRAYER FOR THE DAY
Higher Power, remind me each day that I
am needed. By living well, staying sober, and
helping others through the program of recovery,
I am fulfilling an important purpose in life.

TODAY'S ACTION
When did I last reach out to a newcomer in recovery? Today I will make a plan for how I will share my experience, strength, and hope through the next year to help save someone else's life.

The mind is never right but when it is at peace within itself.

— *Seneca*

There is a joke in recovery groups that goes "My mind is a like a dangerous neighborhood. I had better not go into it alone." During our active addiction, our mind became The Addict's territory. The Addict will still try to grab us and twist our thoughts so that we end up using alcohol or drugs again. How? By stirring up pain, anger, doubt, pride, and other feelings that may lead us to use chemicals.

The way to find peace and to avoid The Addict's ambush tactics is to talk with our sponsors often and to share our thoughts openly with others. There is safety in being out in the open, in sharing our thinking and feelings with our sponsor and other recovery friends.

PRAYER FOR THE DAY
Higher Power, please be with me and guide my thoughts.

TODAY'S ACTION
How will I protect myself from an ambush by The Addict today? I will make a list of the things I will do to keep my mind at peace today. I will read it to my sponsor.

The first thing is to be honest with yourself. . . .
Great peacemakers are all people of integrity, of
honesty, but humility.
— Nelson Mandela

Have you noticed how the long-timers in our recovery programs fit this description? They are peaceful. They are humble. They are honest.

These qualities grow in us with recovery. We gain the respect of others because we are seen as wise, knowing, and successful. We have more and more of these gifts that other, newer recovery members want. The Big Book says that with Step Nine, "We will comprehend the word serenity and we will know peace."

There are other promises too. What they add up to is this: We will be as ready for life as anyone can be. We will know we are doing it right, and we'll be okay no matter what happens. What more can we ask?

PRAYER FOR THE DAY
Higher Power, thank you for the wisdom,
peace, and serenity you are giving me as I work
my program. Help me trust that I have what I
need to live well in this coming year of my life.

TODAY'S ACTION
Are there things that I look forward to happening next year? Today I will make a list. Am I ready for them? I will talk with my sponsor about the things on my list.

People's natures are alike; it is their habits that
separate them.

—Confucius

Deep inside, we are all very much alike. We learn this over and over, the longer we go to meetings and listen to other addicts share their experience, strength, and hope.

We have much in common. We all want to be happy, to be loved. We all want to feel that our lives have meaning. At times, we all feel afraid or inadequate.

The more we get past the details of our lives—our incomes, our jobs, the things we own, the way we spend our free time—the more we find we are all like each other in our hearts. That is why other people are such a big part of our recovery program. There are people who are living happy, productive lives in spite of the damage active addiction caused in their lives. We are not alone anymore. We are not so different anymore—even when we hang out with healthy people!

PRAYER FOR THE DAY
Higher Power, thanks for leading me to this group of
recovering people that is so good for me. Thanks for showing
me that I am not so very different from other people.

TODAY'S ACTION
Today I will list the people whom I was like when I was using. What made me similar to them? Next I will make a list of the people I am like now. What makes me similar to these people?

Celebrate: to observe an occasion with appropriate ceremonies of respect, festivity, and rejoicing.
— The American Heritage Dictionary

New Year's Eve marks the end of one year and the beginning of another. In the old days of our using, we used this day as an excuse to drink, use drugs, and act wild and crazy. We did not really think about honoring the year that was ending or about welcoming the new year.

Some recovering folks spend this evening with their families, playing games, watching videos, and sharing plans for the coming year. Other recovering folks invite recovery friends over for supper or go to a special Twelve Step meeting or a sober dance. Some attend special religious services, perhaps at a church, synagogue, mosque, or sweat lodge.

The ending of the year is an important occasion to celebrate. We are alive, and we are on the path of recovery. It has been an important year!

PRAYER FOR THE DAY
Higher Power, thanks for the good things that have happened this year. Help me stay sober so that I can live the coming year in your love and protection.

TODAY'S ACTION
I will use this night to honor the changes in my life. I will list ten good or important things that have happened this year. I will find time to talk about them with someone tonight as I celebrate. I will remember to have fun, to be sober, and to be safe.

INDEX

A

acceptance, Jan. 3, Jan. 24, Feb. 8, June 12, Aug. 7

Act As If, Feb. 21, Mar. 28, Apr. 17

action, Apr. 10, July 30, Aug. 12, Oct. 18, Nov. 6, Nov. 9

addiction, Aug. 30

advice giving, May 9

amends, Apr. 9, June 19, July 15, Sept. 1

anger, Feb. 11, Apr. 28, Sept. 16, Nov. 25

anonymous, Oct. 28

appreciation, Apr. 15

arrogance, May 12

attitude, Nov. 27

avoidance, July 18

B

behavior, Jan. 23

being a friend, Aug. 10

being a winner, Jan. 8, July 10

being real, Nov. 18

beliefs, June 27

beneath the surface, Dec. 24

better thinking, June 16

blame, May 20

bravery, Nov. 5

C

care, Feb. 6

celebrating, Dec. 31

change, Jan. 25, Apr. 7, May 21, Aug. 17, Oct. 6, Oct. 29, Dec. 5

character, Apr. 21, Sept. 22, Nov. 19, Dec. 15

character defects, Aug. 20, Oct. 30

cheer, Sept. 8

choices, Jan. 18, Mar. 26, May 3, Aug. 6, Sept. 14, Sept. 18, Nov. 13

clutter, Apr. 5

common sense, Nov. 20

compassion, Jan. 6

connection, Jan. 9, Feb. 23

conscience, Apr. 24

control, Jan. 21, Mar. 2, Mar. 25, Apr. 26

courage, Jan. 4, Apr. 8, May 31, July 23, Sept. 5, Oct. 5, Oct. 27, Dec. 7

craving, Sept. 19

crazy thinking, Oct. 26

creativity, Nov. 23

crisis, Nov. 10

criticism, June 20

cruelty, Aug. 27

D

daily living, Oct. 31

death/dying, Aug. 11, Oct. 20

deceit, Jan. 31

decisions, Oct. 19

defects of character, June 1

defense mechanisms, Apr. 13

denial, Feb. 25, Apr. 13

desires, Feb. 4

discipline, Feb. 18, Mar. 31, June 6

discovery, July 21

doubts, July 8, Oct. 22

dreams, Mar. 13, May 27, Nov. 28

E

Easy does it, Mar. 14

ego, Mar. 1, May 12, May 19

emergencies, Sept. 19

emptiness, Feb. 12, Sept. 20

energy, Oct. 9

envy, Apr. 15, July 27, Oct. 16

excuses, Dec. 2

F

faith, Jan. 13, July 25, Sept. 17

fear, Jan. 25, Feb. 24, Mar. 22, May 28, July 25, Sept. 4, Sept. 5, Oct. 18, Nov. 3, Nov. 5

feedback, Apr. 11

fellowship, Apr. 29, June 24, July 6

foes, Mar. 27

forgiveness, Apr. 18, May 7, Dec. 16, Dec. 23, Dec. 25

freedom, Feb. 2, Feb. 29, Apr. 19, May 3, June 8, Aug. 3, Aug. 16

free will, Mar. 4

friends, Feb. 16, Mar. 27, Aug. 10, Oct. 28, Dec. 12

friendship, Apr. 2, May 8, May 11, June 30, Aug. 23, Sept. 15

future, Oct. 15

G

gifts, May 19, Dec. 4, Dec. 25

giving, Dec. 8

goals, July 11, Nov. 8

goodness, Aug. 21

gratitude, Jan. 29, Apr. 22, Apr. 23, May 5, Aug. 26, Oct. 16

greed, Mar. 12, July 2

growing up, Sept. 2

guidance, July 14

guilt, Mar. 10

H

happiness, Mar. 19, May 15, June 2, June 23, Oct. 5, Oct. 17, Oct. 23

harmony, Oct. 31

healing, May 30, Nov. 21

health, Mar. 15, Nov. 15

helping newcomers, Apr. 4

helping others, Mar. 21, May 23

Higher Power, Apr. 25, Oct. 12

holding on, June 14

holidays, Dec. 9, Dec. 17

honesty, Jan. 31, Dec. 18

hope, Jan. 28, Apr. 20, May 16, July 4, Aug. 5, Oct. 4

hugs, Jan. 17

humility, July 3, Sept. 9, Nov. 22

humor, Feb. 26, Nov. 26

hurt, June 7

I

inner life, Mar. 20

instincts, Oct. 2

integrated living, Feb. 5

intimacy, May 4

inventory, Jan. 27, Feb. 3, Mar. 24, Apr. 1, June 29, Aug. 20

isolation, Oct. 10

J

joy, May 6

K

Keep it simple, Apr. 27

kindness, Feb. 9, Mar. 9

L

laughter, June 21, Nov. 21, Dec. 19

learning, Jan. 26, Mar. 29, Apr. 30, Dec. 10

learning from pain, July 26

letting go, Jan. 12, Mar. 6, June 25, Sept. 10

life, May 17

listening, Apr. 3, Apr. 12, Oct. 14

little things, Dec. 11

living, July 20

living in the present, Jan. 14, Jan. 19, Feb. 10, Feb. 20, May 10, May 18, June 10, July 24, Nov. 11

living life, Mar. 18

living our beliefs, June 4

loneliness, Aug. 14, Aug. 31

love, Feb. 14, Apr. 6, Apr. 16, May 14, May 24, June 28, July 19, Aug. 5, Sept. 6, Oct. 3, Nov. 4, Dec. 6, Dec. 14, Dec. 25

loyalty, Oct. 24

M

making a difference, Sept. 12

making a life, Sept. 7

meaning, July 9

meditation, Feb. 17

memories, Feb. 15

miracles, Mar. 23, Oct. 8

mistakes, Jan. 15

N

negativity, May 2, June 20

never giving up, Aug. 2

new beginnings, July 28

O

One day at a time, Feb. 26, Mar. 5, Sept. 26

openness, Jan. 26, May 26, Nov. 18

P

pace of life, Aug. 4
past, our, Aug. 18
peace, Dec. 29
peace of mind, Dec. 28
physical affection, Jan. 17
pleasure, Aug. 15, Dec. 20
power, May 25, Oct. 9
powerlessness, Jan. 1
practicing recovery, Apr. 14
prayer, Aug. 22, Sept. 13
pride, May 5, July 27, Sept. 25
Principles before personalities, Mar. 14
problems, Aug. 9, Nov. 24
Promises, The, Jan. 30, July 24, Nov. 2, Dec. 22, Dec. 29
purpose, Feb. 7, Mar. 18, Mar. 30, June 29, Sept. 27

R

reading, Aug. 25
recreation, Nov. 29
regrets, Mar. 11, July 13
relationships, June 19
responsibility, Feb. 2, July 15, Aug. 16, Oct. 25
rich in spirit, Dec. 22
rigidity, Aug. 24

S

sadness, Sept. 11
secrets, May 29
self-care, Feb. 22, Mar. 15, Dec. 3

self-centeredness, Jan. 22, Feb. 13, Oct. 7
self-esteem, Feb. 19, Oct. 9
self-forgiveness, Jan. 16
self-knowledge, Jan. 10, June 9, Aug. 29, Nov. 17, Dec. 13, Dec. 21
self-love, Mar. 31
self-pity, Mar. 16, Sept. 23
self-worth, Jan. 7, Aug. 28
serenity, July 7, Nov. 20, Dec. 29
Serenity Prayer, Jan. 2, Jan. 3, Jan. 4, Jan. 5, Mar. 3, Aug. 7
service, Feb. 28, Mar. 8, July 12, July 16, Oct. 13, Dec. 27
shame, June 11, July 28
sharing, Apr. 3, May 9, Dec. 4
similarities with others, Dec. 30
slogans, June 22
slowing down, Aug. 8
soul, Nov. 16, Nov. 30
spirit, Aug. 11
spirituality, July 31
spiritual principles, July 20
sponsorship, Aug. 13
Step One, Jan. 1, June 17
Step Two, Feb. 1
Step Three, Feb. 6, Mar. 1, Aug. 3, Sept. 5
Step Four, Jan. 4, Feb. 3, Apr. 1, June 9, Oct. 25

Step Five, Feb. 3, May 1,
    June 9, Sept. 5
Step Six, Jan. 4, June 1,
    Oct. 25
Step Seven, Feb. 8, July 1,
    Sept. 9
Step Eight, June 19, Aug. 1
Step Nine, Sept. 1, Sept. 5
Step Ten, Jan. 27, Feb. 13,
    June 29, Oct. 1
Step Eleven, Feb. 7, Apr. 25,
    Aug. 19, Nov. 1
Step Twelve, Jan. 23, Dec. 1
Stinking thinking, Sept. 29
strength, Sept. 3
surrender, Jan. 24, Feb. 27,
    Apr. 26, June 26, July 17,
    Sept. 24

T
talents, Jan. 11, Oct. 11,
    Nov. 7, Dec. 21
teaching, Jan. 26
thinking, May 13, July 5,
    Nov. 14

those who have gone before,
    July 22
time, June 15
triggers, Mar. 7
trust, Mar. 25, June 3, July 17,
    July 31
truth, Jan. 16, Apr. 16, May 22

U
understanding, Apr. 29, July 29

V
values, Mar. 10, June 13,
    Dec. 22, Dec. 26

W
Walking the walk, Aug. 17,
    Nov. 9
wanting it all, Sept. 20
"we" of recovery, Oct. 22
willingness, Jan. 20, June 18,
    Aug. 19
wisdom, Jan. 5, Feb. 3, June 5,
    June 9, June 17, Sept. 28,
    Oct. 21, Nov. 2, Nov. 12
working a program, Mar. 17
worry, Mar. 3
wounded hearts, Sept. 30

About Hazelden Publishing

As part of the Hazelden Betty Ford Foundation, Hazelden Publishing offers both cutting-edge educational resources and inspirational books. Our print and digital works help guide individuals in treatment and recovery, and their loved ones. Professionals who work to prevent and treat addiction also turn to Hazelden Publishing for evidence-based curricula, digital content solutions, and videos for use in schools, treatment programs, correctional programs, and electronic health records systems. We also offer training for implementation of our curricula.

Through published and digital works, Hazelden Publishing extends the reach of healing and hope to individuals, families, and communities affected by addiction and related issues.

For more information about Hazelden publications,
please call **800-328-9000**
or visit us online at **hazelden.org/bookstore**.

Other Titles That May Interest You

Morning Light
A Book of Meditations to Begin Your Day
BY AMY E. DEAN

Amy Dean brings the comfort and courage offered in her top-selling meditation book *Night Light* to this companion for the morning hours, helping devoted fans and new readers start their day on a bright and positive note. Written in her signature personable style, these sensitively chosen quotations, inspiring reflections, and simple prayers work together to make each day of the year one to look forward to.

Order No. 4897; ebook EB4897

Night Light
A Book of Nighttime Meditations
BY AMY E. DEAN

This meditation classic gives us a serene, reassuring thought as we end our day and face the night—or as we face a dark moment in the course of our day. *Night Light*'s quotations, reflections, and simple prayers ease the loneliness, fear, and anxiety that can burden our nights so we can wake up and meet each new day refreshed and inspired.

Order No. 5030; ebook EB5030

Step Up
Unpacking Steps One, Two, and Three with Someone Who's Been There
BY MICHAEL GRAUBART

Step up to your best life, alongside the millions of people who have embraced Twelve Step programs as a way to gratefully recover from their substance use, alcoholism, and addictions. Author Michael Graubart has been where you are today. With this book, he shows you what it's like to not only maintain sobriety, but to find a different way of life. With honest answers to your most common questions about being part of a fellowship, this book provides straightforward explanations on working the first three Steps of a Twelve Step program.

Order No. 3411; ebook EB3411

Three Simple Rules

Uncomplicating Life in Recovery

BY MICHAEL GRAUBART

For those who are just starting out in a Twelve Step program, the prospect of trying to change drinking, using, or other harmful behaviors can seem overwhelming. The good news is there are just three key things we need to focus on: Trust God. Clean house. Help others.

Three Simple Rules offers a new take on this valuable slogan and explains how these rules can help anyone find fulfilling recovery. Michael Graubart also knows that those six short words are packed with meaning and may not sound so straightforward. Luckily, you don't have to figure it out on your own. Michael uses wit and wisdom gained in more than twenty years of Twelve Step recovery to explain what worked for him so you can figure out what works for you.

Order No. 3655; ebook EB3655

For more information about Hazelden publications,
please call **800-328-9000**
or visit us online at **hazelden.org/bookstore.**

Also of Interest

Find inspiration anywhere, at any time, with Hazelden Publishing's highly rated and well-reviewed mobile apps. Available for iPhone, iPad, iPod Touch, and Android devices.

Touchstones
Recovery Meditations for Men

Featuring all 366 daily meditations from the best-selling meditation book designed for men in recovery from addiction.

Day by Day
Meditations for Addicts in Recovery

Daily inspirational readings that reinforce the Twelve Steps and Narcotics Anonymous principles. Each message also includes a question, a prayer, and a "sentence starter" that help you relate the daily topics to your own life. Use these as inspirations for journal writing or discussions, or type your thoughts right into the app.

Twenty-Four Hours a Day
Recovery Meditations

One of Healthline's Best Alcoholism Apps of 2016 and 2017, featuring all 366 daily meditations from the classic best-selling meditation book for people in recovery from addiction.

For more information about Hazelden's mobile apps,
visit us online at **hazelden.org/mobileapps**.